Modern Manners

FOR

MOMS & DADS

Modern Manners

MOMS & DADS FOR

PRACTICAL PARENTING SOLUTIONS
FOR STICKY SOCIAL SITUATIONS

Sarah Davis, Ed.D.
and Evie Granville, M.Ed.

mango
PUBLISHING GROUP

CORAL GABLES

For permission requests, please contact the publisher at:

Mango Publishing Group
2850 Douglas Road, 2nd Floor
Coral Gables, FL 33134 USA
info@mango.bz

For special orders, quantity sales, course adoptions and corporate sales, please email the publisher at sales@mango. bz. For trade and wholesale sales, please contact Ingram Publisher Services at customer.service@ingramcontent.com or +1.800.509.4887.

Modern Manners for Moms and Dads: Practical Parenting Solutions for Sticky Social Situations

ISBN: (p) 978-1-64250-331-9 (e) 978-1-64250-332-6

BISAC: REF011000—REFERENCE / Etiquette

LCCN: 2020940932

Printed in the United States of America

SARAH: I dedicate this book to my four beautiful children. You dream, laugh, love, and create with me—and it fills my heart every day. I am so lucky to be your mom. To my parents, who have always been my biggest cheerleaders—I love you forever and ever. And finally, to my husband, who gives me strength and always finds space for me to dream.

EVIE: To my parents, who taught me kindness, generosity, and integrity. To my husband, who held my hand along the path. And to my kids, who teach me to surrender to the moment and be conscious.

TABLE OF CONTENTS

Introduction

PARENTING POP QUIZ

Your little one nuzzles close to your chest as you sink into the pillows and blankets that gently cradle your tired body. She's a week old and you're exhausted, but you can't stop looking at this miraculous creature who's made you a parent. Neighbors and friends are dying to meet her, drop off a gift, or snuggle her...but you're not sure you're ready. The phone dings again with your neighborhood bestie on the line: "I have a gift for her! No rush, but I'd love to see her!"

You want to share her with the world; after all, she's perfect. But there are germs, and you're worried about her little baby immune system, and your messy house, and your unkempt hair, and so many other things that are uncomfortable right now. There are just so many calls and texts. You want to say yes, but you also want to say no. You want to be showered and dressed when visitors arrive, but you don't feel like getting out of bed. Can you say "no, thank you" to all these well-intentioned, loving friends? Can't this one thing be on your timetable? And if you say no, for how long can you put it all off? What do you do?

A. Say yes to everyone, even though it makes you super uncomfortable. They all mean well, and you don't want anyone to think you're being selfish or rude.

B. Say no to everyone. They can wait until you're damn well ready.

C. Say yes to your family and closest friends, but put everyone else off with a polite, "I'd love to see you, but I'm just not feeling up to it quite yet. I'll let you know! Can't wait for you to meet her!"

D. Turn your phone off and ignore all the messages. This is your special bonding time, and all of these interruptions are annoying.

Keep reading for the correct answer!

When you start raising kids, you're thrown into so many situations that you could never have dreamed up, let alone figure out on your own. A diaper disaster in the middle seat during take-off or landing. Your mother-in-law posting bath time photos of your naked baby online without your permission. An unexpected gift that leads to a tantrum in front of the gift-giver.

These *What the hell do I do now?* moments crop up at the pediatrician's office, in your new parents' group, at daycare, in church, during travel, and everywhere else. They challenge your relationships with friends (new and old, yours and your child's), family members, childcare providers, teachers, neighbors, and of course, total strangers with judging eyes. And it's easy to feel judged when parenting in public. From social media debates to the threat of your child becoming a meme, there's a reason 82 percent of our surveyed readers said they worry about mom- and dad-shaming!

For too long, parents have been reading books that tell them how to raise happy, healthy, well-adjusted kids. But those books *don't* acknowledge:

1. Parenting doesn't happen in a bubble. It happens at library story time, in the checkout line, at daycare drop-off, and all the places in between. It happens during deployments, pandemics, and natural disasters. Parenting happens out in the world, with all kinds of external factors that you have to take into account! You need skills and strategies to parent confidently, no matter what comes at you.

2. You're raising the next generation of kind, thoughtful, well-mannered citizens. As a parent, you are your child's first and most important teacher, so you have to know what you're doing to set a good example of kindness and composure. There's no dress rehearsal. This is it.

3. Your parenting decisions affect how other people treat and perceive you. If you make choices that reveal you're not really thinking about anyone but yourself and your kids, then you'll earn the reputation that some moms and dads have of being totally oblivious jerks. People—even other parents!—will avoid you. If you make choices that show you're thoughtful and considerate, then you're more likely to draw people in and cultivate meaningful connections—the hallmark of happy parenting.

This is the first book to give parenting a public context and provide real-world, practical strategies for dealing with all those parenting challenges that make you blush and keep you up at night.

REDEFINING ETIQUETTE

Your parents taught you how to chew with your mouth closed, give firm handshakes, and say "please" and "thank you." This book does *not* address that kind of etiquette. You know that stuff already! *Modern Manners for Moms and Dads* thinks about who your actions affect and how they make people feel.

When you become a parent, you show up in the world in so many new ways. Your pre-parent existence might have been limited to simple loops of work-home-work-home, day after day, without much deviation. You might have seen the same people over and over, in the same circumstances—no surprises. But once you have kids, you expand your world tremendously. You join classes and groups. You volunteer in schools and on sports fields. You go to parks, playgrounds, libraries, and so many places you might not have visited since *you* were a kid. Your social circles grow to include new parents, new children, new doctors, new teachers, and new caregivers.

Each one of these people and places becomes a touchpoint for etiquette. When you're out in the world with your kids, you're not just showing them how to behave. You're deciding what kind of world you want your kids to grow up in—one where you think of others and not just yourself. Imagine a world without manners: everyone acting in their own self-interest, no one holding the door for a mom struggling to push a stroller through, no one volunteering to host the preschool's holiday party. Who wants to live in a world like *that*?

Having good manners goes well beyond telling your child to sit up straight and say "please" and "thank you." It's reading your child *and* the room, gauging each unique situation, having strategies in your toolbox, and reaching for the right one. As the architect Ludwig Mies van der Rohe said, "God is in the details." But in order to have the energy and motivation to pull this off, you need to create a strong, impenetrable foundation for your parenting.

OUR PARENTING PYRAMID

Parenthood isn't supposed to be crazy exhausting. Yes, there will be tough days. There will be days when you're counting down the hours to bedtime. But your normal day-to-day routine should be curated for **you,** so you don't get burned out. We don't want you to sink into the couch every night at eight o'clock wondering, *How can I possibly do that all over again tomorrow?* But that *is* how parenting will feel unless you prioritize yourself.

You hear about self-care the moment you leave the hospital with a new baby—sleep when the baby sleeps, eat healthy, and exercise when you can, to name a few. But remember, those initial recommendations make sure you survive the sprint of the newborn stage, not thrive through the marathon that is parenthood! You deserve more. We want you to stop critical self-talk such as, "The kids need me," "I don't need to cook dinner for myself," and "That would be selfish." You can do it. You have to. You know why?

Your daily successes as a parent *directly correlate* with how well you take care of yourself. Researchers have shown that the more your needs are met—what they call "need satisfaction"—the more physical and mental energy you have for parenting and the less stressed you feel. On the flip side, the less often you get what you need—what they call "need frustration"—the less energy you have and the higher your levels of stress, which makes total sense![1] If you're constantly in survival mode and self-care all but disappears from your radar, you won't ever feel fulfilled as a person or as a parent.

The goal is to prevent that level of exhaustion, which is why we talk about mental health in some of the chapters that follow. Maybe you figure that if you drink your water, sleep seven to eight hours, and eat pretty well, you're taking care of yourself. And while, yes, you're *technically* getting the basics, you need to go way above and beyond that pathetic little inch of self-care in order to be productive and satisfied. You need to schedule in the things that keep you sane and whole every single day, whether that's exercise, meditation, a chance to apply your makeup and fix your hair, or a mug of tea in front of the TV.

Check out our Parenting Pyramid.

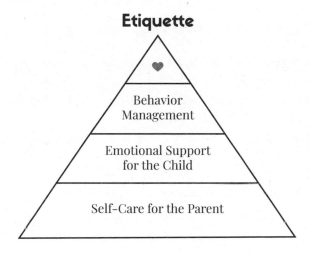

Etiquette

Behavior
Management

Emotional Support
for the Child

Self-Care for the Parent

Self-care is the foundation because, guess what? You're a human being with needs that matter. Maybe the term "self-care" makes you think of meditation retreats, mantras, and other stuff that just isn't your vibe. But hang with us because in this book, we define self-care in ways that people don't traditionally think of as "self-care." And beyond the importance of making time for yourself as a human right, research shows that when you're stressed, you're unable to be in tune with your kids' needs, emotionally or behaviorally.

Citing a number of studies, Dr. Lisa M. Dieleman et al. write, "stress renders parents vulnerable to engage in controlling parenting."[2] Controlling parenting may look like yelling, ordering kids around, shutting down and ignoring them, or even blaming them for things that aren't their fault or responsibility. If you recognize yourself in any of these behaviors, or you can recall an instance when you spiraled down a hole you couldn't seem to climb out of, you're not alone.

When you stop taking care of yourself, you have less patience and less emotional wealth to draw from. You're unable to see things from your child's perspective and you stop being psychologically available to them. When your kids act up and act out, you get overwhelmed and get angry right back. Your emotions cloud your judgment and eat up the energy you *should* be using to look for the root cause of your child's behavior. This just makes them act out more, even if they're just a year or two old.

On the other hand, parents who have greater "need satisfaction" are better connected to their child's needs. These moms and dads are more likely to use a parenting style called "autonomy-supportive parenting,"[3] which emphasizes:

- Developing a child's sense of competence and control
- Taking the child's perspective
- Making them feel loved unconditionally
- Giving them reasonable choices and explaining why others aren't available

Sounds like a great way to raise kids, right? That's why autonomy-supportive parenting is the focus of a lot of research, including a study done by Dr. Aylin Koçak et al. on how parents' need satisfaction relates to this parenting style:[4]

> "[I]t is well known that parents are likely to engage in supportive parenting behaviors when they feel that their needs for autonomy, competence, and relatedness are satisfied.[5] [...] Week-to-week need satisfaction was positively related to both mother-reported[...]and adolescent-reported[...] autonomy support."

Once you're secure in your ability to care for your own needs, then you can tap into your child's needs and become a more patient, deliberate, empathetic parent. You have the energy to coach your child to develop independence and emotional well-being. As you go up the Parenting Pyramid, you'll notice that emotional support comes before behavior. A child can't and won't make good behavioral choices if they're feeling angry, frustrated, or ignored (just like you!). Once your child's needs are met, their behavior will be much easier to manage. In fact, you can pre-empt many behavioral challenges just by stacking the first two pieces of the pyramid!

At the top of the pyramid lies etiquette. When you demonstrate good manners, it means you have the mental and emotional bandwidth to access prosocial behaviors. You can't focus on how your behavior is affecting others without first feeling like your basic needs are being met. Next, your child must be willing to follow your lead because they trust you—because you've shown them patience, compassion, and unconditional love. Once you're there, you're able to teach and model a level of "social competence" for your child that studies have linked to so many advantages in life. As Lauren O. McCay and Denis W. Keyes summarized in their research:[6]

"Studies have linked social skills to resiliency,[7,8] academic performance,[9,10,11,12] and job success.[13,14] Conversely, social skill deficits in children have been linked to delinquency, school dropout, and substance abuse in adolescence,[15,16] and are considered the single best predictor of mental health problems in adulthood.[17,18]"

When you're able to make good manners a priority, you're in your highest, most evolved parenting state. You're balanced and in control no matter what comes up. You're also teaching your child some huge secrets to success, like appropriately expressing their feelings, sharing and taking turns, listening when other people are speaking, respecting others' rights, negotiating, apologizing, and so many more.

Good parenting etiquette is what everyone strives for. When all these pieces of the pyramid come together, you can whisper to your child, "Let's not scream. We're at the grocery store, and your voice is too loud," and not be afraid of them throwing bread at you in response. Instead, your child will hear you and lower their voice, so you'll be able to keep gliding through the store, untouched by chaos. Minor adjustment here, minor adjustment there, and you'll make it through successfully!

This is easier said than done, of course, which is why we wrote this book. We want you coasting through the store confident, classy, and calm!

Naturally, it's not just parents who face these sticky situations with little ones. Grandparents, nannies, babysitters, even teachers—anyone who cares for kids has faced scenarios that left them wondering whether they did the right thing. So even though we'll continue to talk about "parents" in this book, just know we really mean anyone who cares for kids ages zero to five out in the world, beyond the confines of a private home.

The advice that follows comes from our professional backgrounds in child development, education, etiquette, and communication. You can probably tell that we love to dive into the research, so you can feel confident that our advice is rooted in the latest studies. Sarah brings a doctorate in education, a decade of experience teaching kids from Pre-K through eighth grade, and four years working with parents of kids ages four months to five years old. Evie brings a master's degree in education, years in secondary classrooms, as well as professional communication experience in a high-stakes environment. Together, we've coached parents from around the globe through all levels of the pyramid and answered hundreds of super sticky questions on our website and podcast.

As moms to six young kids (three boys and three girls), we've been there, and we get it! We offer real-world, practical advice that is true! We want you to be prepared for everything, because knowing *What to do when...* makes you a happy, confident, and more socially connected parent.

We want you to get invited to playdates so your kid will learn to socialize, and you'll get to make friends who understand what you're going through. We want parenthood to be the thing that helps you lean in and become a model member of your community. We want you to raise kind, considerate human beings who will be the next generation of amazing parents. And we want you to feel good about the decisions you make, so can you walk through life knowing you're a kick-a**, confident rock star.

In the next chapter, you'll get to know more about yourself when you take our quiz and learn how our Parenting Perspective Framework identifies your current strengths and challenges. Ready?

We're so glad you're here! Be sure to keep in touch by visiting our website, www.evieandsarah.com, and tuning into our podcast, *Modern Manners for Moms & Dads*.

Sarah Davis, Ed.D., and Evie Granville, M.Ed.
www.evieandsarah.com

PS: DID YOU ACE THE QUIZ?

This question is all about the foundation of the pyramid—self-care—so there is no one right answer. This parent needs to care for themself in new-parent mode. If that means not taking any visitors or phone calls (**option D**), that's A-OK. And if that means politely welcoming in a select few (**option C**), that's fine, too. This is one of the only times in parenthood that being unresponsive is acceptable—in fact, many new parents disappear into a black hole after welcoming a new baby. It's expected. There are other times when it's *not* okay to ignore social calls, and more delicate language is in order. But don't worry, we get into all that in the next chapters.

CHAPTER 1

Parenting Perspectives

YOU'RE WALKING THROUGH THE AISLES OF
Target with your husband and two little ones by your
side when you turn a corner and hear a spooky howl!

It's coming from the Halloween display. Your two-
and five-year-olds immediately bolt off to look at the
costumes and the wigs, pressing every button in sight.
As you approach, your eyes are treated to a display of
spooky, silly, and tempting buttons with stickers that
read "Push Here" or "Try Me." Your kids instinctively
know what to do.

Before long, shoppers within a five-aisle radius are
assaulted by a cacophony of sounds, your two-year-old
is wearing a Frankenstein mask, and your five-year-old
is tugging at the legs of a hanging skeleton to make
him dance. *What do you do?*

Reach for your phone! You've got to get a picture of
this. Your kids just turned errands into a party, and it's
adorable! But your husband is mortified that they're
touching everything and making so much noise. He
rushes toward them whisper-screaming for them

to "Cut it out!" and "Put that down!" You turn to see whether or not you're offending other shoppers, but the only other person in the aisle is a mom who's letting her kids do the same thing so she can pick out Halloween candy in peace.

These are the moments when your parenting is on public display. The parenting decisions you make when you're out in your community affect your relationships with your kids, partners, friends, and strangers.

If you pull out your phone to scroll through Facebook while your kids play, you may not see the other family entering the aisle looking to actually purchase costumes. You may be in the way with your fun and games and not even know it. That's the most common parenting faux pas: inconsideration by way of obliviousness. If you rush to enforce rigid rules, you may be overlooking a cute, harmless moment and miss the magic of childhood because you're so worried about what everyone else thinks. If you use the experience as an opportunity to check the display yourself while your children break and rip things, your kids may look wild and unruly, and you may look selfish and indulgent.

And when your first instinct in situations like this doesn't align with your partner's, you might find yourselves exploding at each other in the Halloween aisle at Target over whether or not the kids should be allowed to press all the buttons—a ridiculous reason to ruin a day.

What if you'd been running that same errand with a new mom friend who made her kids stand at the end of the aisle, with their hands behind their backs, while kids were getting down with the Halloween aisle? She'd be learning a whole lot about your parenting style, and you about hers. You'd probably both leave wondering if this friendship was meant to be.

THE SOLAR SYSTEM PARENTING FRAMEWORK

After answering hundreds of questions on sticky social situations from our readers and listeners, we realized that there are three types of parents. When we go out in public with our kids, we're all naturally inclined to prioritize one of three things:

1. Our child's wishes and well-being
2. Our own comfort and boundaries
3. The expectations of everyone around us

Recognizing this pattern in parents' choices inspired us to devise a framework that describes and dissects these tendencies. We then developed a quick quiz that sorts each parent into a perspective category and helps them see what's helping them shine and holding them back. Our framework and our quiz are both organized around elements of the solar system (because we're fun like that!). So think of yourself as one piece of the system, with your kids, your partner, and society floating all around you. The piece of the solar system you most relate to—either the sun, moon, or stars—is what we call your "Parenting Perspective."

The way the moon orbits Earth, always at arm's length, waxing and waning over time—some parents metaphorically circle their children to ensure their safety and happiness. We call these parents **Crescents**.

The way the sun is the center of the solar system, offering life-sustaining light to the planets—some parents see themselves as *the* central figure, with others orbiting around them. We call these parents **Fireballs**.

The way the stars gather together in constellations— where no one star is more important than another in the vast night sky—some parents see themselves and their children as just part of a larger whole, in society. We call these parents **Constellations**.

So with which Parenting Perspective do you identify? Don't worry, we'll help you figure that out in just a bit with our quiz. But first, let's tackle the question of why these perspectives matter. Recognizing your instincts when you're parenting in public and learning how to manage those impulses can help you make the best decision for a certain circumstance. Before you rush to react, you can pause to consider the three factors that will help you be a more thoughtful parent, a better friend and partner, and a better community member:

1. Your child's wishes and well-being (the Crescent's natural tendency)
2. Your own comfort and boundaries (the Fireball's natural tendency)
3. The expectations of everyone around you (the Constellation's natural tendency)

Each one of us instinctively prioritizes one of these Parenting Perspectives. Once you discover your Parenting Perspective, you can analyze your own behaviors, identify your strengths, and challenge yourself when your first reaction isn't really the right way to go. You can learn to be more confident about the choices you make, so you don't act in a hurry and feel judgment and shame afterward. You can also view your partner's and your friends' parenting in a new light and gain respect for their "why." Having a plan for *What to do when...* will make you a better, happier, and more self-assured parent.

Let's go back to that scene in Target. Those moms letting their kids touch everything—most likely Crescents—have the right idea! The whole point of those Halloween displays is for people to try things out and on, and fall in love with something that'll eventually end up in their big red cart. But if those items end up on the floor, not back on a rack, or end up broken, then things have gone too far. So long as you leave the aisle as good as (if not better than) you found it, no harm, no foul.

So what about your husband in this scenario—the *uptight* partner who feels like the kids are making a scene? His feelings are valid, and they align with the Constellation Perspective. There are plenty of times when kids shouldn't be allowed to touch everything! But here's where knowing yourself comes in handy. If you recognize that...

- you care more about your kids' happiness and merrymaking than what some cranky lady four aisles down is thinking when she overhears their squeals of delight, and
- your husband hates looking like he doesn't have control of the kids...

...then you can approach him armed with his own logic. "I know you're worried the kids are being too crazy, but right now, they're not breaking anything or getting in anyone's way. If it looks like they're really putting other people out or getting wild, we'll tell them to stop, OK?" Is this a foolproof way to prevent conflict? No, but it sure beats wondering why your partner is so fussy and seems like they're always trying to ruin everyone's fun! Getting to the "why" of someone's behavior is half the battle.

It bears mentioning before we go any further that every piece of advice we offer in the chapters to come weighs these three competing parenting priorities. When we're parenting in public, we can never think *only* of our child, ourselves, or others. It's a delicate balancing act that takes serious discretion. This stuff is complicated, and the stakes are high!

CHANGING PERSPECTIVES IN THE SOLAR SYSTEM

Sure, as parents, we may tell ourselves that we prioritize our child above all else, but that's not 100 percent true. You wouldn't let your son push other kids off the slide just because he didn't want to wait his turn, would you? Of course not! That wouldn't be fair to the other kids, and we believe in fairness over personal gains (at least to this extent). Plus, we're all trying to teach our kids to be good little members of society. We want to raise kids who are kind and generous, who make friends easily, and who get the (social) rules of the game.

We don't *really* prioritize our kids above all, and that's a good thing! By prioritizing the needs of others (like the right of the other kids at the playground to have a safe turn on the slide), we're modeling how we expect our child to act out in the world. It's not always going to be about them, and it's best for them to learn this lesson from us while they're young.

On the other hand, there are times when, as much as we love our kids, we need to prioritize *ourselves*. Even someone who instinctively thinks of their child first may delay naptime and let their infant cry to make a quick pit stop for a cup of coffee. Listen, we're only human! We need to care for ourselves if we're going to be any good to our families, and sometimes that means giving ourselves permission to inconvenience others, including our children. Will the twenty-something working on his novel at the coffee shop appreciate the two-minute crying baby soundtrack? Heck no, but too bad for them.

> "The real job is keeping your cup full so you have plenty of joy and presence to share with your child. [...] You deserve all the tenderness you would shower on a newborn baby. Giving that love to ourselves transforms our parenting—and our lives."
>
> —**Dr. Laura Markham**, *Peaceful Parent, Happy Kids*

These examples highlight something really important: no one favors one Parenting Perspective so strongly that they never deviate. You may *strongly* favor one perspective, even to a fault, but that doesn't mean you only ever act from that instinct. When mama needs a cup of coffee, or to squeeze in a workout, all bets are off! You may be deeply invested in social expectations and making everyone around you happy, but you'll go into Papa Bear Mode when you see your little guy get bitten at daycare pickup.

There's also no "best" Parenting Perspective. The goal is to discover your instinct, so you can figure out when it's a strength and when it's actually holding you back. There isn't a single perspective everyone should aspire to take, especially since perspectives can change over time. For instance, many new parents (especially moms) favor their child's needs above all else, partly because of biology. New moms experience real and measurable changes in their brain that make them especially responsive to their baby's needs. According to an article on this subject in *The Atlantic*:

"[T]he amygdala, which helps process memory and drives emotional reactions[...]grows in the weeks and months after giving birth. This growth, researchers believe, is correlated with how a new mother behaves—an enhanced amygdala makes her hypersensitive to her baby's needs—while a cocktail of hormones, which find more receptors in a larger amygdala, help create a positive feedback loop to motivate mothering behaviors.[19]"

On the other hand, more experienced parents are likely to prioritize their own well-being, recognizing that they're no good to their family if they don't take care of themselves. There is no "right" answer. You shouldn't aim to adopt a particular perspective, but recognize your instincts, assess each situation, and learn to be flexible.

Even though we come at situations and circumstances with different Parenting Perspectives, there's almost always a "right" answer. There's a correct way to react and a logical priority in each situation. If you've got your kid standing at the end of Target's Halloween aisle with their hands behind their back like a little soldier, that's totally unreasonable and unnecessary. That's placing your fear of them acting up—and your fear of being out of control—above their right to play and explore in an environment that was built for a little fun! Just because your instinct is to place society's expectations of perfectly behaved children above your comfort (wouldn't it be *easier* to just let the kids play?) or your child's wishes, doesn't mean that's the right thing to do. *But*, if you found yourself standing in a fine china department, ordering an "energetic" little one to not breathe on anything would be totally justified! There's no one-size-fits-all solution to shopping with kids, or any other situation

WHAT'S YOUR PARENTING PERSPECTIVE? ARE YOU A FIREBALL, CRESCENT, OR CONSTELLATION?

Ready to discover your Parenting Perspective and learn how it's helping you shine or holding you back? Simply answer the questions below, or take the quiz at www.evieandsarah.com/quiz.

1. **Your five-year-old has been invited to a friend's birthday party, which means you'll probably...**

    A. Check in at drop-off to make sure you can leave, and if you can, get out of there!

    B. Hang close to the kids under the guise of taking photos for posterity.

    C. Ask the host if there's anything you can help with, then catch up with the other parents.

2. **What is the first thing you do when preparing your child for a playdate at your home?**

    A. Go over house rules and set both kid and adult expectations. "I'll be here cooking, where will you be playing?"

    B. Talk through your child's feelings and expectations for the playdate, discuss any "triggers," and (if necessary) invite them to put their favorite toys away.

    C. Remind your child that it's important to be a good host by playing the games your guest suggests, and by sharing—the same way your child would want their friend to share if the playdate were at the friend's house.

3. **Which words best describe your parenting?**

    A. Low-Maintenance and Multitasker

    B. Thoughtful and Reliable

    C. Prepared and Passionate

4. **Where would you go on a "first date" with a new mom or dad friend?**

    A. A low-key, neutral location like a playground

    B. Out for dinner or drinks after bedtime

    C. Wherever my new friend suggests!

5. **Which quote speaks to you?**

    A. "Never give from the depths of your well, but from your overflow." —Rumi

    B. "Children are not a distraction from more important work. They are the most important work." —Dr. John Trainer

    C. "Humility is not thinking less of yourself. It's thinking of yourself less." —Unknown

6. **How would you describe your personal style now that you're a parent?**

    A. I wear whatever's appropriate for the given activity.

    B. I choose clothes that are casual and easy to move in.

    C. I use the weekend to embrace my personal style.

7. **What motivates you most often?**

    A. My child's happiness

    B. Doing the right thing

    C. A sense of well-being

8. **What's your first reaction when your four-year-old gets pushed down at the playground?**

    A. I go to comfort my child and ask them what happened. Even if I don't react to the aggressor, you can be sure we're done playing with that kid!

    B. I don't get too upset. This sort of thing happens when you go to a playground. But I always try to find out what happened so I can help my child learn how to avoid situations like that in the future.

    C. I kind of use time at the playground as a chance to breathe, so sometimes I miss things like this. I obviously comfort my child, but I don't stress too much unless they're really hurt.

9. **What's your first priority when scheduling a young child's birthday party?**

    A. First, I look at my child's nap schedule. I

choose a time right between morning and afternoon nap so they'll enjoy every minute of the party!

B. First, I call my VIPs to check their availability (at least a month in advance).

C. First, I check the availability at an experienced kid-party venue where someone else can take care of the details. Less stress, more fun!

10. **Which statement most accurately reflects how you feel about household chores?**

A. I make it a priority to clean and pick up the common areas each day. You never know when someone may show up unannounced!

B. I prioritize the chores that make my home a place I want to be in, and I don't worry about what others may think of my house. This is my personal space.

C. I'll admit, I pay less attention to household chores than I should. But honestly, the dust can wait—kids can't.

11. **What's the first thing you look for in a mom or dad friend?**

A. We get along.

B. Our kids get along.

C. Our families are a good fit for each other.

12. **When you first brought your baby home, how did you feel about visitors?**

A. I invited only my inner circle, who I didn't feel like I'd have to "entertain."

B. I kept most visitors away because it was important to me to have time to bond, rest as a family, and keep germs at bay as long as possible.

C. I ended up hosting visitors when I wasn't really comfortable with it because I didn't want to be rude when people were so excited to see the baby.

ANSWER KEY

Ready to score your quiz? Check your answers against this key to see which perspective you selected most often to determine your primary **Parenting Perspective.** Don't worry about getting a tie, that just means you're one step closer to having that balanced approach to parenting that we're all striving for!

Question 1	A. Fireball B. Crescent C. Constellation
Question 2	A. Fireball B. Crescent C. Constellation
Question 3	A. Fireball B. Constellation C. Crescent
Question 4	A. Crescent B. Fireball C. Constellation
Question 5	A. Fireball B. Crescent C. Constellation
Question 6	A. Constellation B. Crescent C. Fireball

Question 7	A. Crescent B. Constellation C. Fireball
Question 8	A. Crescent B. Constellation C. Fireball
Question 9	A. Crescent B. Constellation C. Fireball
Question 10	A. Constellation B. Fireball C. Crescent
Question 11	A. Fireball B. Crescent C. Constellation
Question 12	A. Fireball B. Crescent C. Constellation

CRESCENT

ATTENTIVE · NURTURING · PASSIONATE
PREPARED · PROTECTOR · HELPFUL
CARETAKER · ADVOCATE

You prioritize your child's wishes and well-being over your own comfort and boundaries, or the expectations of others. Crescent parents are like the moon, orbiting Earth and keeping watch, both night and day—even when they can't easily be seen. You know that you are your child's greatest advocate, so you stay close, always ready to step in and help. But you balance that with wanting them to learn and grow on their own, so you regularly fade out of view.

Crescents are proud of their knowledge and intuition when it comes to parenting. You can anticipate your child's needs and reactions, and you're skilled at minimizing or preventing meltdowns. But it's not just your child that you're looking out for. Crescents are excellent advocates for *all* children. For instance, in an unsafe or scary situation, you're likely the first one to distract or remove kids from the danger.

When parenting in public, Crescents focus on how the world is affecting their child or the children in their orbit at that moment. You'll step in if your child is being hurt or teased on the playground. You'll bring extra snacks in case anyone is hungry on the trip to the museum. You won't hesitate to announce your child's food allergy to the birthday party hostess. And you'll find a crafty, yet kind, way to clear your house of visitors when it's time for baby's nap.

Crescent's Mantra

How are my children (or the children I'm with) feeling right now? What can I do to make them more comfortable in this situation?

Crescent's Auroras:
What's Helping You Shine?

- You're loyal and protective of those you love
- You're trustworthy
- You're an excellent advocate for all children

- You can quickly see and feel when children are becoming overwhelmed
- You're prepared for any situation
- You're the first to scope out the dangers to kids

Crescent's Twilights: What's Holding You Back?

- You can be overprotective
- You can be judgmental of others' decisions and methods
- You might shelter your kids too much from the realities of the world
- You have the sense that you do it "best," and you need to be present at all times
- You feel anxious when you don't have control of a situation

Even though you favor one Parenting Perspective, that doesn't mean you don't consider the other two. It also doesn't mean that your perspective always stays the same. It's actually really important to change perspectives!

Sometimes you need to put yourself first ("No, you can't climb on me like a jungle gym while I'm talking with a friend"). And other times, it's good to check in with yourself. Are you hovering over your child? Is it really necessary to have that one-on-one chat with your child's teacher at open house? Our goal is to help you discover your public parenting instincts and understand which social situations call for a different approach, so we can build your confidence, character, and connections.

FIREBALL

STRONG · OPINIONATED · CONFIDENT ENCOURAGING · MANAGER MULTI-TASKER · SELF-PRESERVER

You prioritize your own comfort and boundaries over the expectations of others or your child's wishes. Fireball parents view themselves as the center of a solar system, with others orbiting around them. You shine bright like the sun and see how your rays help your family thrive. You've learned that you have to fill up your own cup first or you'll have nothing left to give others. You're independent and confident.

Fireballs know that worrying too much about what everyone else wants and needs can be a recipe for disaster. You've learned the fine art of saying no to commitments and expectations that just don't work for you. You prioritize what you value and find a way to get it all done, even if that means delegating things out—from hiring a housekeeper, to taking advantage of before- and after-school childcare.

When parenting in public, Fireballs say, "No, thank you," to the pressure of showing up at school drop-off in the standard Mom or Dad Uniform. You happily ignore that flyer requesting fresh-baked goods for a fundraiser during a busy week. And you build friendships on personal connection, not just by relying on the kids liking each other. You may need to check out for your own sanity, and in putting your own needs first, you're happier and calmer with your children. Instead of stressing about what everyone else is doing or thinking, Fireballs do what feels right for them.

Fireball's Mantra

What is going to be best for me in this situation? How can I set boundaries to make sure I'm not overworked, overwhelmed, or anxious?

Fireball's Auroras: What's Helping You Shine?

- You know you have to take care of yourself first

- You can be a great example to your kids, but you understand that you don't have to be with them all the time to do so
- You understand your own boundaries and embrace them
- You're a high-achiever and goal-setter

Fireball's Twilights: What's Holding You Back?

- You don't often make yourself available to others you aren't close with
- You may struggle to make new friends
- You may need to remind yourself that it's okay for others to have boundaries that don't align with your own
- You can be sensitive about your choices and take others' opinions too personally

Even though you favor one Parenting Perspective, that doesn't mean you don't consider the other two. It also doesn't mean that your perspective always stays the same. It's actually really important to change perspectives!

Sometimes you need to prioritize your child's wishes or the expectations of other people around you. That may mean jumping out of your comfort zone to create a special opportunity for your child, like hanging with strangers at a birthday party so your kid can make new friends. Maybe flaking on Girl Scout cookie sales but showing up for all of the troop's activities isn't a solid plan, because your daughter's troop is relying on you as a team player. Our goal is to help you discover your public parenting instincts and understand which social situations call for a different approach, so we can build your confidence, character, and connections.

CONSTELLATION

NON-COMPETITIVE · THOUGHTFUL ACCOMMODATOR · SELFLESS · RELIABLE EMPATHETIC · TEAM PLAYER · HOST

You prioritize the expectations of everyone around you over your child's wishes and your own comfort and boundaries. Like the countless stars glimmering in the night sky, Constellation parents believe they're a small part of a whole—no one star is any more important than another. You see yourself and your children as valuable members of a community that only works well when everyone shines their brightest. You set high expectations for yourself and others. You always try hard to do your very best and do the right thing, because you know constellations are only as strong as their weakest stars. Just because you're a parent doesn't mean your responsibilities to your community have changed.

When parenting in public, Constellations think about the big picture. You hate when your baby cries on the airplane because it's disturbing other travelers. Your kid's first words will probably include "please" and "thank you." And you feel like Parent of the Year when you navigate an outing with your kids without disrupting someone else's experience. In fact, it totally makes your day when someone compliments your child. After all, you've worked hard to teach them how to handle social expectations!

Constellation's Mantra

How can I handle this situation so that everyone around me stays comfortable?

Constellation's Auroras: What's Helping You Shine?

- You're totally reliable. If a Constellation says they'll do something, they will!
- You're an excellent gift-giver and host
- You look at the big picture of society's needs vs. the "in the moment" needs of individuals

- You're a thoughtful partner and friend who thinks of what their "person" needs to feel fulfilled in a situation
- You're excellent at conflict resolution and diplomatic peacekeeping

Constellation's Twilights: What's Holding You Back?

- You may end up being taken advantage of because you have a hard time saying no
- You can be judgmental about others' decisions
- You probably feel stressed out or anxious in public places
- You can be too accommodating
- You don't think of your own needs frequently enough

Even though you favor one Parenting Perspective, that doesn't mean you don't consider the other two. It also doesn't mean that your perspective always stays the same. It's actually really important to change perspectives!

Sometimes you get so wrapped up in making everyone else happy and fulfilling those supercharged societal expectations that you forget about what you or your children want or need. You may find yourself overanalyzing your choices, sometimes to the point of actual anxiety. You're super self-aware, but sometimes that's not always such a good thing.

Remember, not only is it sometimes okay to put yourself or your children before everyone else, it can actually be the right thing to do! Our goal is to help you discover your public parenting instincts and understand which social situations call for a different approach, so we can build your confidence, character, and connections.

***

Now that you know what you instinctively prioritize when you parent in public, you can start to consider when your Parenting Perspective makes you look and feel like a rock star, and when it does you no favors. Holding on too tightly to one perspective can often lead you astray. The goal here is to honor your instincts while being self-aware enough to step out of them when needed.

For instance, a Constellation hosting a playdate wants to make their guests feel welcome. But someone who can't deviate from that perspective might find it impossible to enforce their house rules with little guests wanting to jump on all the furniture and raid the pantry. For a pure, 100 percent Constellation, that's a terrible conundrum! It'll leave them feeling overwhelmed and resentful. They may not ever want to invite those children over again, and the connection could be lost! But that could be avoided if our Constellation host adds a little Fireball to the mix: "Sorry, sweetie, but we don't jump on furniture in our house. That's our family rule. Let me help you get down."

All they need is a simple interaction—a few words, really—to change the whole dynamic of the visit. Gentle, but firm enough to preserve the order our Constellation needs, so they won't walk their little friends to the door thinking, *That's the last time I have these kids over!*

In the chapters that follow, we'll guide you through the very best approaches to the sticky social situations parents face every day, so you can tackle them with confidence, character, and grace. As you read the quizzes, charts, bite-sized advice columns, and real-life sticky situations, think about how our advice matches up with your instinct in each situation, or how it challenges you to try new strategies.

You'll see we've included quotes and stories from *Modern Manners for Moms & Dads* readers and listeners who strongly identify as Crescents, Constellations, and Fireballs. We've also thrown in stories of our own that show how Evie is a Constellation who sometimes behaves like a Crescent, and Sarah is a Crescent who has learned to adopt a side of Fireball. You'll see how other parents feel about their Parenting Perspectives helping them shine or holding them back, and how they've learned to find balance. We end each chapter by touching on the ways Crescents, Constellations, and Fireballs might approach these areas of their lives differently.

If you want to learn even more about your Parenting Perspective, be sure to visit our website, www. evieandsarah.com. There, you can find a list of our podcast episodes on the best and worst scenarios for each perspective. And don't forget to join our "Talking Modern Manners for Moms & Dads" Facebook group, where we're always dishing on these topics. See you there!

CHAPTER 2

Parenting in Public: There's Nowhere to Hide

MOST PARENTING BOOKS FOR FAMILIES WITH young kids make two assumptions:

1. "Parenting" is something that happens between you and your child without many outside influences; and

2. Your parenting choices don't (or shouldn't) really change based on your environment or circumstances.

Ask anyone who's changed their fair share of diapers and they'll tell you these assumptions are downright ridiculous. When it comes to cleaning your kid's tush in the privacy of your own home, you do what works for you. That may mean changing your child's diaper directly on the white carpet, doing a quick change while your toddler is running laps around the living room, or tossing a stink bomb into the kitchen trash knowing it'll be taken out soon.

But out in public—where the *etiquette* happens—we all play by different rules. We seek out special bathroom stalls with changing tables bolted to the wall. (If you're a dad, this can be damn near impossible, but you try anyway.) We carry bulky changing mats that take up prime real estate in our diaper bags. We slip stinky diapers into odor-reducing baggies. And sometimes, we carry them out of the bathroom with us. Can you even imagine storing a poopy diaper in your diaper bag?? It sounds disgusting, but we've both done it, trying not to leave a long-term stench in a small, one-person bathroom.

Parents go to great lengths to not offend because we all know, instinctively, that:

1. Parenting really *isn't* something that happens in a bubble. Our choices in public can have a huge effect on the people around us; and

2. Parents can often get a bad rap, but we aren't a**holes just because we have kids!

This book is the first of its kind to look at how we "parent in public"—in the spotlight, for all to see and judge, whether in hushed whispers or straight to your face. It's also the first to acknowledge that we might (and sometimes *should*) handle things differently when we have an audience, and when our actions have a direct effect on people around us. Let's face it, taking kids out into the world is inevitable, so we should probably have a plan for those sticky situations to keep you feeling confident in your character and your choices. That's what we're here for!

WHAT DOES PARENTING IN PUBLIC HAVE TO DO WITH ETIQUETTE?

If you listen to our podcast, *Modern Manners for Moms and Dads*, you've heard us answer hundreds of questions that fall into both categories of "parenting" and "etiquette." But if the word "etiquette" sounds as stuffy to you as it does to us, we'll be the first to reassure you that this isn't your grandma's etiquette. This isn't about keeping your elbows off the table or anything fussy like that. When we talk about "etiquette," we mean trying to be kind and considerate *and* giving a damn about it, knowing that our actions affect other people. Of course, when we have kids in our lives, our choices and theirs can have a *huge* effect on others! How you balance the needs and preferences of your kids, yourself, and everyone else is key.

Think back to your first job. Back then, did you know there was such thing as "workplace etiquette"? Nope, you just showed up. It was only after time, trial and error, and maybe a few conversations with annoyed coworkers that you realized your workday's start and end times *weren't* flexible on Fridays, sneakers *didn't* count as "business casual," and heating leftover fish in the breakroom microwave was *surely* social suicide. You had to figure this stuff out on the job, literally!

There's a reason etiquette books on topics ranging from business, to weddings, to weed exist (yes, you read that right). There are certain ways of acting that come off as kind and refined, and others that, well, don't. It's the same thing with parenting. We're betting that you're reading this because you don't want to be the person metaphorically reheating fish in the breakroom. You know hitting the right note when you're parenting in public is incredibly important for your confidence and your connections.

WHAT GOES IN MUST COME OUT

Feeding Your Baby

For some reason, everyone seems to have an opinion about when, where, and *how* moms should feed their babies. Luckily for dads, this one's easier for you: no breasts, no problem! There's no public outcry over all the scantily clad models in the windows of lingerie stores, but a mother breastfeeding her child in public? Well, that's positively indecent! Or a mother pulling out a bottle to feed her baby formula? Oh, how *could* she?

We both breastfed our babies for years. Want to know what all that experience whipping out our boobs in public taught us? There's nothing sexual or exhibitionist about it. It's a totally practical decision to Feed. Our. Babies. If that offends people, they should feel free to look away.

Q. What about breastfeeding in the middle seat of an airplane between two people?

   A. Yup, totally fine.

Q. What about breastfeeding at home in front of your dad/brother/weird Uncle Jim?

A. Also fine, but up to you. If that skeeves you out, do it somewhere else. If it skeeves them out, who cares? They can look away.

Q. What about breastfeeding in front of other people's kids?

A. Yup, you guessed it: fine. Remember, this is just a mom feeding her baby, right??

Q. What about using formula and not using breastmilk at all?

A. Totally fine. You do what works for you.

NURSING COVERS

Do you have to wear a nursing cover when you're breastfeeding in public? Not unless you want to, but you should consider that most people value modesty. There are lots of ways to achieve this, and they don't all include using nursing covers. Here's our advice from personal experience.

EVIE'S Story on Nursing Covers—A Constellation's Perspective

As a new parent, I'd heard horror stories about moms getting chewed out for breastfeeding in totally harmless places. I don't always shy away from telling people to mind their own business, but I knew some weirdo announcing how "disgusting" I was for nursing my baby would send me into a fit of rage worthy of the nine o'clock. So I always wore a nursing cover in public, for my own comfort—to ensure the experience was about feeding my baby, not enlightening less forward-thinking members of my community. Wearing a nursing cover wasn't about making everyone else comfortable, it was about keeping me comfortable and out of the spotlight while I fed my child.

SARAH'S Story on Nursing Covers—A Crescent's Perspective

I wore nursing covers when my babies were really small, but once they were past about six months, I preferred the two-top trick. I pulled one shirt above the top half of my breast and had a tank top underneath that I pulled down. Yes, maybe I was exposed for half a second while the baby latched on, but once they did, I was completely covered up. My babies ate better this way, I was more comfortable, and it took a lot less fooling around with blankets and covers that slipped off anyway.

How about you, Fireballs? You're the moms that probably feel most comfortable breastfeeding in public because, truly, you do you. Does that mean you should feel perfectly comfortable whipping out those milk machines everywhere you go—the playground, in line at the post office, during a wedding ceremony? Not so fast. Discretion is key. If you're in good company (like a bunch of other moms with babies), go for it. Otherwise, remember that a bit of modesty might save you a bunch of headaches.

Diaper Changes and Potty Breaks

While it's hard to imagine why the act of feeding your baby would gross people out, it's easy to understand why people would be squeamish about diapering. That's why our advice hinges on one important rule: anything that involves your kid's bare butt needs to happen in a bathroom.

Can you ever change your kid's diaper in a public place that's not a bathroom?

The short answer: No, never. You should never wipe your child's tush in a place where people could see their private bits or smell the contents of that diaper.

But here's the truth. We've both changed our babies in places that were totally, undeniably inappropriate because we were new moms who didn't have a copy of this book to tell us that was *not* okay, *and* because we didn't see another option.

SARAH'S Story on Her Diaper Change Faux Pas

As a new mom on my very first flight with an infant, I figured I'd thought of everything. I packed everything we needed and more—extra outfits, extra pacifiers, even an extra shirt for me. But then, mid-flight, the baby needed to be changed. This was the kind of dirty diaper where you have to move quickly, and of course, we were twenty rows away from the bathroom. I was in the window seat, my husband was sitting in the middle seat, and yes, there was someone sitting in the aisle. We had two choices: 1) Figure out a way to get to the tiny airplane bathroom, then wait in line for our turn, or ... 2) Change the baby on my husband's lap.

Of course, the best answer here is to go into the bathroom. No one wants to see or smell a dirty diaper. So what did we do? Yeah...we changed him on our lap. We worked quickly to change him, closed up the diaper in a scented bag, and apologized to the woman next to us.

EVIE'S Story on Her Diaper Change Faux Pas

We were on our first family vacation, enjoying dinner at what I thought was a family-friendly restaurant. I munched on a fajita with my nine-month-old at my side, talking with my husband about how we were crushing this parenting thing. Halfway through our meal, I discovered the baby needed a change.

As a first-time mom, I carried a diaper bag packed for every conceivable baby "emergency." So I scooped my daughter up and carried her to the single bathroom of that busy restaurant. When I got there, something was missing: the changing table. There weren't even any countertops. All I found was a pedestal sink, a toilet with no lid, and some truly disgusting floors. I mean, wet, sticky, and obviously filthy. No changing mat was going to keep my extra roll-y baby from touching the nasty bathroom sludge on that floor, and that was a risk I wasn't going to take.

I needed a Plan B. Changing her in the car wasn't an option. We had walked to the restaurant with the baby in a stroller. *The stroller! What about changing her there?* I thought. But then I remembered that we'd packed a little umbrella stroller that didn't recline.

I looked around the restaurant and realized that our table was *way* in the back, my chair was up against a wall, and there was an empty chair next to me. So I did what I had to do: I laid my baby out on the chair, tucked slightly out of sight, and changed her as fast as I could.

It ended up feeling like not such a big deal. Because I was way more of a Crescent back then, my first priority was always making sure my baby got what she needed—in this case, a clean diaper. It wasn't one of my finest parenting moments. Other diners obviously wouldn't have known that I was out of options. They would've just seen some obnoxious mom changing her baby's diaper in the middle of a restaurant, at the table. Disgusting, right?!

But looking back, I'm not sure *what* I should've done. That situation always reminds me to hold off on judging other parents who seem to be doing something totally obnoxious.

NO CHANGING TABLE, NO PROBLEM!

So what do you do if your kid's got a messy diaper but there's no changing table in the public restroom? Here are your options, from best to worst:

1. Do it in your vehicle. Moms and dads get really creative about finding flat surfaces that can serve as changing areas, even if that means sliding the driver's seat *all* the way back and doing it on your lap.

2. Do it on the floor in the handicap stall of the bathroom, but only if you've got a decent-sized changing mat and the floors look clean. Sure, an especially active baby might need a bath when you get home, but a good handwashing will do the trick until then.

3. Do it on the countertop. If the thought of changing your baby on the floor is legitimately giving you a panic attack (we get it!), set up shop by the sink. Hopefully no one will unload on you about how gross that is, but if you do see someone giving you The Look, shift blame: "Can you believe they didn't install a changing table in this bathroom??"

HE LOOKS LIKE HE'S GOING TO PEE!

Eventually you move from the diaper phase to the toilet-training phase, and after a few accident-free days, you venture out in public. Those days are gut-wrenching. *Can we make it through this errand, or through two, without an accident? How many extra outfits do I need to carry with me? What will I do if my kid pees all over the place?* This phase of parenting is particularly traumatic for Constellations. A thousand "what ifs" go through their minds as they rush through their errands to get back home.

You may also be contending with a toddler who's scared to use public restrooms: they're too loud, there are too many people, and of course, those automatic toilets are *way* too scary!

So, let's get confident here! What can you do to make these first few outings manageable, and even successful?

1. Bring a potty with you. We both carried a foldable toilet-on-the-go that expanded into a child-size toilet seat for big toilets. This little accessory may prevent a loud meltdown out of fear of the big toilet and keep public bathrooms peaceful for others using them.

2. Keep your outings short. Go to places where the people won't get too upset if there's an accident. Parent/child classes are wonderful first outings. Places like that are very comfortable with this stage and won't judge or get upset if there's an accident.

3. Always bring an extra change of clothes. Even pack a towel for your child to sit on in your shopping cart, if that makes you feel better.

4. When with friends, do what you need to do! No one faults a toilet-training parent. Don't worry if you have to cut an outing short or keep visiting the restrooms.

Real-Life Sticky Social Situation:
Can My Son Ever Pee Outside?

I'm in the process of toilet-training my three-year-old son. Last week, he had to pee at the library, but he was terrified to go in the public restroom. He ended up peeing on the grass next to our car. Did I make a mistake?

Yes and no. No one wants to see your kid peeing on community property, so that's got to be a last-ditch option. However, if you've run out of choices, better to do that than have him pee his pants. This is the perfect time to reach for that little potty you keep in the car.

The worry with letting him pee on the grass is that he'll start seeing that as an option, and he'll want to pee outside everywhere you go! But you live and learn. If it happened just once, you move on.

WHEN YOUR KID HAS AN ACCIDENT

You're at the library with your baby and your newly potty-trained three-year-old, sitting quietly on the rug for story time, when you notice a puddle forming at your big kid's crotch. Whoops! Now what?

1. Tell the person in charge (if they haven't already noticed). Let them know the rug has been... *soiled*, and offer to bring paper towels back from the restroom.

2. Get your kid out of there. This is probably really embarrassing and disappointing for them! Don't scold your child, try to make them clean it up, or

even apologize. Just get them changed without a huge fuss. There's a reason they call it an "accident."

GOING TO THE PLAYGROUND OR A PLAYDATE

Parenting Pop Quiz

You're sitting on a park bench while your kids play. All of a sudden, you see a little girl push your son into the mud. He looks up, absolutely shocked to find his butt in the sludge. You feel your Crescent instinct kick in, like you're the Hulk about to go green. Your eyes go to the girl who's hiding a giggle behind a cupped hand. What do you do?

A. Rush over screaming, "That is not nice! Shame on you!"

B. Rescue your child from this horrible bully and take him right home for a bath.

C. Scan the playground for the girl's mom. Boy, are you about to have some harsh words with that woman!

D. Wait to see if your son needs your help. It's just a little mud after all.

Keep reading for the correct answer!

Playground Particulars

A playground can be a tricky place for kids *and* adults. Put a bunch of children on equipment they have to share, throw in a few overprotective parents, and add a wildcard like a ball someone won't let out of their clutches, and you've got some serious playground politics to navigate. Here are a few tips to help you ditch the drama:

- **Leave toys at home.** Don't let your kid ride their brand-new, battery-operated car to the playground. You'll end up with ten kids swarming the kiddie car, and it'll be super stressful for you, your child, and the other parents.

- **Skip risky snacks.** Please, please leave peanut butter at home. Save sticky PB&J fingers for private spaces where no one could go into anaphylactic shock. This is not a matter of your convenience, it's a matter of other children's safety.

- **Size matters.** Don't let your baby crawl around a structure for older kids and then act shocked when their fingers nearly get stepped on. On the other hand, don't take your big kids to the tot-size playground where they'll topple toddlers off the bumble bee spring rider.

- **Share without being a pushover.** Got a kid who wants to swing for hours? Go to town! Unless, of course, someone's waiting for a turn. No need to hop off the minute another kid approaches, though. Prep your child for the idea that their turn is coming to an end. "Okay, let's do ten more pushes so this girl can have a turn, too. Ready? Ten... nine... eight..."

✎ **Party-planners beware.** If you're hosting an exclusive event like a birthday party at the park, plan on strangers crashing your party. Parks are community spaces. While you may be able to get permission from your town or city to block off some outdoor tables, the playground will continue to be open to the public.

Parenting Perspectives at the Playground

Playgrounds can be anxiety-inducing for parents who identify as Crescents and Constellations, but for different reasons. Crescents spend time looking for how, when, and where their child is going to get hurt. *Will it be the slide? Is it too hot for their tushy? Will it be that boy who looks like he's a hitter?* Constellations spend time wondering how their kid is affecting other people's experiences. *Does that other kid really want to play tag with my child right now? Am I letting my kid stay on the swings too long? Ugh, my child is climbing up the slide again! Now no one can slide down.* The playground can be a minefield for both of these Parenting Perspectives.

The next time you're at the playground, take a look at that Fireball parent sitting on the bench. Parents who identify as Fireballs view the playground as a time to zone out, read a book, check their phone, or just have some quiet time. They sit on a bench, take a deep breath, and let their children play. Can you lean into that perspective a bit more?

Sure, Fireballs can get a bad rap for being uninvolved, even inattentive, if they're quietly scrolling through Instagram while their kids are running amok on the playground. But excluding those outliers, most Fireballs have the right idea. Unless you have a toddler who really needs you right there, you really *can* sit on the bench! The only exceptions would be if:

- Someone's about to get hurt, or
- Someone's not playing fair. Everyone's seen the bullies or clueless big kids who need an adult to tell them to back off. That's when you put on your Crescent hat and advocate for your kids. Just be sure to talk like a teacher, firmly but kindly. Check page 129 for our tips on exactly how to speak to another person's child.

Don't Cross the Line

Although it might be tempting to help an unfamiliar child at the playground, use caution when touching other people's kids. Children are constantly calling out to the nearest adult for help reaching the monkey bars or climbing the rock wall. Never touch a stranger's child unless you're doing it to make sure they don't get hurt. Like, if that kid is already halfway up the rock wall and screaming that they're about to fall, grab them fast. Just don't stick around for a hug afterward.

When to Step in on the Playground

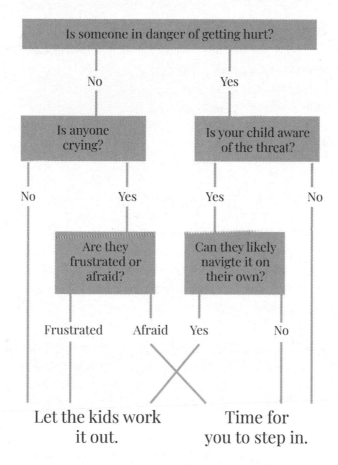

Did You Ace the Quiz?

So what about the girl who pushed your kid down at the playground? Before you rush over, assess the scene. Is your child crying, or wiping himself off without a fuss? Is his instinct to call this mean girl out himself, or look to you for help? Your best choice here is **D. Wait to see if**

your son needs your help. If he can handle it, let him. Then, you might privately tell him to stay away from this girl as much as possible.

If he does need a hand (literally or figuratively), calmly make your way over, even if your Crescent siren is going off at full volume in your head. Help your kid up, then confront the culprit: "That really wasn't nice. Please keep your hands to yourself." Don't worry about her adult chaperone overhearing you. Actions like this require a response.

Playdates at a Friend's House

Whether you're visiting your best friend's house for a super casual playdate or you've accepted an invitation to a new friend's home, here are the first two things you need to do to make a great impression. (Be sure to brush up on your communication skills to ace the visit. See page 108.)

1. **Follow the host's rules, even if they're weird.** No playing inside the house? No using the upstairs bathroom? No sitting on the couch? Whatever it is, go with it. You can have a private talk with your kid about handling ridiculous rules later. (Looking for tips on getting other people's kids to follow *your* house rules? Check our chapter on entertaining on page 178.)

2. **Manage your child's movement around the house.** If there's a closed door or a baby gate, help them understand that it's there for a reason and we don't open it. That applies to pantry and refrigerator doors, too. It's so not cool for kids to go into someone else's fridge searching for food!

PLAYDATES WITH INFANTS

Be prepared to stay for a full eat, play, sleep cycle... so two to three hours. Since babies are pretty flexible about where they sleep, you'll hopefully be able to sneak in some quality time with your friend while the babies do their thing.

- Bring all your gear with you—diapers, blankets, changing mats, extra clothes, whatever. Don't expect to share. New parents are kind of finicky about germs. If you forget something, though, it's okay to ask.

- Lay your baby down on a blanket you brought, maybe even bring your own toys. Babies put everything in their mouths—it's their love language, but it doesn't have to be yours.

PLAYDATES WITH TODDLERS AND PRESCHOOLERS

These usually last about one to two hours and come with some challenges. Sharing toys, meltdowns, fear of family pets, food allergies—all are fair game during a toddler playdate.

- Sharing is hard, but don't run away at the first sign of conflict between the kids. Your host probably put a lot of time and effort into getting ready for your visit. Instead, try to help these young friends navigate sharing. It's hard stuff, but it's a big reason why anyone bothers with playdates at this age!

- *But*, if things are just too intense for you or your kid, it's okay to tap out. Say, "Gosh, it looks like we're coming up on naptime early! I'm sorry we aren't able to stay longer." You could also add,

"Maybe we can do this again sometime soon," if you mean it.

- If you're bringing snacks for your kid (which is pretty common at this age), it's a good idea to check with your host about food allergies in their family. Evie once had someone bring over the very nut her daughter is deathly allergic to!

- If you or your child are afraid of dogs, you can always ask if the dog can chill in another room. "I'm so sorry, we're just a little nervous around dogs. Would it be possible for us to have a visit in a separate space?"

- Set expectations for drop-off playdates. For example, "Are you able to come pick up Clara around four o'clock?"

- Got a gun? It's okay to ask if families have them and how they're stored, especially if it's a drop-off playdate.

- Lastly, don't forget to thank hosting children for sharing their toys. It's a big deal!

THE MILLION DOLLAR QUESTION: DO I NEED TO HELP CLEAN UP TOYS BEFORE I LEAVE A PLAYDATE?

On one hand, you have the Crescent/ Fireball Perspective:

- At the end of even a very successful playdate, you have a tired, cranky toddler who's done and just wants to go home. They probably won't be very cooperative when picking things up.

- There are probably a ton of toys out and you have no idea where anything goes, so your effort wouldn't actually be very helpful.

- Your host is probably ready for the playdate to end as well.

But on the other hand, you have the Constellation Perspective:

- You want to teach your child that it's important for them to help clean up the mess they made, especially in someone else's house.
- Isn't putting things away *somewhere* better than doing nothing at all?
- You don't want your friend to think you're totally inconsiderate by just skipping out on a gigantic mess.

Both sides seem right, don't they? Look to your host! If they say, "Don't worry. We'll be playing all day, and we'll clean up later!" take the cue and go! If they don't offer you any clues, choose one type of toy to pick up, like toy cars. Ask where they go and then quickly show your child what you're doing: "I'm putting the cars away, and then we're going to go. Will you please help me?" Once you've finished that task, gracefully excuse yourself, knowing you did the right thing. One thing to note: once a child reaches about three years old, they can be expected to help clean up, even during the playdate. Expectations do change as kids get older.

A WORD ABOUT PICKY EATERS

Most families with young kids have at least one picky eater: the kid who wouldn't dream of eating foods that other kids adore, who complains that most meals have "too much flavor," who would rather starve themselves than subject their palate to the horrors of normally kid-friendly foods. We both have them in our house, so what we're about to say next comes from experience, not judgment.

As a rule, when you visit someone else's house with your picky eater, it's not the host's job to entertain their every food whim. It's *your* job to feed your child in advance and let them snack on whatever your host offers without complaining about the lack of choice.

Q. Should you ask your host for something other than what's offered?

> **A.** Not unless your child has a serious dietary restriction. Even then, it's probably something you want to discuss before you arrive, so you're not springing this on your host in the middle of a visit.

Q. Should you bring your own food for your picky eater?

> **A.** When you have a toddler, things are more fluid. Toddlers have different eating schedules and may be more adamant about their food choices. It may be easier for each guest to bring their own snacks. Kids who are preschool-age and up are usually expected to eat at least some of the meal provided.

It's important for kids to learn that accommodations can't always be made, and when you're in someone else's home, it's rude to not eat what's offered. Make the best of it—let your child make a meal of dinner rolls if you have to—and just eat again when you get home.

IF YOU INVITE ME OVER, I HAVE TO INVITE YOU OVER TOO, RIGHT?

If your playdate goes well, sure, it would make sense to reciprocate! But just like dating, if you don't want a second visit, don't feel obligated. We always suggest meeting for the first time in a public location to see if everyone gets along before bringing it into the home.

If your new friend is pressuring you for another visit and you want no part of it, cite busy schedules, conflicting nap times, or even pre-scheduled appointments as excuses. Eventually, they'll get the hint.

What Should I Call You?

When your child is interacting with new adults, help them figure out what to call them. We both grew up calling our friends' parents Mr./Mrs. [Last Name], but now it seems more common to go for Mr./Miss [First Name]. Feel free to ask adults what they'd like to be called, so your kid doesn't end up looking rude for assuming they're on a first-name basis!

Running Late and Last-Minute Cancellations

Parents are perpetually late! We get it. But because we're all beholden to little ones and busy schedules, it's especially important to follow a few simple rules.

- Call or text to explain if you're over five minutes late. Anything beyond a half hour and you may want to cancel entirely.

- Kids are unpredictable, but try to be reliable. If you're the one who's never on time, people will start to get annoyed and the invitations may stop.

- It's inevitable that you'll have to cancel plans at some point. Kids get sick, things break, whatever. Try really hard not to make it a habit. If playdates make you anxious, tell your friends or find something you prefer, even if it's going to a movie where there won't be talking. That way, you don't have to cancel out of sheer panic.

Real-Life Sticky Social Situation:
Saying "No" to Neighbors

How do you keep your next door neighbor's child from always inviting herself over to play? This little girl always watches my three kids, and asks if she can come and play. We feel it's too intrusive. What should we do?

There are a bunch of factors to take into consideration when coming up with a plan for a sticky situation like this:

1. How well do you know this child? Is this a kid who's spent a lot of time in your house or with your kids in the past? Have you somehow given him the impression that he's welcome pretty much whenever? If so, you've got to let him down easy. Pull him aside and tell him you still like having him around, but you're trying something *new*: "Special Family Time." From now on, you'll tell him whether or not you're having Special Family Time when he sees you outside. If you are, then you'll set up another time to see him; if not, he's welcome to come over.

2. How well do you know the parents? Would it be possible to speak with them? If you're very, *very* close with the parents and telling them their kid was coming on a little strong wouldn't offend them, that might be the way to go. They could be more direct with their child. But most parents can get *super* defensive about something like this: "Why on earth wouldn't you want our child at your house?"

3. Are there other neighborhood kids who always seem to make their way over to your house? It's really tough to exclude one child if he's noticing that another kid from down the street is always there. Make sure that if you're setting rules about Special Family Time, you're applying them fairly. That way, he understands this is about your family having time together, not about him. It lets him know you'd like to see him, but on your terms, not his.

Keeping Kids Healthy

New parents have a reputation for being germaphobes, and for good reason. We want to protect our babies from getting ill and feeling miserable. Plus, we know how awful it is to be up all night with a sick baby. But it's weird to go around asking others personal health questions, so instead of having uncomfortable conversations, we disinfect toys after playdates, wash little hands over and over, and just pray that each interaction won't end in illness. Or at least that's what we used to do.

During the coronavirus pandemic of 2020, the whole world changed, and so did our etiquette. We started asking questions that, until then, would've been considered pushy, overbearing, or rude. "Has anyone in your house had a fever or any other symptoms?" "Who else have you been seeing?" "Where have you gone in the last two weeks?" It became socially acceptable to ask really personal questions to protect your family. If you're a Crescent or a Fireball, you were probably already a rock star at this. If you're a Constellation, the pandemic gave you permission to ask tough questions and go with your gut when something didn't feel right, rather than worry about offending others.

One topic related to kids' health that has always been especially controversial is vaccines. People can be so passionate about the choices they make for their family. This can make for some super sticky situations when people choose not to vaccinate, or are unable to do so for medical reasons.

As etiquette experts, our advice is to not get into huge debates on the topic of vaccines, especially if you feel strongly one way or the other. However, it is okay to ask if a child you'll be spending time around has had all their shots, especially if your child can't be vaccinated due to a medical condition. If you don't get the answer you need, politely decline the invitation. You can state your reason if you'd like, but avoid further discussion. Something like this would work: "We're saving our visits with families who aren't vaccinating until the baby has had all their first-year shots."

THE DOS AND DON'TS OF SHARING GERMS

- Do teach all kids, but especially sick kids, to wash their hands before they eat, after the bathroom, and after coming home.
- Do teach kids not to share cups or utensils with friends.
- Do teach kids to cover sneezes and coughs with their arm instead of their hands.
- Don't freak your kids out too much. Kids will get sick from time to time, and that's okay!

Want a cute little rhyme for teaching your kids to cover their mouths? Check out Aunt Matilda Rabbit!

Aunt Matilda Rabbit, when she wanted to sneeze ...
Did she cover her eyes? No!
Did she cover her knees? No!
She covered her sneeze! (Dramatically cover your
nose with your inner arm.)

HOW SICK IS TOO SICK?

Can you leave your house if your child has a bad cough?
Do you have to cancel a playdate over a runny nose?
Can a sibling of a sick child go to a birthday party?
Should you take your children out to run essential-ish
errands if they're feverish?

We're obviously not medical professionals, but we are
experienced moms who've had more than our fair
share of opportunities to pick up sicknesses from other
families. We're not here to tell you how to treat a sick
child, only how to be considerate when you've got one.
So here are our rules:

Is your Kid Too Sick to Leave the House?

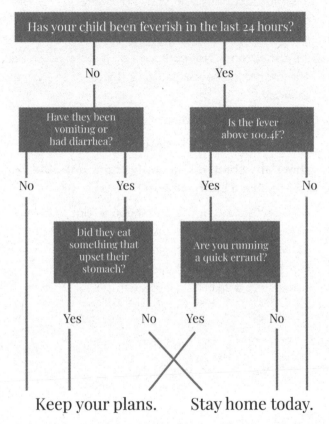

Has your child been feverish in the last 24 hours?

No   Yes

Have they been vomiting or had diarrhea?

Is the fever above 100.4F?

No   Yes   Yes   No

Did they eat something that upset their stomach?

Are you running a quick errand?

Yes   No   Yes   No

Keep your plans.   Stay home today.

Q. What if my child has a stuffy nose or cough?

A. Do they have a fever? If so, cancel your day. No fever? Carry on, but if you've got a playdate planned, be sure to mention that runny nose or cough to the other parent (and be prepared for them to cancel on you).

Q. What if my child has a rash?

A. Do they often have rashes, such as eczema or allergic reactions? If so, you can totally go out! Be prepared for some stares and have an answer at the ready: "I know, it looks pretty bad, right? Thankfully, it's just eczema. Not contagious!" If rashes aren't a common occurrence, call your doctor to see what they say.

Q. What if my child has lice?

A. Oh please, please STAY HOME!

Q. What if my child has an easily communicable disease, like a stomach bug?

A. Keep that kid home! But if you've got to take a sick child out to get medicine, just keep to yourself, get in and get out, and get home as quickly as you can. Try not to touch too much, and wipe down the surfaces you do touch, if you can.

Real-Life Sticky Social Situation:
Sick Kids at Playdates

Last week, I invited my neighbor and her toddler over to play. We play outside all the time, but this was an invitation to play at my house on a rainy morning. When she arrived, she told me in passing that her two-year-old had a cough and a runny nose, but no fever. I felt really uncomfortable. I think she thought that because our kids always play together outside, it wasn't that big a deal, but I really didn't want a sick kid all over my house touching my kid's toys and coughing all over everything. I didn't ask her to leave but I really wanted to. Could I have asked without ruining the friendship?

You definitely could have! But take her perspective into account for a moment—she probably thought it wasn't that big of a deal. Some toddlers spend entire winters with a cough and runny nose! Next time you plan on having her over, send her a quick text the morning of: "Are we still on for today? Everyone healthy and feeling up to it?" If she writes back telling you about a runny nose or anything else that makes you uncomfortable, ask to reschedule.

If your friend and her child get to your house and you see that her kid looks sick, you can say something like, "I know this might seem a little paranoid, but I'm thinking we should reschedule for another day when everyone's feeling healthy. Would you mind?" If you say it kindly and make it more about your comfort than how snotty her child is, hopefully your friend won't be upset. Make sure to invite her over again in the near future, though, so she knows it wasn't personal.

ADULT OUTINGS...WITH YOUR KIDS

So you think you're actually going someplace that's not a friend's house, a playground, or a school? You want to take your kids to a place that's meant for...*adults*? We're talking the bank, the post office, your dentist appointment, your cousin's wedding, and all those other places that don't come with seat-belted shopping carts or cushioned play areas. These are the outings that give new parents indigestion! But don't worry, we've got you covered with some dos and don'ts for successful adult outings.

Dos

- **Do prepare like a Crescent.** Stock up that diaper bag with snacks, toys, and anything else you'll need to keep your kid comfortable and entertained while you run your errands. And don't even think about leaving your house without a sippy cup!

- **Do set expectations like a Constellation.** You're probably thinking, *Do I have to tell my kid to use their inside voice every single time we leave the house?* Yes, you really do. Before you walk into any adult environment, talk about what's allowed and what's not. Don't expect your kids to naturally pick up on these things. You've got to spell it out for them every time.

✎ **Do plan your escape like a Fireball.** If you know you're heading into a long religious service, wedding ceremony, or other event geared entirely toward adults, find a seat near the exit. Don't sit in the middle of a long row! Make it easy to slip away quickly and quietly.

Don'ts

✎ **Don't rely on screens.** If you give your kid your phone every time you need them to behave, you're doing them a *huge* disservice. How are they supposed to learn to wait patiently in line at the post office if you never teach them how to do it? Is it fun? No. Is it exciting? Not really. But kids *can* learn to be bored and patient. It's good for them. We promise. (PS, this needs to be said: You shouldn't be playing on your phone and ignoring your kids either. Intermittently checking it is okay. Staring at your screen isn't.)

✎ **Don't let your kids take over the show.** If you're bringing kids to a place of business, a place of worship, a fancy restaurant, or a wedding, don't let them break into song or rehearse their ballet routine. Sure, they're adorable, but this isn't about them. Sometimes kids really do need to be seen and not heard too much.

✎ **Don't freak out.** If things don't go as planned, don't be that crazy person screaming at their kids, whacking their little behinds, or dragging them around by the arm because they're acting like kids. Set expectations *knowing* that your kids won't always live up to them. And when they don't—when things go terribly wrong—take a breath, leave, and try again another time.

3 Behaviors to Prioritize

When your kids are in their toddler and preschool years, that's the perfect time to teach them what kind of behavior adults expect in most public spaces. Here are the big three:

1. **Use your inside voice.** Maybe you've noticed, but kids are *loud*. Speak at a volume you want them to imitate. Are you in church where you whisper, and only if you really have to? Or are you at the grocery store where an excited "Woohoo!! Check out this deal on cupcakes!" is A-OK?

2. **Control your body.** To kids, everything is a playground. The tables at restaurants are for hiding under. The bottom rails of the shopping cart are for joy rides. And the cushioned benches in the pediatrician's office are obviously trampolines. Of course, kids have lots of energy, but helping them expend that energy before you have to enter a quiet environment is one of the best strategies for success in quiet public spaces.

3. **Stay with me.** Tell your kids that they're not allowed to run away from you. A) It's not safe. B) It's easier to manage children who are within arm's length and speaking distance from you.

Places Young Kids Don't Belong

- Funerals
- Bridal showers, baby showers, weddings, and Bar/Bat Mitzvahs, unless you have explicit permission from the guest of honor
- Your pap smear
- Movies and performances for adults
- Your two-hour hair appointment

Embarrassing Questions Your Kid Will Ask

- Why does that lady have such a big heinie?
- What's that chair she's pushing herself around in, and why are her legs so small?
- Is that a man or a lady?
- What happened to that guy's hair?
- Why does that old lady have a mustache?
- Why is that adult as small as a kid?
- Why is that person's skin so black/white/freckled/spotted?
- Why does that person stink?

PREVENTION

An excellent way to prevent many of these questions is to educate your child about diversity and celebrate it early on through books, media, and conversation. Take a look at your child's books and the shows and movies they watch. Do they include people of various cultures, races, ethnicities, religions, financial means, and physical abilities? Encourage conversations that celebrate differences while you're at home and you'll probably field fewer questions in public. You'll also be raising a kind child who embraces differences and accepts others for who they are. Awesome, right?

DAMAGE CONTROL

So what if you're doing your damnedest to talk to your kids honestly about all the different ways of being in the world, and it's still Twenty Questions each and every time you encounter something new?

You can answer most questions factually: "Bodies come in all different shapes and sizes, but it's not polite to talk about other people's bodies." Or just simply, "Yes, some men wear dresses." "Some people use wheelchairs." "Some people have dark skin, some people have light skin."

Other times, you've just got to tell your kid to zip it until you can talk in private. Whisper, "Let's talk more about that later." Then, when later comes, talk about whatever your kid saw and answer their questions with honesty and sensitivity, so you won't have a repeat of that situation. This is an awesome opportunity to show your child how to express empathy in tough situations.

Personal Space

Most adults get it: don't touch other people without explicit permission. But once in a while, someone either forgets the rules or hasn't learned them yet. This can really throw new parents off, so keep a close eye on your curious little one and remind them not to lean over into someone else's stroller to kiss their baby's cheeks. Sure, it may be very sweet to you, but to that new parent, your little angel is just a germ factory!

And what if you're on the receiving end of too much touching? How do you tell someone to back off? Depends on how well they can read your cues.

1. Give them the "teacher look." It says, *Oh, I know I didn't just see you do that!* Sometimes just glaring at someone is enough to get them to back off.

2. Step away. Move your body (or your child's body) out of reach.

3. Use a sign. No, seriously. Take advantage of those "Please don't touch the baby tags" parents hang on car seats.

4. Say something. Here's a good start: "Sweetie, please don't touch the baby. I want him to stay healthy, and the more people touch him, the more likely he is to get sick." Firm but kind.

Real-Life Sticky Social Situation:
Public Temper Tantrums

I was in Target with my two kids this weekend when my three-year-old had a huge temper tantrum. We were in the store making returns when we passed by the toy aisles. I remembered we needed a gift for a birthday party, and I thought we could just pop over really quick to find something, but that turned into a screaming fit of "Why can't I get a toy, too?" It was so embarrassing! I'm talking on the floor, kicking, shouting—the works. I did my best, but it was almost impossible to hold a flailing child while pushing a cart with a baby in it. I was completely torn about whether to let him scream it out right there on the floor, try to make my way to the cashier, or just abandon the cart full of stuff I actually needed. What's the best way to handle a temper tantrum in a store?

As awful as it is to manage a public temper tantrum, running out of Target empty-handed is not the answer. You worked hard to get those kids to the store and pick out the things you needed. Plus, if you literally drop everything when your kid has a fit, he'll learn something really important: "If I don't feel like being here, I can just scream and kick and thrash around, and then we'll leave instantly." *Poof!*

No, it's better to stay right there in the toy aisle, where people are completely accustomed to hearing kids scream, and work it out. There's no need to be mortified. Target is as kid-friendly a public setting as you're going to get! And no one can fault a mother with a full cart for trying to calm a screaming child so she can pay and get out!

Next time, don't feel badly about sitting down on the floor right there next to your big kid. Empathize first. Tell him you know how sad he is that he can't pick out a toy today. There are so many great toys! It's totally normal for a three-year-old to freak out about this, especially when they're tired. Let him know you're close, and ask if he wants a hug. When the screaming subsides, give him options: "Would you like me to carry you to the front of the store to check out, would you like to walk, or would you like to ride on the cart?" Give him some control over what happens next.

If the tantrum is going on for a lot longer than you're comfortable with, or past five minutes, consider taking your child out of the store to let him calm down outside. You'll feel less pressure to keep him quiet, and he may even calm down faster in the fresh air. When you're both ready, you can either return to your shopping or go home.

As for worrying about what everyone else thinks while your kid is freaking out, it's time to put on your Crescent hat and forget about them. It's important for other adults to see that you *know* your kid isn't behaving well and you're trying to do something about it. So if you've chosen to sit right there with him, speaking calmly, you're already doing everything you can. Carry on with confidence!

Prevent the Meltdown before It Even Starts

1. Avoid the toy aisle unless you really need something.
2. If you're going into the land of toys, set expectations with your child. "We're going to pick out a toy for David's birthday. Do you want to help me? We're not going to pick out anything for you today, because it's David's birthday." Make sure your child hears you. If they're old enough, have them repeat what you just said.
3. Let your child hold the chosen toy all the way through the store.
4. If they find something they love, offer to take a picture of it with your phone so you can remember it for another time.
5. Finally, if your child can handle it, let him look and touch the toy display for a few minutes. Give him a two-minute warning, and then leave.

Eating at Restaurants

Going to restaurants with young children is like yoga: it's a practice. It takes time to master the art of eating out with kids. Start with quick, low-key restaurants, practice your skills, and work your way up. Within a few years, your kids *will* be able to sit through a ninety-minute restaurant experience at one of those ritzy places.

Before you enter the restaurant, ask yourself, *Do I have ...*

- Crayons? You'd be surprised which restaurants don't offer them.
- A couple of quiet toys for infants and toddlers? Preferably things that won't roll off the table.
- The menu? Bring it up on your phone if you can, so you'll be ready to order as soon as you're seated.

Next up, pre-emptive conversations are *always* an etiquette do, even with toddlers! Focus on three big rules:

1. Use "walking feet" (no running)
2. Use inside voices
3. Stay in your seat

Set expectations. If your child can't follow these three rules, you'll have to leave. Eating out is a privilege!

One little white lie we've both used? "Your food won't come unless you're sitting quietly." Works every time!

SUPER IMPORTANT RESTAURANT SECRET!!

Always, always ask for your child's food to be brought out *with* the adult food. Often, servers will bring kid food first, thinking that they're doing you a favor. They're not! Kids will be done and ready to leave before you've even taken a bite.

EVIE'S Rant on Every Server's Worst Nightmare

Years ago, when I was waitressing, one of the groups I hated seeing in my section was families with little kids. They took forever to order, they had a thousand questions, they made special requests for extra forks and napkins and refills, and they always, *always* left a huge mess. No, thank you!

Now, when we eat out as a family, I try to remember how much I despised mopping some messy toddler's milk off the floor only to discover that their parents had been cheap with my tip. If your family is extra sloppy or extra needy, and your server meets those demands with a smile, remember to tip them well as a way of saying thank you!

SARAH'S Rant on Using Screens in Restaurants

Here's an unpopular opinion: parents shouldn't bring tablets to restaurants. Will it make your life easier to set your kid up with a screen in the moment? Absolutely. Parents can give a one-year-old a phone while waiting for food and then, magically, there's peace at the table.

But it's merely a band-aid. You think you've won, but you haven't. You've actually made things a thousand times harder on yourself, and you've set your child up for lots of restaurant drama in the future. Does that sound melodramatic? It really isn't.

In the short term, the next time you go to a restaurant, your baby will cry because they know what they want: that screen. You'll want to say no, and you might be able to...if you've only used a screen once or twice. But if you've created a habit, it'll be next to impossible to stop it. If you don't give your child the screen, you'll likely face a public, epic meltdown. Before you know it, that screen is a must-have when you go out to eat.

Is this really that big a deal in the long term? Yes!

1. Restaurants offer so many opportunities to teach social skills, like conversation, patience, awareness of surroundings, and body control in their seats. Your child will watch you order food. They'll engage in conversation, or maybe even take a break and go outside with you for a moment. If they have a screen, they'll miss out on all of that. They won't even be able to observe it, as their eyes will be locked onto their entertainment.

2. The ritual of eating as a family and learning the social skills around a table are important to many families. If this is a priority to you, you can start teaching these skills early! Go to family-friendly restaurants at first, start small, and set age-appropriate expectations.

Honestly, many of those early outings won't be pleasant—your child may be bored, hungry, or impatient. But the pay-off is huge! By allowing your child to feel these uncomfortable feelings, they learn about their environment *and* gain patience. It's okay for your toddler to be unhappy and uncomfortable—this is how they learn coping skills. As they get older and are faced with other "boring" environments (like doctor's waiting rooms), they'll be ready to handle them with a good attitude and strategies for entertaining themselves. See? Hard in the moment, but massive pay-off down the road!

And while we're at it, you should put away your phone, too. Set a good example.

Traveling

"Traveling with three- and four-year-old boys is like transferring serial killers from a prison. You have to be constantly aware."
—**Jim Gaffigan,** comedian and father of five

PARENTING POP QUIZ

You're on an airplane by yourself with your six-month-old and preschooler. Your big kid has to pee and you're 30,000 feet in the air. What do you do?

A. Ask them if it's *really* an emergency. Can they hold it for just forty-five minutes longer?

B. Pick up your baby and bring both kids to the restroom. Struggle through balancing your baby in your arms and convincing your preschooler they won't fall into the sky if they pee in the scary metal potty.

C. Ask a flight attendant to hold your baby while you take your big kid to the bathroom and hope your baby doesn't scream the whole time.

D. Look for another parent who might give you a hand.

Keep reading for the correct answer!

TRAVEL DOS

✐ Bring *way* more of everything than you think you need. Do you normally carry one spare outfit? Bring two or three. Usually have three diapers on-hand? Bring ten! Seriously, what would you do if you ran out of diapers?

- Pack an extra shirt for yourself. A rolled-up t-shirt will take up practically no space at all, but you'll be so glad to have it when your kid's vomit is running down your back!

- Wear slip-on shoes, so you don't have to sit down to tie your laces after the security check while your kid totters away.

- Ditch the diaper bag *and* your purse, and pack everything into a backpack instead. This way, you'll have your hands free for lifting kids, pushing strollers, or holding little hands.

- Take your travel game to the next level with babywearing. Your baby will be happy being close to you (read: less screaming). Fellow travelers will thank you for not trying to push your bulky stroller through the crowds, and you won't have to figure out how to collapse your stroller and push it through the X-ray machine while holding a baby.

TRAVEL DON'TS

- Don't let your kid kick the seat in front of them. Surely, it's happened to you. It sucks. And it gives people the impression that: 1) you're not paying any attention to what your kid's up to, 2) you don't care, or 3) you *do* care, but you can't control your kid. All bad options.

- Don't get lost in your own little world. Travelers in airports, train stations, bus depots, and rest stops want to go, go, go! People get super annoyed when families with young kids stop the flow of traffic in a crowded terminal. Be a Constellation and ask yourself, *Are we in the way?*

✎ Don't use "outside voices" in very "inside" environments. Before you even board that plane, train, or bus, remind your kids about keeping their voices down. Talk about how their voices will sound so much louder to everyone because you'll all be together in a tight space. Once you're on board, keep talking in your most exaggerated whisper as a reminder.

✎ Don't let your child bring their own suitcase. It's hard enough to herd kids through terminals during travel. Giving them luggage just means they'll be that much slower, more distracted, and in the way of others. Pack a backpack for your big kid instead.

CONSTELLATION ANXIETY DURING TRAVEL

Being on the road with young kids can be especially stressful for Constellations, who take normal travel stress and add a heaping dose of anxiety over how their kids are annoying others. They know being out of their routine makes kids *and* adults cranky, unpredictable, and quick to anger. Travel becomes an intense juggling act of what will keep both their kids and everyone else happy.

Guess who ends up completely burned out in this equation? The Constellation parent! If this sounds like you, we're giving you permission to let go of the following travel stresses:

✎ **Crying during takeoff and landing.** Babies and toddlers often cry because of the change in air pressure. Do what you can to give your kid a drink, a lollipop, or a piece of gum, but don't freak out if they're fussy. As long as you look like you're trying to deal with the crying, people will cut you some slack.

✎ **Letting little ones get up to stretch their legs.** If the aisles aren't overcrowded with people or food carts, and the fasten seat belt light is off, your kid is free to roam as long as you're with them, they're not being loud, and they're not touching everyone along the way.

✎ **Taking too long in the airport "family" restroom.** No one except families with young kids should be using this bathroom, and they're the ones who will understand why your two-year-old needs fifteen minutes in the bathroom!

DID YOU ACE THE QUIZ?

So what do you do when you're traveling solo with a baby and a big kid who's just told you they need to use the potty? First, you think, *Didn't I beg you to do that* before *we got on the plane?!* Then, you consider your options:

Option #1: Did you remember your baby carrier? Pop your baby back in there and bring them with you (**modified quiz answer B**).

Option #2: Scan the plane for another mom or dad (**quiz answer D**). Not a parent with babies, but someone with big kids and screens in front of them. Head over with both your kids so they see exactly what you're dealing with and ask if they'd hold your baby so you can hit the bathroom. It's not like they could steal your baby or do something terrible in view of all those other passengers, right?

Option #3: Find a friendly flight attendant and beg them to help (**quiz answer C**). Is it possible they'll say no? Uh-huh. There isn't any rule that says they *have to* hold your baby. That's why this is option #3.

Tools to Keep Kids Happy, So You and Others Can Have a Pleasant Trip

- Dollar store coloring books
- Triangular crayons or washable markers
- Reusable stickers, sticker activity books
- Magnetic playsets (They're a thing. Look them up.)
- Snacks. Lots of snacks.
- Bottle of water
- Lollipops or gum for popping ears and motion sickness
- Change of clothes, including socks and underwear
- Tablet loaded with their favorite shows, movies, and apps, *plus* headphones (so everyone doesn't have to be subjected to it)

PUBLIC PARENTING AURORAS AND TWILIGHTS

How is your Parenting Perspective helping you shine or holding you back when you're parenting in public?

Crescent

When it comes to taking your kids out in public, you're well-attuned to their needs and you focus on them. You plan playdates around your little one's nap schedule so they'll be at their best. Your vehicle and diaper bag are stocked with extra outfits, snacks, and clean toys. When you run errands, you consider what's going to entertain your child and what's going to overstimulate them.

Watch out for: Opportunities to be flexible. Of course, your child is your first priority, but there are times when it's okay for your child's needs to take a back seat. Your best friend is hosting a birthday party that'll keep your little one out later than you'd like? Attend anyway. Maybe you'll decide to not bring your kid's favorite snack to the party and let them eat whatever's there.

Fireball

Your parenting motto is, "Do your best and don't worry about the rest." You don't freak out about potty-training accidents or public tantrums. You know that trying to please everyone in a public setting *and* meeting your child's every need is a recipe for serious burnout, so you take another approach by asking the question, *What works for me?* That may mean sitting back on a park bench while your kid navigates playground politics, or letting your child play with the (previously organized) sugar packets on the restaurant table so you can eat in peace.

Watch out for: Taking the easy way out and overlooking the effects. There's real power in not worrying too much about everyone else's impression of you. Just don't go *too* far in that direction. So you let your kid play with the sugar packets? No problem! Just make sure you put them away and don't leave the job to the poor server. Keep an eye out for circumstances that might make your life easier, but someone else's life harder. Years ago, as a new mom, someone told Evie, "Being a parent isn't an excuse for bad manners." And it's so true. Make sure your Fireball instincts align with your character and values.

Constellation

You know that taking kids out into the world is a great big balancing act, and you and your child are just two actors on the public stage—no more important than any other. You take time to talk to your kids about what is kind and considerate when you're out in public. You teach them to hold doors and say "please" and "thank you." And you take great pride when other people notice your well-behaved little ones.

Watch out for: Worrying too much. Parenting in public can be a real struggle for Constellations like you who are anxious about inconveniencing people and getting dirty looks. Kids can be loud and wild and totally unpredictable, which can make you feel out of control. You know how to behave, but you can't always get your kids to! Cut yourself a break. Nearly all adults get that kids will be kids every now and then. It's not a reflection of your parenting.

CHAPTER 3

Communicating: It's like Dating All Over Again

SARAH'S Story on Meeting her Best Friend

It was only six thirty in the evening. The chair creaked as it tilted back and forth. I stared out the window at the energetic summer air and rocked my toddler slowly. His eyes whispered and closed, and I held him longer than he needed it. It had only been a few weeks since we'd arrived in our new city. It had only been a few days since I'd dropped my husband off at the airport for his ten-month deployment to the Middle East. The days were long, beautiful, and hard. I looked for a routine in the mundane. Gym, grocery shopping, mommy-and-me gymnastics. I could get through the day, but at night, as the sun set, the panic set in. Who would I call if something happened? Who could I call to hang out with at the playground? How would I make friends here? Where would I even find these friends?

I'd seen her a few times, putting away groceries, eating dinner with her husband on our adjoining balconies. She had a toddler, too. And that's all I knew about my next-door neighbor. So the next day, after I prepared my son to swim in the neighborhood pool, I hoisted my pool bag over my shoulder and my toddler onto my hip and walked the five feet to her door.

"Hi! I'm Sarah and this is my son. We just moved here a few weeks ago. I noticed you have a baby around his age. We're on our way to the pool. Want to join us?"

"Hi! I'm Evie. Actually, yes, we'd love to! I'll meet you there in ten minutes!"

And that was the day I met my best friend.

MAKING FRIENDS IS MORE IMPORTANT THAN EVER

Friends make us happier, fulfill our social needs, and give us a support system as we struggle through the daily, exhaustive impossibilities of early parenting. When Evie and I first met, we took a walk around the neighborhood every day. We'd meet after breakfast, in yoga pants and sunglasses, and walk and talk for almost an hour, pushing strollers. Everything was fair game, from the daily sleep training struggles to the ever-present feeling of being lost and undervalued as a brand-new stay-at-home mom.

Stay-at-home parents can go days without speaking to another adult. Isolation and loneliness can contribute to anxiety, depression, and low self-confidence. Of course, working parents face their own obstacles. They often go from work, to mom/dad, then back to work, and may not have any chance for social relaxation. Whereas stay-at-home parents can be isolated and lonely, working parents can be inundated with stimulation that isn't necessarily the kind they need to recharge.

If you're an extrovert and you gain energy from people around you, making friends is probably at the top of your priority list. If you're an introvert, maybe that desire for being out with a bunch of parents at a playgroup is low, but you still long for a friend or two who just "gets you." Most of us are desperate for a community—a safe place to go where we can be ourselves—whether that's a couple of people or a huge group. According to the Mayo Clinic, a friendship circle helps to increase your sense of belonging, boosts happiness, reduces stress, improves self-confidence, and can even reduce your risk for health problems.[20] Subconsciously we know this, and so we crave community.

WHAT DOES COMMUNICATION HAVE TO DO WITH ETIQUETTE?

Communication and strong relationships go hand in hand. You can't have friendships or strong family ties without communication, and you can't have good communication without good etiquette. Excellent communicators make friends wherever they go. They're good listeners, good observers, and have a knack for "reading the room" and making the right social choices.

Even though many of us have excellent communication skills before we become parents, they don't necessarily translate well into the next phase of life, when our time and bandwidth are largely monopolized by our kids. Our focus and attention change, our interests and availability change, and our relationships change. We don't relate to any of our existing friends, family, or acquaintances in quite the same way. Many of us build new social circles to connect with people who are beginning their parenting journeys at the same time as we are.

Making friends, making plans with friends, and not scaring off friends is all brand-new again. *How do I pick up a new friend at the playground while also chasing my toddler around? Would it be totally gross to tell a new mom friend my birth story? Is it totally self-centered of me to call my friend during her toddler's naptime?* The game has changed, and so have the rules.

Then, of course, there are new relationships in your life that require a whole new level of tactfulness. How do you keep relationships with babysitters, nannies, and caregivers healthy when you need to be working as partners, but don't always see eye to eye? Do you know how to have that tough chat when you need to say, "I don't like the way you do this"? How do you know if you're over-managing your child's babysitter?

Lastly, you have to recalibrate your family relationships to establish new boundaries and expectations. How do you tell your mother-in-law to stop feeding your toddler sugary treats? Can you skip that thank-you note to your parents for your toddler's birthday present?

There are so many nuances of communication that become more complicated when you're a parent!

BEYOND THE SMALL TALK

Now that you know how important your friendships are in your parenting journey, let's talk about how to identify and communicate your needs to curate that perfect social network. First of all, you may be a parent 24/7, but you are still *you*. You still have likes, dislikes, and dreams, and talking about those with someone who really gets you is fulfilling. It's not fulfilling to have an "I'm more tired than you are" conversation about sleep training every time you hang out. While that may be cathartic at times, it's not going to help grow a friendship. It'll keep you as acquaintances at best, and you'll quickly outgrow each other.

So, next time you're scanning the room at a playdate, you need to know who to zone in on. Who is like you? Who could be the Sarah to your Evie? Take a look at the following statement and reorder the list based on your priorities.

When making new friends, I look for...

1. Kid connection
2. Adult connection
3. Similar parenting styles
4. Similar schedules
5. Proximity

Constellations prioritize 1, 4, and 5: Constellations want their friendships to feel easy. You don't ever want to feel like a burden to your friend, so you prioritize similar schedules and proximity. You don't want to have to worry about asking friends to rearrange their days to suit you. Plus, if your kids get along, your visits can be conflict-free.

Crescents prioritize 3 and 4: Crescents look for symbiotic philosophies. You like to know that the person you're spending time with is going to understand and validate your decisions, even if at times you're overprotective. And because you prioritize your child's needs, finding a friend whose schedule aligns with yours is a must.

Fireballs prioritize 2, 4, and 5: Fireballs look for adult connections, plus convenience in scheduling and location. These relationships aren't all about the kids—they may not involve the kids at all. They're about leaving space for a bond *outside* of parenting, like a wine date after bedtime at that hot new spot in your neighborhood.

***

OK, you're at a playdate with lots of other parents, hoping to leave with a few new phone numbers. How do you use that time efficiently, so you have the biggest chance of walking away with a new friend?

Round One: Always start with easy questions to collect some data. "How many kids do you have?" "Do you work outside the home?" "What do you like to do for fun?"

If you find out that your new acquaintance has four kids, and you've just given birth for the first time, you may have a hard time finding common ground (not that it's impossible, they just may not be who you need at this stage in your life). If this person's always at work during the week and you work weekends, unfortunately, that friendship will never have time to get off the ground. Find some common data points. Evie and Sarah both had one-year-olds, husbands who worked a lot, and had both been teachers before becoming moms. A trifecta!

Round Two: If Round One is successful, think back to your top priorities from the list above and listen carefully to what your new acquaintance is saying. Do they talk almost exclusively about their child and draw a total blank when you ask about their interests? Or do they keep bringing the conversation back to topics totally unrelated to the kids? Also, how do they interact with their child? Are they very hands-on and attentive or are they more laid-back, sitting on the sidelines? Does that matter to you?

If you ask the right questions and listen carefully, you'll soon know whether this person is looking for a playground buddy, a Saturday girls' night date, or neither because their social circle is full. If you made it past Round One and your new friend has your same priorities, you may be on your way to an actual friendship! Be sure to at least get a phone number before you part ways, so this budding connection can keep growing.

Can You Become Friends with Someone Who Doesn't Share Your Parenting Perspective?

The short answer is yes, but only if you can be flexible and a little open-minded.

SARAH'S Story on Becoming Friends with a Fireball

A few years ago, after yet another move, I met a woman at a moms' group playdate. She was smart, funny, and stylish. However, our kids weren't quite the same age. I was an uber-Crescent, so I couldn't fathom having a friend who didn't have kids the exact same age. What would we even do together? Up until I met her, all my friend time was "kid time" disguised as quality time for the grownups.

She sent me a text asking if I wanted to meet her at the YMCA for a chat and leave the kids in the free babysitting they offered. I was stunned. She wanted to meet without the kids? That was the first time anyone had ever suggested that to me. But the Y was somewhere I went all the time anyway, so I agreed.

We were alike in so many ways, as we'd discovered the first time we met, and I wanted to spend more time with her. But in her invitation to meet sans kids, I realized our Parenting Perspectives didn't match. She was a comfortable Fireball. She knew something I didn't at the time, which was that it's important to put yourself first—to have friendships that are not kid-centric. She pushed me on that boundary, and because I was so excited to get to know her, I was willing to try something new. Our friendship grew over time, and we had lots of meaningful and enjoyable conversations. We actually made that YMCA chat date a weekly thing, and it went on for over a year until she moved away. It became one of my favorite parts of the week.

Sarah's Super Strategies for Finding Friends

As a Navy wife of over ten years, I've had to start over many times in new places. I know that in order to make friends, I have to put myself out there. It's scary to have "first date" after "first date" with a bunch of new people, hoping you'll connect, but that's how it works. Really, as a Crescent, I'm protecting myself and my kids by strengthening our social network. I know how depressed and anxious I can get if I don't have geographically close friendships.

So from the moment we arrive, I start actively searching. Being alone isn't an option for me—it will end with me swirling around in my head way too much. We aren't always in one place for a long time either, so I have to cut through "small-talk acquaintances" and look for real friends right away, which means I've gotten really good at it over the years. I'm going to share my *best* friend-making secrets with you:

1. **Be comfortable with discomfort.** You may get asked to join in on a trip to a farm that's thirty minutes away, or asked to have lunch at a trendy, not-so-kid-friendly coffee shop. Go, even if you'd never participate in that activity otherwise. If it's a total disaster, you can leave early. But give it a try first.

2. **Find the people.** One of my best tricks? Go for a walk around the neighborhood as the buses arrive in the afternoon and make a point of introducing yourself to the other parents you see.

3. **Give yourself a year.** The first people you

socialize with aren't usually the ones who become your besties. However, they may be the gateway to your best friend. Those first relationships help you get a hand on the culture and environment around you, so you need these early connections to learn the lay of the land.

HOW NOT TO SCARE OFF YOUR NEW FRIENDS

Honestly, there aren't too many things you wouldn't share with your bestie or close friend. With new friendships, though, you'll want to tread carefully on those classic, must-avoid topics, like politics, finances, sex, and religion. But that doesn't mean you can't dish! New mom friends love to share their birth stories, with all the gory details. If that's the way the conversation is going and you want to share, jump in!

New parents also love to touch on topics like how tired they are and how they aren't getting enough help from their partners. That's totally fine and actually very cathartic. But you may want to steer clear of big family drama or personal financial issues right away. You don't want to bring down the whole room with stuff that you're not sure anyone else can relate to. As your relationships grow, take time on these tough topics that reveal who you are and what you believe.

Don't Be That Parent

Even though it seems like most topics are ok to bring up, there are absolutely some that'll send your new friends running off the playground. Here's who *not* to be. We know there's someone like this in your playgroup!

- **The One-Upper:** If your friend just told you how hard it is to be a parent of one, please don't start your next breath with, "Wait until you have three!" They may never have three kids. This is their current reality. Leave them alone.

- **The Oversharer:** No one needs to know your favorite sex position. They just don't.

- **The Bragger:** Everyone thinks their kid is the best. Give your kid a compliment and move on.

- **The Diagnoser:** Even if you're a board-certified child psychologist, leave categorizing unusual behavior to someone else of the parent's choosing.

- **The Self-Loather:** Don't speak poorly about yourself. Self-deprecating topics force other parents to either agree or disagree with you, and both are awful positions to be in! Unless you're talking to your best friend, it's not another parent's job to convince you that your child *isn't* being bratty, or that you really *don't* need to lose those last ten pounds of baby weight. These conversations make everyone uncomfortable.

- **The Inappropriate Inquisitor:** These people sure can ask some cringeworthy questions. Some friendly advice:

  - Don't ask a woman if she's finished having babies.
  - Don't ask if—or even imply that—a mother of multiples used IVF to conceive.
  - Don't ask insensitive questions of adoptive families, like...

- Someone's reason for adopting, or whether they have any of their "own" children.

- Details about the adoption process ("Where did you get that baby?" "How much does adoption cost?").

- Information about a child's biological parents or background. That's private. If you want to adopt as well, you can respectfully ask an adoptive parent (who's already your friend) if they'd be willing to share their story privately so you can learn from their experience.

HANDLING ANNOYING ADVICE AND COMMENTS

You've got a baby and everyone's got an opinion. So what do you say when people in your life feel like they know way more than you do?

- Accept friendly suggestions (ahem, criticism) with a quick, "I'll have to think about that."

- If they keep pushing their opinions on you, we like, "Thanks. That may work for you, but it's not really our thing." The less you engage, the less they'll have to say! One-sided conversations are no fun.

The Perfect Comeback

But what about when someone's being rude? Maybe they have good intentions, or maybe they're being passive-aggressive. Either way, you want to: 1) identify their intention, and 2) have the perfect response ready, so you won't walk away thinking, *I should have said something better!*

We present to you The Perfect Comeback Chart, for finding just the right thing to say in an uncomfortable or insensitive situation.

If Someone Says...	They Probably Mean...	So You Can Say...	Ick Factor (1–10)
You look tired!	You look awful!	If you're not tired, say, "Do I?" If you are tired, say, "Yes, I've been up a lot recently with the baby. We've had a tough week."	**8–10** It depends on who it's coming from. What's the point of this statement? To make you feel bad about yourself? The only times that may not be the case are if it's coming from someone who really loves you, or from someone at work. Your mom or best friend might be expressing genuine concern. A colleague might be telling you to put a little more effort into your professional appearance. Still yucky, but possibly constructive.
Wow, you have your hands full!	Your life looks like a hot mess!	Smile and say, "We're good right now!"	**2–3** If this comment is said in solidarity by a parent whose been in a similar situation. However, if someone's trying to make you feel bad for wrangling your brood in public, it's a higher ick factor!

Way to go, Dad! I'm so impressed that you're out with the kids by yourself. You're Dad of the Year!	How are you possibly out in public with your kids... without your wife?!	"Thanks! I've got this!" or, "We have a great time together! I love my time with the kids!"	10 This is gross. Why do people automatically assume that dads can't parent? Why can't they just say, "Your kids are so cute"?
Oh, you're bottle feeding?	Why aren't you breast-feeding?	"Yes."	10 Feed your baby. It's no one's business how you do that.
Wow, you have triplets? How did that happen?	Did you have IVF?	People know how babies are made, so just smile and say, "I had three babies!" That should shut them up.	6–8 Some people are just trying to find something to say and don't mean any harm—they get a pass. But those looking for dirt on exactly how those babies ended up in the uterus are totally icky.
Where is your child from?	Your child is obviously not of the same race as you, so are they adopted? Is your partner a different race or culture than you?	If you feel comfortable disclosing your child's race or culture, you can answer honestly. If the child is adopted, say, "He is adopted. His mother is Mexican."	7–8 People are fascinated by mixed-race families and adoptions, and that's often why they ask. Sometimes they're just trying to start a conversation. If they keep prying, you might educate them on the inappropriateness of this question.

If Someone Says...	They Probably Mean...	So You Can Say...	Ick Factor (1–10)
Wow, you have three boys/girls? Aren't you just dying for a little princess/man?	You must be devastated since you only have children of one gender.	"We're very happy with our family!"	About a 6 This one is bad, but much worse if the children are listening!
Are you having twins?	You're huge!	"Nope! Not as far as I know!"	9 or 10 Super ick. The only appropriate thing to say to a pregnant woman is, "You're beautiful!"
Isn't your kid too old for that?!	What's wrong with your child? Why can't you stop that behavior?	Smile. If you find you can't contain yourself, you can say, "He's okay. He'll calm down soon." You don't owe it to anyone to disclose a diagnosis, a trigger, or any of your own private business.	10! This is an awful thing to say! A comment like this doesn't take into consideration that some children are neurodiverse and can be triggered by public environments. These comments are insensitive and rude!

CAN MOMS AND DADS BE FRIENDS?

There he is each Friday at the parent/child gymnastics class. He comes in carrying an infant car seat with a baby girl nestled inside, his two-year-old son trailing right behind. Out comes the baby carrier, and he clicks his infant in as he gets his toddler ready to go into the gym. He's just like all the moms arriving to take the class. He plays with his son, runs off to change a diaper, and gets into some fun chats with the other parents about sleep training and wonder weeks. But when a few of the moms decide to grab a quick coffee on the way home, they scurry off without inviting him. Everyone can see this dad could use some friends, but no one invites him to things. Why? Because he's a dad.

Parenting little ones is lonely and exhausting. Not including dads just because of the misguided idea that women and men can't be friends is not cool. The thing is, dads are everywhere now. Gone are the days when most, if not all, women were the primary caregivers. Now more than ever, there are two working parents, and dads share in many of the caregiving responsibilities. According to the Pew Research Center, by 2016, dads made up 17 percent of all stay-at-home parents, up from 4 percent in 1989.[21] That's a huge jump!

That statistic doesn't even include the dads who share drop-off/pick-up and general school/kid responsibilities. "In 2016, fathers reported spending an average of eight hours a week on childcare—about triple the time they provided in 1965."[22] Unfortunately, many parenting groups are still female-centered, and aren't open-minded about including dads or non-traditional families. Being a parent—mom or dad—can be isolating. Including that dad in a "moms" group, or inviting him and his children to the next park playdate is kind. Plus, you never know if you might totally hit it off and build a friendship with someone who brings a different flavor to your life.

FRIENDS WITHOUT KIDS

Most of us have one or two friends who don't have kids. Does that mean those friendships are doomed? Absolutely not! This is when you've got to tap into that Fireball part of yourself! Don't say goodbye to those friendships just because you have kids and they don't. Talk to that friend on the phone, maybe even steal a weekend away—but do your best to keep them in your life.

Be patient with these friendships, especially if you just became a parent. There will be transition time, and you'll both need to adjust your expectations. Your friend may not call when your little bundle first arrives, and that may frustrate the hell out of you. But maybe you weren't the most present for them in the last nine months either. Celebrate the friendship for what it is. They may be right there with you when you take the kids to the zoo, or they may be the kind of friend who knocks on the door after bedtime for a glass of wine. Both sound great, right?

Fireballs are probably the best at maintaining pre-parenting friendships, so the rest of us need to take a page from their self-care notebook. Remember that pyramid? Self-care is at the foundation for a reason. Fireballs will find time to meet their college buddies for a drink on a Friday night, or brunch on a Sunday morning. If those friends make you feel like "the real you," or make you feel young and carefree, make time for them. You might not have the ability to sneak away for a big getaway right now, but keep up with them on social media so that, when you're ready, they won't think you fell off the face of the earth.

STAYING IN TOUCH

Parenting Pop Quiz

You've met your perfect match. You're *so* excited. This could be the friendship you've been hoping for. Throwing caution to the wind, you decide to text your new friend to make plans, even though you got together just yesterday.

> Hey! It's Jen...Ryan's mom. So fun to meet you yesterday! Hope this isn't too early, but wondering if there's any chance you're free today to play? We're around most of the day.

You watch for a response, but nothing comes. You find yourself picking up your phone every few minutes.

A few hours later, a quick message appears.

> Hey Jen! Sorry—just saw this! We're really busy today. Maybe some other time soon though!

What do you do?

    A.   Text her again the next day, asking her to make

plans. If she doesn't respond, then maybe it
wasn't meant to be.

B. Text her asking, "Did I do something wrong?"
You really thought the two of you had made
a connection.

C. Let her make the next move.

D. Realize this probably wasn't meant to be and
move on.

Keep reading for the correct answer!

Texting Tips

Texting is the best way to get in touch with a
quick, "Hello, how are you?" or a question with a
straightforward answer. If you've got a hysterical (but
lengthy) story to share, leave an audio message (love
that feature!), or save it for your next face-to-face chat.
If you need someone to listen to you complain about
the absolute horror that is potty-training, pick up the
phone. Texting is great, but it doesn't take the place of
someone hearing your voice, or you hearing theirs.

✎ Don't forget to include your name if you're
texting someone for the first time. "Hey—loved
meeting you!" takes on a totally different tone if
the recipient has no idea who you are or where
you met!

✎ Don't have a one-sided chat, as in, don't send
a stream of ten messages to their zero! If they
haven't responded to the first two, take a breath
and wait.

✎ Don't freak out if you don't hear back right away.
It's probably not that your friend didn't see
your message, or didn't think it was important.

They've just got other stuff going on. Waiting twenty-four hours is a good rule—check back in then.

✎ Do take time to respond. Do you have to respond to a text right away? No way! Think about what you want to say and respond when you're ready. As long as you don't wait more than about a day, you're good!

✎ Guess what? None of these rules apply to your bestie. If they haven't responded within their normal limits, give them a call! Don't be afraid of the phone. It still works.

EVIE'S Confession on Being a Terrible Texter

I'm just going to admit it: I'm terrible about texting. I have this habit of seeing a text come in while I'm busy, and then tricking myself into thinking I'll remember to respond later. But by the time "later" comes, the original message is buried under a bunch of others. I often forget to respond to texts for *days*, until something jogs my memory (usually in the shower, where I can't respond and will probably forget again). You know that "Mark as Unread" feature we have for emails? That's what I really need for texts. So if I owe you a reply, I apologize!

WHEN IS TOO EARLY OR TOO LATE TO TEXT?

Unless you're texting your child's teacher, their babysitter, or your boss, you can pretty much text anytime. Most people turn their phones off at night, so if they really don't want to be disturbed, they don't have to be. But many parents awake with young kids welcome a middle-of-the-night check-in! If it's your child's teacher, your boss, or a more formal relationship, wait until about eight in the morning during the week, and no text messages after nine o'clock at night unless it's a true emergency.

SARAH'S Story on Midnight Texting

When I was a new mom, I used to fill my husband in on new friend information at five in the morning when he woke up for work. He'd always ask, "When did you talk to your friends? How do you know what happened overnight?" My answer, "We talk all night during feedings!" How's that for news traveling fast?

DID YOU ACE THE QUIZ?

So what do you do about that text exchange that makes you feel like you're back in high school? You don't want to come on too strong. A second text the next day would be too much. A "Did I do something wrong?" text? No, that would come off as too needy.

More than likely, she's really busy and doesn't have the free time in her schedule you thought she did. A possible solution? **A combination of options A and C.** "No problem! I'd love to get together. We're free most days. Let me know a good time for you." Now the ball's in her court. If she wants to make plans, she will. If not, the old adage is true: she's just not that into you.

Here's another little secret about this quiz. What you're seeing here is a Constellation's communication conundrum. She's terrified of making her new friend uncomfortable in this brand-new stage of the friendship. But could she have taken her power back in this interaction? Sure! She could have picked up the phone and asked if her new acquaintance was available later in the day. That would have saved her *hours* of angst as she waited for a response.

Constellations can feel paralyzed in unfamiliar social situations. They certainly don't want to interrupt anyone, or offend anyone, or overstep, so they can be timid. The irony is that Constellations thrive in social circles once they get comfortable! So if you're a Constellation or have one in your life, know that this is a challenge specific to their Parenting Perspective (putting everyone else's needs above their own), and they may need a little reassurance from friends and family to know they're not overstepping.

Talking on the Phone

PARENTING POP QUIZ

You're on the phone with your doctor's office trying to make an appointment. Your children realize this is the perfect opportunity to begin fighting over who shall be the sole owner of the hot pink crayon. Both kids are screaming while you try to make an appointment to get more birth control. Oh, the irony. What do you do?

A. Close yourself in the bathroom and finish your call.

B. Ask the office to wait one minute while you gently mediate between your children.

C. Scream at your children, then hide in the pantry to complete your call.

D. Tell the doctor you'll call back later.

Keep reading for the correct answer!

Because talking on the phone requires both callers' almost-complete attention, it's many parents' least favorite mode of communication, and of course, the one with the most rules.

According to an informal survey conducted by yours truly, most parents prefer to text, saving phone calls for their BFFs and parents. However, there'll still be times when you have to pick up that phone to schedule appointments, talk to an urgent care nurse, or check in with a teacher. Unfortunately, kids always wait until you're on the phone to fight, scream, and ask you to wipe their butts.

LET'S PLAY TELEPHONE. WHAT ARE THE RULES?

- If your kids are around when you're making a call, set specific expectations. "I'm going to call Aunt Theresa. What will you be doing during that time? Coloring! OK, great. When I'm done, we can go play outside. But while I'm talking with Aunt Theresa, I won't be able to talk to you." This won't work every time, but it will set their expectations. If your kids do well, tell them how awesome they were when your call is over!

- Check your watch before picking up the phone to make a "just saying hi" call. If it's near dinnertime or bedtime, don't even bother. That's just chaos disguised as "family time." And unless you're familiar with a family's schedule, try not to call before nine in the morning or after nine in the evening. (Again, totally not a rule for your bestie!)

✎ If it's a new friend and you want to chat, send a text first to see if you're catching them at a bad time, or start the phone conversation by asking, "Is this a good time?" After a few calls, you won't need that anymore—you'll get more comfortable.

✎ If you call a friend while your kids are around, make sure you have the kind of relationship where you're comfortable saying, "I've got to call you back," even if they're mid-sentence. You don't want to get stuck listening politely while your three-year-old creates a marker masterpiece on the walls.

✎ Avoid having side conversations. If your child interrupts a few times, that's expected. But if you need to have a conversation with another adult in the room, hang up the phone and call back later.

✎ Thinking of leaving a voicemail message? Don't bother. Send a text instead—they'll get it faster. Unless it's their birthday. Then, use that unicorn opportunity to record your best rendition of "Happy Birthday." Maybe they'll keep it forever.

✎ If you're one of these people that just doesn't listen to voicemail messages, change your recording to say just that: "Hi, thanks for calling! While you can certainly leave me a voicemail message, I may not get a chance to listen. The best way to reach me is by text. Talk soon!"

DID YOU ACE THE QUIZ?

So what do you do about all the screaming during the call with your doctor's office? It's really hard to call a doctor back when you're mid-scheduling. So if you have a baby or toddler, you may just have to stick them in their crib or pack 'n play for safety, and then walk away to finish your call. If you have older kids who won't stop screaming, use the **A and B combo**: excuse yourself for ten seconds, mute the call, and tell your kids to stop. Let them know that you're going in the other room to finish the call, and not to follow you. When the call is over, talk through expectations again and even roleplay making another call if they need practice.

Email Etiquette

Maybe you avoid email as much as you can. There's still no getting out of it entirely! Your child's teacher probably prefers email over text because it's more formal and creates a professional boundary between you and them. Parents also love being able to send party invitations by email.

Check your inbox and try to respond on a daily basis. (For personal communication, you can stretch the twenty-four-hour rule out to a couple of days before you're in danger of seeming inconsiderate.) If you get an invitation via email, make sure to open it and respond by the date the host requests. This is one of those things some people don't think is a big deal until they try to host a party themselves and have *no* idea how much food to buy because no one RSVP'd. So here's the rule: You have to RSVP, even if you click "Maybe."

If you're one of those people whose inbox is overflowing with thousands of messages and it's just too much for you to handle, you can always tell new friends that the best way to contact you is by text. That'll lessen your load. Just don't think you're off the hook for what still ends up in your inbox!

Thank-You Notes and Birthday Cards

Becoming a parent usually means receiving boatloads of baby gifts, home-cooked meals, and well wishes. Most people go out of their way for new parents and babies. All the more reason you need to make sure to say, "Thank you!" That's an absolute must. The question is how? When do you *need* to write that thank-you note? When will a social media shout-out suffice? How about a call or video thank-you?

A handwritten thank-you note is necessary when:

- The gift-giver loves to receive them.
- The gift-giver sends them to you.
- The gift-giver is of an older generation when thank-you notes were expected.
- The gift is for a formal event, such as a baby shower.

A social media thank-you is okay (sometimes in addition to the thank-you card!) when:

- You want to give a shout-out to your generous friends and show your family enjoying the gift.
- The gift-giver enjoys social media attention.

A video text or phone call is okay when:

- The gift is for your child and he's too young to write, or doesn't write for any reason.

- You and the gift-giver have a reciprocal understanding that videos are the perfect way to appreciate gifts.

- The gift-giver has explicitly told you, "You don't have to write me a note!"

- You're going to send a thank-you note, but not for a week or so. Call or text to acknowledge your initial excitement about the gift. That way, the giver can relax knowing that you got it!

The bottom line is that you have to say "thank you" in some formal way. You must put thought into your thank-you, because your gift-giver put thought, time, and money into your gift.

Q. Should I write the thank-you note or have my kid do it?

    A. When your child is the recipient of the gift, get them involved in the note writing if possible. Even if they just contribute by writing their name or scribbling a picture, you're starting to instill manners in them early.

Q. How quickly do I need to get thank-you notes out to gift-givers?

    A. Unless you're talking about a 250-person wedding, thank-you notes should be tackled within two to three weeks of receiving a gift. But if you miss that "deadline," better late than never. You can always include a little note in your card apologizing for its late arrival. It'll still be appreciated even if it's coming six months after you opened the present!

Q. Why does it always feel like moms are in charge of thank-you notes??

A. The sad truth is that there are higher expectations for moms to write thank-you notes. When dads don't do it, no one seems to notice... or they blame mom! So here's a challenge for you, dads. Want to score some major manners points? Write some out yourself! They will be unforgettable, for sure.

How to Write the Perfect Thank-You Card

1. **The Greeting:** "Dear Auntie Sue,"
2. **The Opening:** "Thank you so much for the handsewn baby quilt!"
3. **The Acknowledgment:** "It was so thoughtful of you to remember how much I admired your pinwheel quilt the last time we visited."
4. **The Proof:** "We've got your masterpiece hanging above the baby's crib. It got tons of compliments when we had friends over last week."
5. **The Repeat:** "Thanks again for your thoughtful gift! We just love it."

Sending Birthday Cards and Gifts

When do you have to send birthday cards and gifts to long-distance friends and family? This topic isn't cut-and-dry.

If your brother loves to get mail for his two-year-old, send his little one a card, even if she's too young to understand. If your brother doesn't care about these sorts of things, you can get away with waiting a few more years. Many new parents love to receive mail for their kids, and it often goes straight into their baby books! If you know a parent who'll appreciate a card, send away.

In terms of gifts, if you receive a gift each year for your child, you should reciprocate. If you don't, you can decide what you'd like to do based on your budget and your relationship.

Real-Life Sticky Social Situation: Backing out of a Long-Standing Gift Exchange

My friend and I have been friends since high school—almost fifteen years! She has two kids and I have one. Since the kids were babies, we've been exchanging gifts on their birthdays and at Christmastime. It was cute when the kids were little, but now that they're in school, I'm having a hard time figuring out what to get her kids. We never see them and I have no idea what they like. How can I gently back out of this gift exchange?

We totally understand this dilemma! You could approach your friend and explain that at this point, maybe this exchange is more for the two of you and less for the kids. You could definitely suggest just exchanging gifts with each other, if you really want to. If the relationship is really between the two of you, that would make sense.

HOW TO TALK TO OTHER PEOPLE'S KIDS

- **Always** say hello! "Hi Evan! Hey, you've got a new toy truck. That's awesome! Would you show me what it can do?" Greeting kids is just polite, plus you earn brownie points you can redeem later when Evan is jumping on your newly upholstered sofa and you tell him to cut it out.

(Check out our chapter on entertaining for more tips on handling bad behavior on playdates!)

- **Always** thank children for sharing their toys. Sharing is hard!

- **Always** assume kids are listening. Just because they're deeply engrossed in a fairyland tea party doesn't mean they're not hearing you divulge all the ugly details of your divorce, or their new ADHD diagnosis. Save adult conversations for adult time, and don't discuss your kid like a specimen. They can hear you.

- **Never** ask or force a child to talk to you or touch you.

But What If You Need to Put Someone Else's Kid in Their Place?

If you have to speak with someone else's child in a critical way, ask yourself, *How would I want my child's teacher to speak to them?*

- Firmly
- Authoritatively
- Kindly

What does that actually sound like?

"I think it's probably safer if there's only one friend on the ladder at a time. Next time, do you think you could stand here on the ground until your other friend reaches the top?"

"I'm going to help you come down off the couch and jump onto the floor with me. In our house, we don't jump on couches because I don't want anyone to get hurt."

Real-Life Sticky Social Situation:
Too Many Interruptions

I have a really great friend who I see all the time. I love her and I'm so excited we've gotten to spend all this time together. The problem is our kids. We meet at the playground about four times a week with our three-year-olds, but the kids are constantly needing us or interrupting. Honestly, I feel super stressed by the end of the playdate. I feel like I've been trying to start the same sentence like 1,000 times and we haven't actually had a REAL conversation. Is this normal? How are we supposed to feel like we've talked when we're constantly being interrupted?

This is totally normal! We had this exact experience when we were on playdates with our toddlers. It's really hard to cultivate a strong friendship when you can't finish a sentence. At three, your kids are old enough to learn how to wait their turn to talk. Maybe you can suggest that your child touch your arm (without actually saying anything) if they need you when you're in the middle of a conversation. You can set your hand on top of theirs to let them know *you* know they're waiting patiently for you. Make sure they understand this is their way of asking you to pause, but it might not happen right away. Of course, heap praise on the kids when they actually pull this off!

You can also build your friendship outside of playdates. Even if you and your new friend aren't together, sometimes the best way to build a mom friendship is over the phone. You can text while you're parenting, and if you're interrupted, your friend won't notice!

COMMUNICATING WITH INDIVIDUAL CAREGIVERS

> "We're artful distractors, as teachers, nannies, and parents. That's correlated to the Crescent in me—being able to diffuse any kind of sensitivity and mood swings."
> —**Laura,** Crescent, mom of one and professional nanny of twenty years

Most great caregivers are natural Crescents. They're protective, empathetic, and nurturing advocates. As Laura stated above, excellent caregivers are "child whisperers"—they're excellent at recognizing a child's mood and diffusing any tension before it gets worse. Their talent is children. Remembering this nugget of information will help you tremendously when you speak with anyone who cares for children. Keep their sensitive nature in mind. The ideal parent/caregiver relationship is a partnership in which both parties share similar goals, so respect their opinions as well! They usually have unique insight into your children since they're with them for hours at a time.

> "I'm open-minded and I ask parents to be the same and be honest about everything. I really appreciate it when they ask my opinions about something because they know I can give them another point of view of the situation."
> —**Debora,** Crescent, full-time nanny

Always approach your caregiver with respect and kindness. If you have to correct something they're doing, give a specific compliment first! They're much more likely to change if they know you appreciate what they're doing well. Pre-empt confrontation by having an in-depth hiring process. During your interview:

- Be upfront about expectations, hours, screen-time boundaries, house rules, and your kids' personalities. For example, if you have a baby, specifically ask if they're comfortable giving baths and changing diapers.

- Communicate about what will happen if someone gets sick. Are they comfortable watching sick kids? What happens if the caregiver falls ill? This is a two-way partnership.

- Negotiate a rate up front. If they'll be driving, cooking, and/or taking care of multiple kids (especially a baby!), they should be compensated fairly.

- Explain where to find your contact information, emergency contact numbers, and any medical information your caregiver may need, including medications (accessible only to the adult in charge). Always provide clear, written instructions for how to use emergency medications.

Give your caregiver a rundown of your essential house rules, but expect things to not go exactly as they would've if you'd been there. Babysitters are generally fun for kids because the kids can get away with more, and that's okay! If it's a full-time nanny, they'll probably need to be more on top of rules. But even then, things will be different, just as they would be with two parents in the house who have different rules. Remember that disciplining other people's children is difficult and can be awkward for your babysitter.

For more on managing challenges and conflicts with childcare providers, check page 265.

When Your Childcare Provider Is a Family Member

Paid: If this person is paid, provide expectations just like you would with any sitter. However, your communication will have to be much more friendly and loving. "Could I ask you to help me with limiting Mabel's TV time to two shows a day? I've noticed she gets cranky if she watches more than that." Your relationship with your family member extends way beyond the childcare they're offering, so be aware of this whenever you're offering criticism.

Unpaid: If you've called on a family member for a *big* favor, like watching the baby while you're working the night shift, you've basically lost your leverage to complain about their methods. If it's a one-time favor, don't say anything negative unless you think your child is in some kind of danger. Don't complain about the baby watching *Sesame Street*. Don't complain about the baby eating a regular banana instead of the organic variety you prefer. Too many complaints and you might just lose your free childcare. If this is a regular babysitting job, you can set boundaries. But try not to be bossy and demanding, since this person is ultimately doing you a favor.

Real-Life Sticky Social Situation:
Setting Boundaries with Your Mother-in-Law

When I went back to work, my baby was three-months-old (she is sixteen months now) and my mother-in-law became our full-time, paid babysitter. This was a great set up for us because she comes to our house and is one-on-one with our daughter. I trust her more than any stranger to take care of our baby. When she first started, we wrote out instructions for everything. As my daughter has grown older, things have changed and we have verbalized new instructions. However, since the very beginning, we have had trouble with her following our wishes. For example, Please don't hold her until she falls asleep. Please don't shake the bottle of breastmilk before you give it to her. Please don't feed her chocolate pudding before she is a year old.

Any time I work up the courage to ask her to stop doing something, she gets defensive about it and makes me feel bad for asking. The thing that really bothers me now is that she always plays music and props the door open during nap times, even though we have specifically asked her not to do those two things. My husband says he has reminded her twice, but it keeps happening, and he gets frustrated with me because it's "not that big of a deal." But it is a big deal to me simply because it's not what we have asked her to do. I don't want to make a big deal of things that don't matter, but I am also tired of her

> *doing things her way and not ours. I said I wanted to put sticky notes out with specific instructions (like, "please, no music during naps" on the Google Home in her room) but my husband said no. What would you do? Should I just let it go?*

Ultimately, it's important for her to follow your rules because you're paying her to do a job. That being said, you have to be very gentle about it. Start any conversation about things you'd like her to change with gratitude, to help prevent feelings of defensiveness ("Thank you for taking such good care of Rachel. She's so lucky to be with her grandma all day"). Once she's feeling positive, use language that gets grandma's buy-in ("Could I ask for your help with something?"). Next, explain exactly what the problem is without assigning more blame than you need to ("I've noticed that when Rachel's door is open while she's napping, she wakes up early because she hears the dogs bark when I get home, and then she's super cranky in the evening. Would you mind keeping her door closed?").

You may have to let some of the little things go in order to focus on the things that really matter. If you give your mother-in-law control over what she's doing with the baby 95 percent of the time, she'll be more likely to follow your big rules once you've really explained your reasoning. Just know that some people won't follow rules until they know why they exist in the first place.

COMMUNICATION AURORAS AND TWILIGHTS

How is your Parenting Perspective helping you shine or holding you back when it comes to your communication style and skills?

Crescent

A Crescent wants to protect their words. They usually prefer to have big conversations in person. They'll want to use body language and non-verbal cues to gauge how a conversation is going, and may get very anxious if someone wants to have an emotionally charged chat over text. They'll have to fight the urge to pick up the phone. Crescents are also rock stars at communicating with kids, because they're natural kid advocates and can usually predict and understand kids' emotions well.

Crescents will probably want to know things about their new friend's parenting style. Do they vaccinate? Do they spank? They'll want to be on the same page about some big parenting things before they take the adult friendship any further.

Watch out for: Being respectful of other people's needs. Some people prefer to have emotional conversations over text because it's easier to hide intense feelings or think through what they want to say. While that can be supremely uncomfortable for a Crescent, it's important to acknowledge that not everyone wants to talk face-to-face. Also, a Crescent who works with a childcare provider needs to watch their control factor. When two Crescents talk about children, sparks can fly, since both people are strong advocates and have passionate opinions. Keep an open mind and know that the other person is coming from a loving place.

Fireball

Fireballs know who they are and what they like. They may have discovered long ago that they're never, ever going to listen to voicemail messages. They may have an inbox with 50,000 messages and not care a shred. A Fireball has narrowed down the communication method that works best for them. It streamlines things, and they stick with it. They're skilled at making their needs and preferences known to caregivers, partners, and friends.

In friendships, Fireballs are the people who organize getaways because they prioritize adult connections, regardless of what stage of parenting (or life!) those friends may be in. Fireballs may steer chats right to their own interests and lives outside of their children. If you've got big differences in your parenting styles or the ages of your kids, Fireballs may not care, and that can be awesome! The biggest predictor of a successful relationship is the two of you have other things in common.

Watch out for: Times when you should give in a little. Because Fireballs are so clear on what they need, they may assume that others are, too, and that they will ask for it. But pair a Fireball and a Constellation together and things can get lopsided. One says exactly what they want, and one will try to offer something even if it's not what they want at all! The trick is for Fireballs to step back and encourage others to voice their opinions and preferences.

Constellation

Constellations can be slow and thoughtful communicators. They try to choose their words carefully so they don't offend anyone. They can be very sensitive to other people's words and reactions. On the other hand, they may have a hard time communicating when someone else has overstepped and offended *them*! Constellations will go out of their way to communicate with each person in the method of his or her choosing. That may mean that they make way more phone calls than the average person, or that they have fifteen messaging apps on their phones. It might also mean that they use a ton of emojis to try to convey their tone via text.

Constellations may let others lead the conversation. Just don't make the mistake of thinking they're hanging on your every word. They may be politely listening to all the details of your latest juice cleanse while mentally planning their escape. Make sure to throw them questions that get them talking, too.

Watch out for: Overanalyzing and getting in your own way. Constellations can agonize over the exact wording of a message before sending it, when it might just be better to pick up the phone and use the communication method that works best for them. They also need to give themselves permission to push back when something's not working for them, like unwanted advice. Constellations may have a hard time confronting caregivers. Being eager to please and worried about others' feelings, they may struggle to make a change.

CHAPTER 4

Entertaining: You Can Put Away Your Fine China

PARENTING POP QUIZ

Your big kid is turning five! To celebrate, you're shelling out some serious cash to invite his entire class to his favorite bounce house party venue. The package you purchased covers twelve kids, just the number who RSVP'd "Yes." Perfect! But the day before the party, a couple of parents text you to ask if they can bring a sibling along. You call the venue and learn that each additional kid will cost you $20 more. Yikes! You weren't planning on *that* expense. What do you do?

A. Suck it up and say yes. Sure, it'll cost you an extra $40 and you'll need extra pizza, cake, and party favors, but how can you say no?

B. Say yes but ask the parents to chip in toward the cost of the sibling attending. It's not a big deal for extra kids you've never laid eyes on to come, but it shouldn't cost you any extra money.

C. Say no with a polite explanation of the venue's limit on the headcount.

D. Say no, with no explanation. They should know better!

Keep reading for the correct answer!

There's something about having a baby that transforms people from guests to hosts. For many it starts during pregnancy, with the desire to celebrate and be celebrated. You gather friends and family to reveal the gender of the baby. You're showered with gifts to help you prepare. Once the baby arrives, you invite friends and family to join in christenings, baby naming ceremonies, adoption celebrations, and other cultural traditions. And before long, you're hosting birthday parties every year. Even if you never thought of yourself as the entertaining type, everyone tries their hand at it once they're parents.

Then, there are those who relish their former glory as the "Host with the Most." Maybe you used to take pride in handing guests a signature cocktail as they walked in the door. You curated the perfect playlist for each event and guest list, and beamed when friends gushed over your delicious dishes. You had the house everyone wanted to visit.

You might not be the host you once were with a toddler hanging from your leg, or you might be a reluctant new host. Either way, it's time to embrace this new era of entertaining.

WHAT DOES ENTERTAINING HAVE TO DO WITH ETIQUETTE?

Of all the topics covered in this book, entertaining is one of the most *etiquette-y*. Humans have a surprisingly long history of hosting, with feasts going back tens of thousands of years. Parties have always been a way of demonstrating wealth, power, and privilege. And even back then, there was a formula for hosting success: lots of food, music, dancing, and alcohol. These days, you can visit any bookstore or library and find tons of stuffy, old-fashioned books on Entertaining with a capital E that'll coach you on formal place settings and keeping a well-stocked bar. But for parents with young kids, entertaining isn't about acquiring social status. It's about connection.

We host playdates so our kids can play dress-up with their friends and learn to share their toys. We host parties to honor a child's birthday or an expectant friend. We even host book clubs with other parents because we're desperate for friends of our own. When we host, we're asking people—busy people, *with kids*—to take time out of their schedules to be with us. We accomplish that by finding a balance between showing kindness and hospitality to our guests and setting boundaries that prevent us from feeling used up and burned-out by the hosting experience. We want to be welcoming and accommodating without making ourselves crazy or resentful. *This* is the fine art of entertaining.

EVIE'S Story on Entertaining to Build Connection

When my kids were very young, my husband and I decided to leave the life we'd built in Northern Virginia, just outside of Washington, DC, for a new adventure in Houston, Texas. It was a tough decision to make because we had lived in Northern Virginia for ten years and loved it there. Both our babies were born there, and we'd built careers and a strong network of friends who were like family to us. But because the cost of living around the capital was so incredibly high, it made more sense for us to move.

It was the right choice in many respects, but one thing I hadn't factored in was how hard it would be to start from scratch socially. When we arrived in Houston, we knew exactly one family who lived on the other side of town...not exactly a recipe for immediate social success. By month three, I was desperate for connection and truly depressed, so I tried to do what I'd done in Virginia—I joined a mommy group. When I'd given birth to my first child, I was a part of an amazing group of women who'd all welcomed babies within a few months of each other. We'd been so tightly bonded by the experience of entering motherhood together. But this time, the chemistry just wasn't there. I realized that experience just couldn't be replicated.

I racked my brain trying to figure out how to rebuild my friend group and settled on the idea of launching a book club for moms with young kids. We'd read books under three hundred pages (who has time for more than that?) and meet once a month in the evenings after bedtime, at a restaurant where we could all enjoy a proper meal without interruption. Launching this group ended up being the best thing I could've done. It gave me a reason to get together with other smart women at the same stage of life, and it gave us something to talk about so the conversation never stalled out—that hot new novel with the twisted plot, or the best-seller about transforming your life. It was the perfect recipe for a new social circle.

There was just one problem: I wasn't seeing these new acquaintances often enough to get them into friend territory. I had to up the ante, and I did that by entertaining. I launched the group in the fall, and by December, I was hosting a holiday party at my house. Welcoming those women into my home was a huge step forward. It gave them an opportunity to see where and how I lived. It gave me a chance to be hospitable and make them comfortable in my home. That night, I exchanged phone numbers with most of the women—who I'd only been emailing up to that point. We started texting about playdates, found each other on Facebook, and even formed a writing group fueled by our passion for reading. Hosting that holiday party changed everything. I love that entertaining has the power to build bonds that strong.

"Entertaining is about sharing generously and creating an atmosphere where friends feel welcome."
—**Annie Falk,** author and entertaining expert, in an interview with *Architectural Digest*, October 2015

CURATING YOUR GUEST LIST

The first step is figuring out who to invite, and if you're managing a party for young kids, this can be especially complicated. When you're party-planning for adults, veteran hosts learn to expect some extra plus ones. But hosting young kids may mean a single five-year-old getting dropped off at your doorstep, or a family of five crashing the party. That's why you need to plan ahead.

If your headcount is limited by your budget or your venue, keep the guest list smaller than you can actually accommodate so day-of unexpected guests don't put you in a bind. Plan for at least one adult per child since kids this age rarely fly solo (and thank goodness for it, a drop-off party for a dozen two-year-olds would put most of people over the edge!). Lastly, keep in mind that the younger your guests are, the more likely you are to have extras. A two-year-old is much more likely than a five-year-old to end up attending a party with Mom, Dad, and Baby Brother.

When you host a party for a one- or two-year-old, you're *really* hosting a party for the adults. Kids and parents are a package deal at that stage. But once kids are old enough to make friends of their own at school and daycare, you'll find yourself hosting parties with kids you barely know and adults you've never even seen before. That's when it starts to get weird for entire families to show up. The transition is slow and implicit—no one's going to tell you that you *can't* bring your whole family to a party for a five-year-old that's in your kid's class; eventually, it becomes an unspoken rule. Hosting younger party guests means larger headcounts, especially if the party takes place on a weekend or evening when families are typically together; hosting older guests means you can expect fewer extra people.

Parenting Perspectives at a Party

If your guest's parents are Crescents, you can bet they're going to attend, especially if you're unfamiliar or the party includes any activity that might lead to injury or conflict. The parents dropping their kids off with reasonable confidence: Fireballs. They figure that you're an adult with kids of your own who's willingly taken on the responsibility of hosting, so you've probably got this. They'll use that time to go run an errand.

EVIE'S Story on Invitation Etiquette

One of the most powerful things I've learned about kids is that having them forces you to embody the mantra, "The show must go on." Sometimes that means bringing a joyful event to an end, like forcing yourself off the dance floor at your brother's wedding because it's way past your kids' bedtime. Sometimes that means planning a child's birthday party despite the fact that your city was just devastated by a natural disaster.

One month before my daughter's birthday, Houston was hit by Hurricane Harvey, which had an effect on so many aspects of life, both big and small. Among the smallest was our needing to find a new venue for her party when the sweet little pottery studio we'd chosen had flooded, along with so many other spots we loved. I didn't want my daughter's birthday to be *another* thing Harvey had ruined, so I kept looking for another venue until we stumbled upon the idea of a party at the movie theater in our neighborhood (the one that had been spared by the rain). It seemed like a great solution, until I saw the theater's pricing. Let's just say it was *way* above our budget. But short on options, we caved.

With the least expensive party package, we could host fifteen people total, including our family of four. We were given the option to pay extra for additional party guests, but we couldn't swing it financially, so we needed to be deliberate with our guest list. Further complicating matters was the fact that the kids were at an age where some parents would feel comfortable dropping them off, while others who'd never met us before surely would not. How do you plan for that? How many invitations do you send out in a case like this?

We decided to email invitations to seven families with a note that said: "Feel free to drop your child off in the party room and pick them up at 4:00 p.m., when the movie is finished. If you would like to celebrate with us, you're welcome to do so! Please just let us know so we can include both of you in the headcount."

That was my way of trying to tell parents that both they and their kids counted toward our total number, which isn't usually the case for kids' parties. We also used an online invitation that allowed guests to RSVP with the number of adults *and* the number of kids who would attend, rather than just a simple "Yes" or "No."

Ironically, we didn't end up using all fifteen spots because most parents opted *not* to stay for the movie. We also didn't send out a second round of invitations after the first RSVPs came in because I didn't want to create the perception of their being "B-list" friends. Having unused seats felt a little bit like throwing money away, until we wrapped up the party and a theater employee handed me three free movie vouchers for the seats we hadn't used. Keeping the guest list small and in-budget, and communicating clearly to parents, worked out after all!

Real-Life Sticky Social Situation:
Reciprocating with Invitations

At the beginning of the school year, one of the kids in my daughter's class invited all the students to her birthday party. My daughter went even though she isn't especially close to this child. Now, it's our turn to plan a party and we're trying to keep our guest list small. I asked my daughter if she wants to invite this child, especially since she went to her party a few months back, but she said no. Would it be rude to leave this child out?

Remember, kids who celebrate birthdays in September and October are usually still making their friends for the school year when their parties roll around, so it's possible this family invited the whole class for that reason. Maybe they just had a big budget to work with and wanted to be generous, or maybe their child is a social butterfly. No matter the circumstances, you're not obligated to reciprocate. Would it be nice to do? Sure, but if you're trying to keep your guest list small, don't worry about inviting someone just because your child attended their party.

ALL ABOUT INVITATIONS

The party's on, you've got your guest list, and now it's time to fill everyone in on your big plans! This is another aspect of entertaining little guests that can get surprisingly sticky—from lost invitations, to their wording, to tracking down RSVPs.

Paper vs. Electronic Invites

Your little Eliza is turning four. You'd like to invite the girls in her class to a spa party at a local kids' salon. Should you send paper invitations to school with her, or email the parents? Let's break this down!

	Paper Invitations	Electronic Invitations
Pros	They're super cute and kind of a charming throwback in this digital age. Kids love receiving an envelope and a paper invitation just for them! They give parents something to hang on their fridge with all the details. You have something for your child's baby book.	They're free and easy to send and receive. They're a discreet way of distributing invitations, especially when not everyone's invited. Most electronic invitation services will email guests event details and RSVP reminders as the date approaches.
Cons	There's usually some cost associated with them. You may have to ask a teacher to help you distribute them (which some schools won't allow, while others require that the entire class be invited). They may result in hurt feelings if you aren't inviting everyone. They may just get lost in the shuffle of life with young kids!	You may have to ask a teacher to help you collect parents' email addresses or phone numbers (some schools have a policy against this). You're assuming parents even check their emails (which—newsflash—many don't!) or open unfamiliar text messages.

Regardless of how you distribute invitations, remind your big kid not to blab about the party to friends and acquaintances. Sure, you invited their whole class, but what about the neighborhood kid who didn't make the cut? If you've got a four- or five-year-old, it's worth talking to them about how they'd feel if they discovered they weren't included in someone else's party, so they understand why it's better to be quiet about the whole thing. A super mature three-year-old might catch on, too, but typically with younger kids, you just have to hope they don't spill the beans!

SARAH'S Story About Lost Birthday Invites

There've been so many times that I've found rogue birthday party invitations at the bottom of my child's backpack *after* the party has happened! This was especially a problem when my children were in preschool, because the teacher would slide the invites in the folder and somehow they would make their way to the little crevices at the bottom of the backpack. I always felt so badly, because not only did we miss those parties, but the parents thought I didn't RSVP. This was especially difficult when the whole class was invited, because I was that one parent who couldn't take time out of my schedule to RSVP. Ugh! I've found that if the parent follows up in the drop-off or pickup line ("Hey, did you get our invite?"), it can fix this particular issue before the party happens.

What Information to Include

Whoa, whoa, whoa, before you skip this section because you *think* you already know what to include on an invitation, take a minute. Of course, there's the obvious stuff, like date, time, and location. But there are other important details you might forget to include that can absolutely ruin your guests' fun!

Think of this: you send out invitations without a plan for what you'll actually do during your kid's party. Winging it, you figure you'll just buy some puffy paints and cheap t-shirts for the kids to decorate. Bonus: instant party favor! But wait, you forgot to tell the parents to send their kids in play clothes they can ruin with permanent paint. *Whoops.* That little girl who gets paint on her favorite party dress is going to be devastated, and her mom (who spent good money on it) isn't going to be very happy with you either.

What do your guests need to bring or know about the activities? If it's a pool party, will you be supplying the towels and sunscreen, or should your invitation start by saying, "Bring your favorite bathing suit, beach towel, and sunscreen for a dunk in the pool..."? If it's a bounce house party, could you please remind parents to bring socks so they don't have to buy a pair at the door for three stinkin' dollars?

How and when do you want people to RSVP? If you're giving out your phone number on the invitations, do you want guests to call or text you? (Hey, some of us almost never answer our phones, some of us lose text messages, and some of us haven't listened to a voicemail message since 2014!) And how early do you need those RSVPs? It's always a good idea to cheat and say you need them a couple of days earlier than you actually do!

And one little tip on what *not* to include on the invitation: Don't ask guests to bring any materials they'll need for a project you'll complete during the party. If you can't source the materials yourself, pick a different project altogether.

Could You Please Not Stay?

Can you ask parents to not stay behind after dropping their kids off at a party? Not really. With kids in the five-and-under set, you've really got to leave that decision up to the parents. However, if you're hosting a few kids at your home for some benign activity—say, cupcake decorating—and you'd really prefer that it be kids-only, you can include language in the invitation that gets your point across, like "Adults are welcome to join us for the fun or return at 3:00 p.m. for pickup." They'll know what you mean.

Timing

How long should your party or get-together be? Plan for one and a half to two hours for families with young kids. That's about as long as everyone can hold it together! Plus, your party isn't the only thing on everyone's schedule for the day.

If you're hosting an event with an open-door policy, where guests are free to come and go within a window of time, be sure to say that on the invitation so they don't feel compelled to stay at your party for four hours! For a baby shower, you might say something like, "Swing by anytime between 10 a.m. and 2 p.m. Melissa will be opening gifts at noon."

Once you've got the details nailed down, get those invitations out to guests two to three weeks before your event, even longer if you're planning an adult gathering. You want to give people ten to fourteen days to look at their schedules and decide whether or not they're able to squeeze your event in.

RSVPs

So your RSVPs are due today, but you still haven't heard back from half of your guests. What gives? Don't take it personally. It's not that your party isn't the most eagerly awaited event of the year among the preschool set, it's just that...well, actually, that's exactly it. Sure, this party is a big deal for you (the time, the effort, the expense), but it's just a blip on everyone else's radar.

If you have people's contact information, feel free to reach out on the day RSVPs are due (remember, this should be a couple of days before you *actually* need them) with a friendly reminder: "Lucas is so excited for his birthday party on the 12th! We're really hoping Cooper will be able to come. Let me know if you can make it when you get a chance."

SARAH'S Story of Missing RSVPs

When my son turned four, I invited everyone in his class to a party at the YMCA. A few days before, I had only four RSVPs! I actually called every parent in that class asking if they were coming to the party, and the funny thing was, they were completely stunned I called! "Oh, that birthday party? Yes, of course we'll be there!" What?? I was completely confused. They were planning on attending, but not planning on letting me know. Was I just supposed to order food for fifteen kids on a hope and a prayer?

Did You Ace the Quiz?

So what about that last-minute RSVP with the request to bring an extra kid or two to your party? Should you say yes? Think it through.

Are we talking about a twelve-year-old that's probably going to do everything in their power to make themselves invisible at your kid's "baby party"? Will including one or two more kids simply mean a few more juice boxes and a couple extra slices of cake on your end? If it's really not a big deal to let an extra kid or two tag along, go with option **A. Suck it up and say yes**. You never know what's going on in a family that would make it impossible for that parent to come up with another plan for that tag-along kid. Maybe it's a single parent family, maybe the babysitter cancelled, or maybe this family doesn't have the budget for a babysitter.

But what if the ask is bigger than that? "Can I bring my two extra kids to jump in the bounce houses at a cost of $40 to you, the host?" Well, can you afford it? Are you feeling generous? Is this a person with whom you're really close or hope to cultivate a relationship? If not, choose option **B. Say yes but ask the parent to chip**

in toward the cost of the sibling attending: "You can definitely bring your son along! The only issue is that we're up against the venue's headcount, so there'll be a separate admission fee, which you can pay when you arrive. Does that work for you?"

Should You Say Yes to Extra Party Guests?

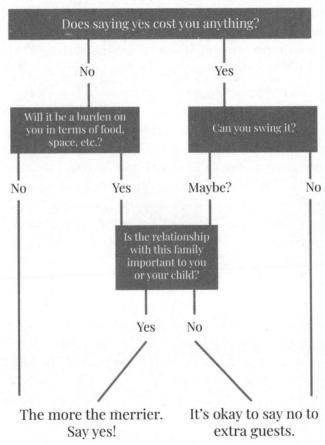

Does saying yes cost you anything?

No — Will it be a burden on you in terms of food, space, etc.?

Yes — Can you swing it?

Will it be a burden on you in terms of food, space, etc.?
- No
- Yes — Is the relationship with this family important to you or your child?

Can you swing it?
- Maybe?
- No

Is the relationship with this family important to you or your child?
- Yes
- No

The more the merrier. Say yes!

It's okay to say no to extra guests.

COME HUNGRY

In Mediterranean culture (Evie's Greek and Sarah's Italian), the *worst* entertaining mistake you can make is letting your guests leave your home hungry. That would mean you were inhospitable—or worse, *selfish*—in the presence of people you invited into your company. Oh, for shame! For us, food is everything.

That's not to say that when you're entertaining with young kids in the mix, you have to prepare a full spread of hot, homemade dishes. Not at all! Food just can't be an afterthought, and you want to have plenty of it.

Start by filling your guests in on what the food situation is going to be. Your invitation may say that you'll be serving pizza and ice cream at a kid's birthday party, or you may simply text your girlfriends saying that you'll have coffee and pastries for them when they come over for your baby playdate. Let people know whether to expect a meal or a snack, so they can prepare with an empty stomach or an almost-full one. If you're offering more than a simple snack, give your guests an idea of what you'll be serving.

Let's say that you're hosting a new family at your place for a barbeque, only you didn't tell them your plans ahead of time. Just as you're about to fire up the grill, your guests announce that they don't eat meat! *Uhhhh...buns and ketchup for dinner?* When you give people a heads-up about your plans, you give them an opportunity to raise concerns—a privilege most people won't abuse. Food is very personal and no two families eat the same way, so laying out the basics of your food plan saves you a headache and ensures that your guests will have a great time.

Lastly, plan for the number of people you think will show up, plus a few more. If you're serving mini-croissants with coffee, assume each person will eat two. Don't just grab a container of them, actually count how many are inside!

May I Offer You a Drink?

Should you serve alcohol to your adult guests at an event for families with young kids? You sure could. Glasses of wine amongst friends or beers at a family cookout are totally fine. But are you obligated to have alcohol on-hand? Definitely not, although Constellations are more likely to feel obliged, and Fireballs are more likely to want to enjoy an adult beverage!

What about Feeding Adults Who Tag Along to a Kids Party?

Do you have to feed the adult chaperones of your *true* guests, the kids? Not necessarily. If you're hosting a ninety-minute birthday party with people you barely know, don't double your pizza order just because one or two parents may grab a slice. As your kids get older, parents know that they're just hanging around for crowd-control; they're not really guests at these parties. You might offer a room of ten adults a slice of cake, and one or two *might* say yes. Plan to have a *little* extra food on hand, but not the amount you'd normally need to entertain these same adults in an adult-only context.

If you want to go above and beyond, consider creating a coffee station for parents, even if that means grabbing a box of coffee on the way to the party. It's a little way of acknowledging the adults in the room without too much effort or expense, and that little pick-me-up in the middle of all the kiddie chaos will be very much appreciated!

Party like A ...

- 🖊 **Crescent by anticipating your youngest guests' needs.** Stock up on juice boxes and apple slices. Keep lots of paper plates and napkins on hand for snacking. Plan a few easy activities and games. And don't stress about the messes—they happen!

- 🖊 **Constellation by making your guests feel at home.** Show your guests around the areas of your home that you've prepared for them. Hang their coats, offer them drinks, smile, thank them for coming. These little niceties don't have to disappear just because there are kids in the room!

- 🖊 **Fireball by sneaking in a treat for the adults.** While the kids are eating goldfish, let the adults snack on baked brie and uncork a bottle of Merlot. No eating scraps off your kid's plate when you party like a Fireball!

Real-Life Sticky Social Situation:
Accommodating Allergies

We're hosting a birthday party for two of our kids this weekend. I love making elaborate cakes for my kids, and really want to make sure that all the guests are able to enjoy it! But that's taken some creativity because the guest list includes so many different food allergies. For example, if I use almond milk to make the frosting safe for the child with dairy allergies, then the child with a nut allergy can't eat it.

I was at another party where a little girl cried because the cake was chocolate and she couldn't eat it, and it made me so sad for her. Fortunately, I like baking and I have twins, so I have to make two cakes anyway. It's not a terrible amount of extra work to make sure that one cake is nut-free, and one cake is chocolate-free and dairy-free.

When I mentioned this to my co-workers, some were shocked that I would bother accommodating every single child. They said things like, "The party won't be ruined if one kid can't eat cake," and, "Can't you just buy one of them a separate cupcake?" So I'm wondering what you think the etiquette standard is for this type of situation. Is it the host's responsibility to ask all guests about allergies and buy or make a cake accordingly?

EVIE'S ANSWER

As a mom to a child with a severe food allergy, I can't tell you how much it means when another parent even *remembers* your kid's dietary restriction. To know that you remembered the restrictions and prepared multiple cakes to accommodate all the kids is downright saintly! To me, your coworkers' response that "the party wouldn't be ruined if one kid can't eat the cake" is short-sighted and inconsiderate, because a kid with a food allergy is faced with this disappointment all the time. It's not just one kid at one party; it's the same kid being singled out for disappointment time and time again.

For the sake of all the kids' safety, it's a good idea to announce if a food item at your event has a common allergen in it. But to be honest, parents who face these concerns typically know to ask in advance. They're also good about making accommodations for their child, because it's an ongoing issue in their lives. When my daughter went off to preschool, we were asked to bring in a stash of nut-free cupcakes for her. These were stored in the freezer, so that when the other kids were eating the treat provided by the family of the birthday child, my daughter could participate with a food item that was safe for her.

As sweet as it was of you to make two cakes to ensure everyone would be able to enjoy a slice at your children's party, you aren't required to do this as the host. In the future, you could simply touch base with families that have dietary restrictions to say something like, "I realize some of our party foods might not work for Andrew, so I wanted to reach out before the party to make sure we coordinate a safe treat for him in case he isn't able to eat the cake." Nine out of ten parents will take that as a reminder to bring a treat for their child, rather than place that burden on you.

A Word about Hosting Picky Eaters

Of course, playing host means juggling unpredictable situations as they come up, sometimes during your party and sometimes before anyone's even arrived! So what should you do if you're informed that one of your little guests has a picky palate?

Scenario 1: You've got a whole kid-friendly menu planned for your gathering. A few days ahead, you get a text from a parent saying, "So I know this might be weird, but can I bring a jelly sandwich for James when we come to your house? He's really fussy and I'm afraid he won't eat what you have."

Even if you're cringing inside, text back saying, "Sure, that's fine! Totally understand." Your guests will be way more comfortable, so you'll all enjoy the visit more.

Scenario 2: You're mid-party, so the finger foods are gone and the main course (something you really worked hard on) is out. Someone says, "I hate to ask, but would it be possible to take the cheese and crackers back out? I'm not sure Julia's really going to eat anything but that."

This is frustrating, especially if you've taken time to think about the kids in planning your menu. So say something like this: "Some of these dishes are really kid-friendly! Want to try a little of this first? If you don't like it, I can take the other food back out."

Scenario 3: You're hosting a friend whose child has a severe food allergy or sensitivity, and you're freaking out thinking that you're going to mess something up and make the poor kid sick!

Don't be afraid to ask your friend what their child can and can't eat, and express concern about meeting those needs. This will be music to their ears! They'll guide you on what will work best. If one of you is truly concerned about cross-contamination, you can even suggest that your friend bring food for their child. Better safe than sorry.

GOODY BAGS

If you're a regular on the kids birthday party circuit, you've probably noticed that goody bags are kind of a *thing*. They usually come filled with candy, stickers, bubbles, and other inexpensive plastic toys purchased in bulk. But are they a *good* thing? To the kids, they're *ahhhh-mazing*...for about twenty minutes. After that, all that stuff gets forgotten. To the parents of your guests, your goody bag may be appreciated entertainment for the car ride home, or unwelcome sugar and clutter.

Whether or not you opt to make goody bags is totally up to you, but don't feel compelled to do it. In a community poll, we found that the majority of parents said goody bags are *not* necessary at kids' birthday parties!

"So when parties first started with my kids, I did goody bags. As we got invited to parties, we kept getting goody bags. I now find it to be the most annoying thing on the planet because it's usually filled with small pointless things that I end up throwing away from off the floor in a week anyway. I don't think I'm going to supply goody bags for my daughter's next birthday, because when I think about it, I will be supplying the place for the birthday, the activity, the pizza, the cake or whatever we choose to do, and drinks. That's enough!"
—**Chloe,** Fireball, mom of two

CREATE THE PARTY VIBE

Have you ever been to a party where you didn't know anyone and the vibe was kind of...*lame*? You probably drift around, making small talk with strangers and watching the clock, wondering if it's time to leave yet. No one wants to throw a party like that, but how do you avoid it?

Don't make the mistake of thinking you can just invite people over for any reason—a birthday party, a baby shower, a playdate, whatever!—and everyone will walk out having had an amazing time. There's probably nothing more disappointing than spending days grocery shopping, tidying up, preparing food, hosting, and then cleaning up afterward, only to feel like your party wasn't a complete success. So what's the secret to hosting a great gathering? Ask yourself, *What's the point of the party?*

Let's start with something easy: a kid's birthday party. If you were going to invite a class of five-year-olds to your house for two hours, you wouldn't just buy a cake and assume the rest would take care of itself. You might plan a quick craft, purchase a pinata, and set up an outdoor obstacle course. You'd schedule things into the event to keep the flow. And let's not forget, most five-year-olds come with an adult chaperone—those same activities you plan for the kids keep the adults moving, talking, and relating to each other, too, which means no clock-watching.

Does that mean you've got to schedule the party down to the minute? Not at all! It's great for little guests to have a chance for free play, and grown-ups don't want to feel overly managed at something as low-stakes as a kid's birthday party. But having a structure for the event that matches your goal (activities your child enjoys) really does make things more fun and rewarding for you, the host.

What about a more adult event, like a baby shower? At this stage of life, we can end up attending, hosting, and being honored with baby showers or baby sprinkles multiple times each year! So think back to the most entertaining showers you've attended. What was the structure? Did they go something like this:

1. A little time to mingle and snack as guests arrive

2. A few silly games to loosen up the group

3. And a chance to bring the focus back to the expectant mother and her new gifts?

Yup. That's because it's a formula for success, no matter what type of gathering you're organizing.

GRACIOUSLY RECEIVING GIFTS

As the host, you're occasionally in the position of knowing that you or your child will be receiving gifts, which can lead to a bunch of awkwardness! Here's a little Q&A to keep things from getting ugly.

Q. Can I share a "wish list" or gift registry with my party guests?

> **A.** If you're hosting a baby shower for someone else: yes, please do share the mother-to-be's registry information! However, if you're requesting anything untraditional, such as cash, used items, or a meal train as part of the registry, be very clear with guests about what you're requesting and how to accomplish it. That way you don't leave them with lots of questions and research to conduct. If you're hosting a type of event that doesn't normally get a registry, especially a birthday party, tread lightly. This is a hugely divisive issue, even for us!

Benefits of a Registry

- You have some control over what's coming into your house. Sometimes, you'll receive gifts that aren't *exactly* the sort of thing you'd buy for your own kids. Maybe it's something that's messy (like finger paints), or maybe it's something you're opposed to (like guns).

- You remove the guesswork for your guests. Picking gifts for other people's kids can be hard, so creating a registry saves time and...

- Money! When you buy a gift off a registry, you know it's something your party host really wants. You can pick something they won't have to return or regift!

Drawbacks of a Registry

- It can come off as kind of presumptuous to place your child's birthday party right up there with other major life events for which registries are much more the norm, like weddings and baby showers.

- Your child needs to learn to be gracious about receiving any and all gifts. Sure, some of the presents your friend's parents picked out may not be your favorites. You may even end up with duplicates. But there's a special lesson here: It's the thought that counts.

- You may inadvertently be sending your kids a message about their own entitlement by helping them set up a registry. It's one thing for a parent to create a registry for a child who's young enough to not even understand the concept; it's another for an older kid to hand-select specific toys for his birthday.

Our final verdict: While there's convenience in setting up a birthday party registry, you're sure to rub lots of people the wrong way, so save that wish list for your closest relatives who ask for gift ideas.

"I love [birthday party gift registries]! I am the person who stands in the aisle forever, trying to figure out what is age-appropriate, what the child will enjoy, trying to remember if they have said item, *and* figuring out the budget!... Tell me what you want so I can buy it, the end! Also nice to know where the kid/parent shops, so if I hate everything on the registry, or there is something big on there, I can just buy a gift card towards said item!"
—**Andie,** Crescent, mom of one

Q. How about the whole "No Gifts" thing?

A. We all know that people who request to *not* bring gifts have their hearts in the right place. It's an acknowledgment that their kid really doesn't need a thing! It's just that most people have been conditioned through childhood and adulthood to recognize that you *are* supposed to bring a present to a birthday party. So then you're in the uncomfortable position of either...

- Going against your wishes and bringing a little something, or

- Showing up empty-handed and probably feeling sheepish, only to discover other parents broke code and brought gifts.

Either way, it leaves your guests with the sense that there's no good option. We suggest avoiding the *No Gifts* request, but if you really feel compelled, be prepared to accept any gifts your guests graciously bring!

Q. Can you offer *any* kind of direction on birthday gifts then?

A. Actually, yes! You can offer a very general gift theme for people to work from. Sometimes you do this inadvertently: host a princess party and you're bound to end up with a stack of princess tiaras and costumes, princess crafts, and princess books. The only other way you can work this is if you're requesting something very broad and really inexpensive, like books or craft supplies. You can add a line to your invitation that says something like: "A copy of your child's favorite book would be much appreciated!" That way, the gift is meaningful to the gift-giver, useful to you, and doesn't need to cost more than a few dollars.

Q. Should we open gifts at the party?

A. If we're talking about a baby shower, yes! Traditionally, shower gifts are opened in front of guests so they can *oooh* and *ahhh* at all the adorable baby gear (and congratulate themselves for stocking you up so well). But again, when it comes to birthday parties, we like to do things a bit differently.

Opening presents in front of the other kids can be totally fine, but there are some pretty compelling reasons *not* to unwrap gifts with an audience:

1. First and most importantly, older kids are savvy enough to compare their gift to others. Some families might send flashy gifts that the big kids know are pricey. Other kids might show up with small tokens from the dollar store. You certainly don't want anyone feeling badly about the value of their gift.

2. What's in those wrapped packages is as big of

a surprise to you as it is to your kid. You can't always prepare the birthday child for what to say or how to react to a gift they don't like or already own.

3. Plus, if your party is only ninety minutes long and you spend twenty minutes eating and twenty minutes opening presents, that means these kids are sitting around for half of your party—probably not the most fun.

On the other hand, opening gifts in front of others is an important skill that requires tact and consideration, and it's something everyone should learn to do well. It's wonderful for kids to have the opportunity every so often to practice in front of loving family members who won't take offense at a little slip up. Before just such an occasion, act out some appropriate responses so your child doesn't say:

- "I don't like this!"
- "How much did this cost?"
- "Can we return it?"
- "I already have one of these."

Of course, your kid might still embarrass you. If they do, make it right by overriding their comment. If your child says, "Ewww! This is *not* what I like," say really loudly, "You're going to love it! This is going to be so much fun!" Classic case of modeling the behavior you want to see.

Q. Do we have to send thank-you notes?

A. Check out our guidelines for gracious thank-yous on page 125.

Q. Is it ever okay to regift?

A. Yes, but if and only if the gift-giver will never, *ever* notice that: (1) you no longer own their gift, and (2) the gift they gave you is in someone else's hands. This really only works with generic gifts from out-of-town gift-givers. Regifters, beware!

Q. I have twins. How can I suggest that guests provide a separate gift for each child (even if they're inexpensive!) instead of one to share?

A. People who don't have twins often see this as a great gifting strategy, even though we've heard from twin moms that it's better for both children to be acknowledged separately. If you have toddlers, you may receive gifts meant to be shared, and that's probably OK at that age. But as your kids get older, you could have a party with two themes to give your guests the hint that your children have separate likes and dislikes. If someone asks you what they like, you could always give two answers: "Ben loves cars, but Josh loves dinosaurs."

For Gift-Givers

How much you spend on a gift is a very personal decision. For a child you barely know, and on a tight budget, you may spend $3 or $4 on a coloring book and crayons. For your best friend's baby shower, you may spend $100! It totally varies based on your family's finances and the nature of the relationship. The only important caveat of gift-giving is that the value of your gift should loosely correspond to the number of people in your family attending the party. Just one kid going to the party?

A smaller gift will do. Two or more kids, plus adults? A bigger gift is best.

The fact is, gift-giving is complicated—probably more so at this stage of life than any other. We'd need a whole other chapter to cover the complexities of the topic! Tune in to our podcast, *Modern Manners for Moms & Dads*, to hear us tackle lots more sticky gifting situations.

HOSTING IN YOUR HOME

If you're entertaining at home, preparing for guests can be a special challenge. While you're wiping down the bathroom, your toddler's dumping out five hundred blocks. While you're folding the laundry that's been living on your coach for three days, someone's spilling their sippy cup on the rug. Getting ready for guests can feel like you're on a hamster wheel!

That's why we've broken down what to prioritize in your home (and what to let go of) in the next chapter (check out "Priorities When Preparing for Guests" on page 212). We'll give you all the details you need to get your home ready for guests, plus a surprising rationale for keeping your home tidy on a regular basis, not least of which is that you won't have to call in professional cleaners when it's time to entertain! For now, let's dive into handling sticky situations while guests are at your house.

Managing Messes

When you open your house to guests, you accept a certain amount of risk. Maybe it's a toddler squeezing the entire contents of a juice box onto your brand-new couch, maybe it's a poopy diaper change gone terribly wrong, or maybe it's an adult whose red wine ends up on your white carpet. It can make us crazy to have the reward for entertaining be damage to our home.

If something does go wrong, try to erase that look of terror from your face. Your guest is probably as horrified as you are about the mess they (or their child) made. Do your best to not make them feel badly about an honest mistake. Clean-up and get back to the party as quickly as possible. On the other hand, you don't *have to* serve things or set up activities you know to be messy. If the thought of tomato sauce on the upholstery makes you want to cry, don't serve it! Your house, your rules. When Evie had white carpets, she *never* served red wine. Sarah never serves things with tomato sauce when there are kids involved.

It's especially true that you shouldn't stress about the mess when it's the type you should anticipate. A house full of people can create a mountain of dirty dishes, for instance. Don't spend your time at the sink when you should be hosting. What would that say about your priorities? Stack dishes in the sink, enjoy your friends' company, and manage the mess later. (On the other hand, if your guests are overstaying their welcome, starting on the dishes sends a pretty clear signal that it's time for them to go!)

> "A good upbringing means not that you won't spill sauce on the tablecloth, but that you won't notice it when someone else does."
> **—Anton Chekhov,** playwright

Should You Ask Guests to Help Clean Up?

What happens if you've hosted a playdate at your house and by the end, it looks like a tornado tore through the toys? Should you encourage, or outright *ask*, your guests to help you tidy things up before they go? It depends.

Think of it this way: if you were hosting an adult dinner party, would you ask your guests to wash the dishes at the end of the evening? Of course not. When you're hosting people with toddlers and you ask "the kids" to clean up, you're really asking the adults to do the job of the host. And now, not only are you asking them to put toys away in a house that's unfamiliar, you're asking them to do it at the end of a playdate, when their temperamental two-year-old is rolling on the floor on the verge of a meltdown.

On the other hand, if your living room ends up a total disaster and the clean-up can be tackled by a couple of currently smiling five-year-olds, then you can ask for help. By the time children are four to five years old, they're perfectly capable of cleaning up on their own with a little bit of guidance. "Would you please help me put all the cars in this bin while Lilah puts the books back on the shelf?"

Of course, the best strategy for these messes is a proactive one—one that doesn't even allow for the *possibility* of all toys coming out at once. Just because you're hosting a playdate doesn't mean the kids can have free rein over everything in your house. It's actually a good idea to pull together some toys for your visit and store others away (especially those with lots of pieces or parts).

Getting Kids to Follow Your House Rules

So you're having big kids over? How brave of you! Get ready for some fun *and* some unique challenges, as you try to find that perfect balance of being cool and laid-back without letting your house turn into a zoo. It's time to put on your big girl panties—or big boy undies, as the case may be—because you're going to need to lay down the law.

This can be especially awkward if your little guests have an adult chaperone (or if you're a Constellation who struggles to make sure guests feel welcome). Maybe your house rule is no running inside. Totally reasonable. But what if your new little friend is a runner, and their adult isn't asking them to slow down? Can you say something? Absolutely! Here's how:

Grab your child and their friend for a little chat. Get down on their level and say, "Can I talk to you both about something really important for just a minute?" Slide your foot against the floor. "Do you see how slippery this floor is? If we run on this floor, do you know what's going to happen? Yup, we're going to fall down and get hurt. And what's going to happen if we get hurt? That's right. We aren't going to be able to play anymore. So what should we do? Use our walking feet in the house so we can keep everyone safe and keep playing!"

Ta-da! Is that other parent going to think you were out of line for speaking to their kid when they were standing right there? No, because you made it all about the trouble with your floors. Your visitors don't know your floors are slippery, and they certainly don't know your house rules. Just use our favorite trick and talk like a teacher would: get down to the children's level, use a calm but authoritative tone, and move the conversation in a way that makes the kids feel like they came up with the brilliant idea to follow your house rule!

It's Okay to Be Weird: OK, moms and dads, we know most of you have at least one weird rule in your house. Maybe it stems from a pet peeve, or maybe it comes from past experience. No matter your reasons, don't be embarrassed about enforcing even your weirdest rules with guests! Want to know ours?

SARAH'S "WEIRD" RULE

I don't let my children's friends in my bedroom, and they're not allowed to play on my kids' beds either. I view my room as a private space, and in my mind, it's kind of gross for other kids to be playing where my kids sleep. My kids have grown up with this rule, and now they enforce it on their own.

EVIE'S "WEIRD" RULE

When my kids were babies, I had a problem: I didn't like bugs entering our home to eat the nearly endless supply of crumbs, but I also didn't like having an exterminator spray chemicals all over the house. I got crazy about food staying at the table—no food on the couch, no eating on the run. The only place my kids were allowed to eat was sitting at the dining room table, and when my little ones were finished eating, I'd vacuum after each and every meal. Crazy, I know. Now that my kids are older, we've kept the rule that food stays at the table, even when friends are over. I can tell some kids think I'm a maniac for not letting them eat their crackers on the couch, but that just doesn't work for me.

Sharing Is a Skill

For the kid hosting the playdate, having to share their toys can be *maddening*. How would you like having a friend over and letting them rummage through all your favorite stuff? Then again, helping your child learn to share is one of the best reasons to entertain! Here's how to prep your child before their friends show up:

1. Ask them what happens when they go to a friend's house. Are they allowed to play with their friend's toys? Yes, of course! What would it feel like if they *weren't* allowed to play with them? Should they let their friend play with their toys today?

2. Give your child permission to tuck a few things away, like favorite toys and loveys, and make them off-limits to guests. Just make sure to explain that your child can't play with those items during the visit either!

3. Reiterate that sharing your things can be super hard, but it's only for a little while.

During the visit, be patient with your child and prepare to help manage scuffles. If your child needs a little break from the visit, give them a chance to step away to a quiet room for three to five minutes before rejoining the group. Kids this young are still learning all the social skills needed to navigate these interactions, especially in their own home, and it's okay to take a break!

Telling Your Guests It's Time to Go

If you're in the middle of a playdate and you absolutely *need* it to end, you can say so. If the parent is there, say something like, "I'm so sorry, but I think we're coming up on naptime a little early today. Could we continue this another day next week?" If you need to ask an adult to come pick their kid up, go with: "We're wrapping things up over here a little earlier than expected. Would you mind swinging by when you can?"

But what if there was actually a problem with your guest's behavior? What if this kid you had over for the last two hours without their adult was jumping off the couches and tearing through the house like a wild thing, and wouldn't slow down no matter how many times you asked? That's when someone becomes an "outside friend," as they say in Sarah's family: someone who you visit with in your backyard or around the neighborhood, but not in your home. Could you bring up the behavior to the child's parents?

Sure, but they probably already know their kid's speed and: (1) don't mind it, (2) don't care enough to change it, or (3) can't change it (hey, maybe this child has other issues going on that you just don't know about). Plus, it's hard to criticize another kid's behavior at your house without sounding totally biased. *Of course my child was an absolute angel, but yours was a beast!*

As a last resort, if you really can't make that friendship work, you might have to back away from it, and that's okay. Sometimes, friendships just aren't meant to be.

SPECIAL GATHERINGS AND THEIR QUIRKS

Baby Showers

Q. Can I throw my own baby shower?

A. Well, not really. This is one of those topics where there are some long-standing etiquette rules that people still follow pretty closely. Because the point of the shower is for guests to "shower" the parents-to-be with gifts, most people feel that it's tacky for expectant parents to host their own party. On the other hand, it is supposed to be a celebration of the baby, so you could argue that it isn't much different than a parent hosting a birthday party for their child. It's not like the parent-to-be is *dying* to receive diapers at their shower—all the gifts are for the baby.

So here's the deal. Your shower should fall somewhere in your last trimester. If no one has offered to throw you a shower once you hit that six-month mark, start to put out feelers. Maybe even ask the best hosting candidates if they think it would be weird for you to throw your own shower. Once they realize you don't have anyone to do it, they might decide to step up.

If you're truly in a situation where that's just not going to happen, weigh your options. Hosting is a responsibility and an expense of its own! A shower is supposed to be fun for a new parent. Can you host and still have fun? Maybe. Will you come out ahead in terms of the money you'll spend on the party vs. the amount your guests will spend on gifts? It sucks to have to come down to math, but it's something to consider. In the end, if you decide you want to host your own party, go for it and do your best to make your guests' experience a pleasant one in terms of food, drinks, and games. Thank them profusely for the gifts at the party and get those handwritten thank-you notes out within the next couple of weeks to end things on a classy note.

Q. Is it appropriate to host a baby shower for a couple or individual who's adopting or using a surrogate?

A. Definitely! If the family is using a surrogate, ask them if they'd like to include her in the party and check the best time for the festivities. As for adoption, uncertainty is par for the course. Check with the soon-to-be parents about whether they'd be more comfortable celebrating once the baby arrives.

Coming to See a New Baby

Q. We just welcomed a baby and lots of people have asked about coming over to meet her. Should I say yes?

A. Welcoming a baby can be joyous, but also totally overwhelming. You can feel confident putting off seeing visitors until you're ready. While you're in the hospital, task family and close friends with letting people know that you need some time to rest and recover. If people ask to meet the baby once you're back home, you can tell them you're "not quite ready for visitors," but that you'll let them know once you are. Take the time you need and don't feel pressured to host.

Overnight Guests

Q. We've got family with young kids staying over for a few days. What's the best way to prepare?

A. Check with your guests about their needs—food, space, schedules, and otherwise.

- Is there anything you can pick up at the market that would save them a trip? Evie and Sarah's first babies both had dairy allergies, so they always needed a supply of soymilk on hand. Without the help of their hosts, the grocery store would've been their first stop after any flight.

- What sort of sleeping arrangement can you offer, and how does that match up with your guests' needs? For instance, does this family co-sleep or will they need a separate area for the baby?

- Do you have any gear you can let them borrow? Do you have a playpen you won't need during the visit so your guests don't have to travel with one? Bonus points for putting a clean sheet on it!

ENTERTAINING AURORAS AND TWILIGHTS

How is your Parenting Perspective helping you shine or holding you back when you entertain?

Crescent

While you might love entertaining, you always have an eye toward setting boundaries that work for your child. That might mean scheduling get-togethers around naptime, or helping your child hide their lovey before friends come over, since there's no way they'll be able to share it. You're great about considering the gathering from the children's perspective, with fantastic activities, entertainment, and snacks.

Watch out for: Opportunities to let your child ease out of their comfort zone. Having friends over and having to share your home and belongings is a special skill that can be really hard for kids to master. While your instinct might be to swoop in and save your child from the frustrations that come with having friends in your home, encourage them to be flexible.

Fireball

For most Fireballs, your home is your sacred space, so opening it up to others can take you right out of your comfort zone. Even when entertaining doesn't necessarily mean inviting others over, it can feel like a whole lot of work for very little obvious reward, especially when your littlest guests can be demanding and prone to making messes. When you do entertain, you're great about remembering the adults in the equation. You might host a princess party for your five-year-old in the living room while the adults gather in the kitchen around a spread of their own, dishing over cold beers.

Watch out for: Missed chances to build bonds by entertaining. So if entertaining in your home makes you feel crazy, think about organizing a girls' night out by making dinner reservations or scoping out that new wine bar. Or, coordinate a playdate at the park and bring some simple, on-the-go snacks for the kids—a $5 to-go pizza could even do the trick!

Constellation

You really give a lot of thought to the way you're perceived in everything you do—from parenting, to the appearance of your home, to hosting a party. So when it comes to entertaining, you make hospitality a priority. You want your guests to feel at home and really enjoy themselves, so you're likely to think of all the little details that'll make the visit special.

Watch out for: Overdoing it and feeling burned-out. It's okay to set boundaries and enforce them (even around rules or preferences you know are a little unusual). It's okay to keep things simple. It's even okay to ask your guests to head out if your child has just had enough. Don't put so much pressure on yourself that entertaining becomes unmanageable.

CHAPTER 5

Home Is Where the Mess Is

PARENTING POP QUIZ

The dog starts barking. You look out the front window to discover your mother-in-law pulling into your driveway. Crap! You just got the new baby down for a nap and were hoping to hop in the shower. Instead, you'll be treating your mother-in-law to a real scene: a sink full of dirty dishes and baby bottles, dirty (but sorted) laundry piled on the living room floor, and the scent of un-scooped kitty litter wafting through the air. And PS, the front door is blocked by a pile of shoes and your stroller. What do you do?

A. Run and hide. Don't answer the door! The doorbell may wake the baby, but at least you'll save yourself the embarrassment of your mother-in-law seeing you and your house like this.

B. Call for backup. Find your husband and have him stall outside. If only you had twenty minutes to fly around the house and whip things into shape!

C. Accept the inevitable. She's here now. Nothing you can do about it. Hopefully, she's coming over to help, not to judge. Push the stroller aside, welcome her in, and don't point out how messy things are.

D. Call her cell *before* she approaches the front door and ask her to run an errand for you, to buy yourself enough time to get things under control.

Keep reading for the correct answer!

DO YOU LOVE COMING HOME?

When you walk through the door, does your home feel warm and inviting, like a sanctuary from the chaos? Or does your home feel like the center of it?

Before you have kids, you refer to your home as your "nest." You curate Pinterest boards with perfect paint colors and glitzy kitchen hardware. You thumb through magazines with spreads of stylish interiors thinking that someday you'll have a home like that, too. But there's a reason these beautiful photos are in magazines— they're a fantasy.

When you bring home a baby, your whole house changes. Your kitchen turns into a sanitizing/drying station for bottles, nipples, and pacifiers. Your living room evolves into a rainbow-colored baby paradise, filled with bouncers, rockers, playmats, playpens, and swings. Your bedroom becomes a breeding ground for dirty laundry and dirty diapers. And before long, those little babies grow into toddlers who seem to thrive on creating chaos. We're talking blocks scattered across the floor, bookshelves emptied of their contents, and stickers on any surface those little hands can reach.

All of us have had that moment of surveying our once-presentable home and wondering, *What the hell happened here?* We're not slobs, but our kids sure make us look like them! And our attempts to contain the chaos usually feel futile, because while we're mopping the floors, someone's probably crushing Play-Doh into the carpet. That's why so many of us just kind of...give up.

We relegate ourselves to messy homes that make us irritable, unsettled, embarrassed, and unlikely to entertain. Just think, when was the last time you walked into a home with young kids and the adults *didn't* apologize for the mess? Or, when was the last time you walked into a home with young kids and you weren't slightly grossed out by something you saw? Are parents just doomed to live this way? No, but working against the norm is a choice.

TOO MUCH STUFF

If you ever looked around your home after welcoming a baby and realized that tiny creature somehow brought with it an avalanche of stuff, here's a statistic for you: in 2013, Americans spent over $23 billion on "baby products, including toys, grooming, formula, and durable goods like cribs."[23] With 3.9 million births registered in the US that year,[24] that's roughly $5,900 worth of baby stuff per kid! That's insane, right? So why so much spending? Some people think it's linked to the way we parent:

> "Today's parents are spending more per baby. Why? Today's children are deemed more worthy of protection than they used to be. For Xers, this is out of guilt: "What if I could have prevented my child from getting hurt?" For Millennials, this is out of shame: "What if others think I'm a bad parent?"[25]"

But the spending doesn't stop with baby gear. Researchers at the University of California, Los Angeles's Center on the Everyday Lives and Families (CELF) actually spent years studying the homes and possessions of suburban families, and their findings are filled with commentary on the glut of toys we buy for our kids. "The United States has 3.1 percent of the world's children, yet US families annually purchase more than 40 percent of the total toys consumed globally."[26] But why so much stuff?

Those same researchers speculate that "[d]ual-income parents get to spend so very little time with their children on the average weekday, usually four or fewer waking hours. This becomes a source of guilt for many parents, and buying their children toys, clothes and other possessions is a way to achieve temporary happiness during this limited timespan."[27] Part of the reason our homes are overwhelmed is because consumerism makes us feel like good parents. But to be honest, it's not just our kids' stuff that's overwhelming.

No, we're guilty of over-purchasing for ourselves, too. A dollar bin mug here, a nifty little gadget there, and you end up with a home cluttered to the point that the vast majority feel is more than they can manage. "[N]ot only is 54 percent of America overwhelmed by the amount of clutter they have, but 78 percent have no idea what to do with it or find it too complicated to deal with so they let it build up, taking over their homes and offices."[28]

What Now?

If the rise of minimalism among parents is any indication, everyone's feeling a bit overwhelmed by the contents of their homes. From capsule wardrobes, to no spend challenges, to "sparking joy," more and more of us are questioning the need for all this *stuff*. If we really want to live in homes that are comforting and inviting to us and others, it starts with our possessions: what, how much, and where.

Even if minimalism isn't your thing and the name Marie Kondo sends shivers up your spine, cultivating a practice of reflection on the things you own (or want to own) and helping your kids be mindful of their possessions can set you up for less clutter and less wasted money. And less clutter means less cleaning— there's no downside to that!

Appealing "Clutter"	Unappealing "Clutter"
Plants	Mail and other paperwork
Neatly organized collections	Dirty dishes, napkins, tissues
Holiday decor	Piles of unfolded clothes, clean or dirty
Framed family photos	Electronic device cords
Stacks of books	Random toys without a permanent home

THE RESEARCH: HOW YOUR HOME AFFECTS YOUR HEALTH

There's actually a lot of research on how the state of your home can change the way you think, learn, and feel. In one study out of the University of California, Los Angeles, researchers recorded wives giving self-guided home tours, then studied the words the women used. People who talked about their homes as cluttered or unfinished had "increased depressed mood" and "flatter diurnal cortisol slopes."[29] For those of us that didn't go to medical school, the latter is associated with poor health in so many measures, including fatigue, cancer, obesity, and depression.[30]

"Well, maybe those particular women were just neat freaks," you say? Nope. The researchers even controlled for marital satisfaction and "neuroticism"—their term, not ours. It turns out, people who live in houses they see as messy works-in-progress are actually less happy *and* less healthy. What's more, clutter has another negative side effect for both kids and adults: it makes it difficult for everyone to focus. Researchers at Princeton University found that when your eyes have to take in too much stuff, all demanding your attention, it's hard to focus on a particular task:

> "Multiple stimuli present in the visual field at the same time compete for neural representation by mutually suppressing their evoked activity throughout visual cortex, providing a neural correlate for the limited processing capacity of the visual system.[31]"

That's science-speak for a cluttered environment equals a cluttered mind. And the same is true for kids, whose mental capacity for learning decreases in environments with more distractions. Here's what researchers at Carnegie Mellon University found:

> "We placed kindergarten children in a laboratory classroom for six introductory science lessons, and we experimentally manipulated the visual environment in the classroom. Children were more distracted by the visual environment, spent more time off task, and demonstrated smaller learning gains when the walls were highly decorated than when the decorations were removed.[32]"

And in case you needed more motivation, it's important to know that it's not just the *state* of your home that affects your mental health, but also the work you do in it. Research out of the University College London actually confirmed that heavy housework is "independently associated with lower odds of psychological distress."[33] The very act of cleaning is good for you!

In fact, a poll by the National Sleep Foundation showed that people who make their beds "every day or almost every day are more likely than those who do so less often or not at all to say they get a good night's sleep every day or almost every day (44 percent vs. 37 percent, or a 19 percent difference)."[34] Taking care of your home helps your body, your mind, and your mood.

WHAT DOES YOUR HOME HAVE TO DO WITH ETIQUETTE?

So far, we've talked about how much a clean and tidy home benefits you and your family. But is this really an etiquette issue? Aside from the personal benefits of a cleaner, tidier home, there are social benefits that we don't usually like to admit or discuss, and *they* make this an etiquette issue.

As parents, we all experience moments when our home is downright dirty—grimy bathtubs, muddy floors, gross toilets. It's usually not because we like living in bachelor-pad-level squalor, but because we're overwhelmed by life. Maybe it's a stomach bug going around the house, or sixteen-hour days at work, or a brand-new baby. It happens. When you live with kids, even houses that can normally withstand a white-glove inspection get gross.

But there's a serious difference between *your* gross and everyone else's. It's like your own kid's runny nose versus another kid's: you'll totally wipe *your* kid's snot with your sleeve, but the thought of touching another kid's slobber makes you gag. Same thing with your home: your dirty toilet is just an afterthought during a busy week, but so much as a stray pubic hair on an otherwise pristine toilet in someone else's house will make you want to hold it in till you get home!

Normally, our homes are private spaces, where a little bit of dirt doesn't kill anyone. But when we welcome guests into our homes, we're opening up our most personal spaces to build connections. The critical question is how might opening your home help or hinder the connection?

We've all been in someone else's house and seen something that made us cringe. This isn't because we're looking for reasons to be critical, but because our eyes see things the homeowner has stopped noticing, whether it's a moldy shower or crusted food on the kitchen floor. And when there are kids in the equation, the degree of scrutiny skyrockets. No one wants their baby crawling on someone else's dirty floors, and most moms and dads would be squeamish about snacks prepared in a kitchen adorned with mouse traps.

Can a dirty home affect your social life? Heck yes! If you're the type of person who likes to host, but your guests are a little queasy about the sandwiches you're serving after seeing your cat on the counter during food-prep, that's a problem. Or maybe your home is so overrun with stuff that there's no place to sit. That's no way to make your friends or your kids' friends feel at home.

WHICH HOME WOULD YOU RATHER VISIT?

Think about this scenario: You're invited to a new friend's house. You've met a couple of times at the playground, but this is the first time you're visiting with each other in a home setting. Which of these two homes would you rather visit?

Home 1	Home 2
✔ Living room: comfy couch adorned with throw pillows ✔ Toys: tidy and organized in bins and shelves ✔ Changing table: stocked with diapers, wipes, and a clean (unstained!) changing mat	✔ Living room: unfolded laundry covers the couch, so you resort to sitting on the carpet ✔ Toys: broken and littered across the floor ✔ Changing table: unusable! Dirty diaper forgotten on the stained mat, and the whole room smells awful

Now, we can just hear you naysayers with your "I'd rather see laundry on the couch, because that means they're keeping it real!" Yeah, yeah, yeah. We're all for that with our besties. But the problem with laundry on the couch when a new friend comes over is that it shows them how little an effort you made to get ready for their visit. You're showing them that they were a total after-thought—you couldn't even be bothered to clear a space for them to sit!

The idea here is effort. When your home is clean and tidy, you're telling visitors, "I knew you were coming, and you're important to me. I want you to feel comfortable in my home, so I put in a little extra effort to make you feel welcome." Does that mean you have to stress-clean your disorganized closets or clear out cabinets under the bathroom sink? Heck no! No one should be poking around there anyway. But think about the things that would make a visit to someone else's home most comfortable for you:

- A place to sit
- A clean place for the kids to play
- A clean, stocked bathroom
- And maybe a snack, because who doesn't love snacks?

Guests learn lots about you when they visit—not just whether you're a neat-freak or a pack rat, but also the significance you place on their visit.

YOUR HOME IS A REFLECTION OF YOU

Just like the way a person looks says a lot about who they are, so does their home. Come on, just admit that walking into a house that's neat and tidy gives a totally different impression of a family than stumbling through broken toys and dirty wrappers. When you really put thought and effort into the way you present yourself out in the world, it's like you're announcing your own self-worth. You're saying, "I matter enough in my own life to set aside time to shower and change out of my pajamas every day."

When you take care of your home, you're also telling people about your priorities. You're saying:

- I know my house is one of the only environments where I have near-complete control, and I choose to use it wisely.

- I know creating order makes me focused, calm, and happy, and I choose to give myself that mental and emotional boost.

- I know the act of cleaning keeps my body, my mind, and my family healthy, and I choose to make that a priority.

If this is what you communicate when you spend time caring for your home, what are you saying when you stop prioritizing your home—not in the short term, but in the long term? *I don't matter. My life is out of control. I give up on my house, my life, myself.*

Even if you think you don't care what people say about your messy house, you should care what your messy home says about you. And not just what it says about you personally, but about the pride you take (or don't) in your possessions. When your stuff is carelessly tossed around the room, it doesn't exactly say "I cherish these things."

Listen, we know that trying to keep your home presentable when you're parenting young kids feels like a war of attrition. It's so much easier to pretend to embrace the chaos than it is to fight it! But the research is clear: we aren't our best selves when our home is overwhelming and out of control.

A HAPPY MEDIUM

Nobody's home is perfect all the time, especially not a home with kids in it. If you were to pop into our homes right now, you'd see that they're lovingly imperfect. As we write, Evie's kitchen has been taken over by a hoya plant, it's ceramic pot, and a whole lot of dirt because she's trying to save her little friend from overwatering. Sarah's downstairs bathroom may or may not have dried toothpaste all over the sink from the kids brushing their teeth this morning. Would these make flattering scenes for pop-in visitors? Not especially.

If you think we're suggesting that your home be photoshoot-ready at all times, this is a good place to take a breath and get real. Homes like that are not only unrealistic, they're also sad. Anyone would recognize that the adults in those houses were stressing way too much and stifling their kids. On the other hand, not worrying at all about the state of your home can have a real impact on your health, your happiness, and your social life. That's why you need reasonable goals for yourself, the other adults in the house, and your kids. That means prioritizing and sharing the work.

EVIE'S Problem Area in Her House

We have this section of our kitchen counter that juts out into the entryway. Unfortunately, it's the spot where everything gets tossed when we come in, and then quickly forgotten. From business cards to coloring pages, and paperwork to pencils, we just can't seem to keep this area clear of clutter. I hate that it's one of the first things you see from the front door, so it's a constant battle against all the real-life stuff that ends up in our house without an obvious or immediate home. My only real strategy here is to organize things into stacks. A stack of papers always looks less overwhelming than an explosion of them!

SARAH'S Problem Area in Her House

With four young kids, laundry piles up faster than we can wash it. My kids are supposed to put their laundry in the hamper, which is upstairs, but I always seem to find stray pants, socks, and shirts lying around. It drives me crazy to have piles of clothes everywhere, dirty or clean! I started a chore chart with my kids, with putting clothes in the hamper as one of the top responsibilities. And I try to separate the clothes as they come out of the dryer and give my three older kids (ten, seven, and five) their baskets of clothes to hang and put away.

IN A HOUSE FULL OF WORK, HERE'S HOW TO PRIORITIZE

Address immediately	<ul><li>Clean up bodily fluid or excrement</li><li>Address foul odors (garbage, food, bathroom, or any others your family might produce)</li><li>Tackle anything unsanitary (toilet water, raw chicken, etc.)</li></ul>

Address within a few hours	• Wash and put away dirty dishes and pans • Make beds
Address daily	• Fold and put away clean laundry • Wipe kitchen table and counters • Sweep or vacuum kitchen floors (keep those bugs at bay) • Tidy toys and books • Address clutter (mail, projects, school papers, etc.)
Address weekly	• Dust surfaces • Clean toilets, bathtubs, and bathroom counters • Vacuum or mop floors (including the kitchen) • Take out trash (more often when smelly) • Sort and wash laundry (probably happening much more frequently than this—just don't wait longer)
Address monthly	• Deep clean (refrigerators, windows, under furniture, air vents) • Check baseboards, fans, and other easy-to-overlook areas • Replace blown out lightbulbs

EVIE'S Story on Dealing with the Mess

Most days I can live with a certain degree of messiness. I don't expect perfection, even though I'd like it because I'm crazy like that. But eventually I reach my breaking point, and it's usually not very pretty. Like all kids, mine bring new things home day after day without so much as a thought of tossing the old stuff. And when I do ask them to purge, they're reluctant. Why would they get rid of all this perfectly good stuff?

I can go for weeks looking at the same messy kids' rooms—books and stuffed animals and papers and party favors tossed around—before I get totally overwhelmed and snap. Sometimes, snapping involves making a bag of things to donate while the kids are at school. One time, "snapping" involved showing my girls an episode of *Hoarders* so they could see what houses look like if you never throw anything away.

I'll never forget the look of horror on my children's faces. They had no idea people lived like that, with stuff up to the rafters and narrow paths carved through rooms swallowed up by junk. We talked about how hoarding is a disorder, but you can train your brain to let things go when you no longer use them or they're not important to you. And, not everything can be important.

Did watching *Hoarders* scare my kids straight? No, but I don't regret giving them a visual of how life could be if I weren't here to nag them about purging every now and then.

SARAH'S Story on Dealing with the Mess

About once or twice a week, I go around my house with a trash bag. Not necessarily for toys, but for things that don't have a home. I'm talking clothing tags strewn on the floor, little stickers that have been fastened to the wall, broken crayons on the ground, extra papers from school, or little toys from fast food restaurants that no one's playing with at all. I find that by walking through the house on a regular basis I can keep up with the clutter a little more. With four little kids, my house is definitely not pristine, but if I can keep the common areas presentable, I feel better.

THE CASE FOR GIVING KIDS CHORES

Even if housework is just about your least favorite thing, most parents get that it's actually great for kids to be assigned certain age-appropriate chores. First and foremost, it builds personal responsibility. Most of us grew up doing chores and would agree that they helped us become self-sufficient, capable adults who grasp that housekeeping is a team sport. In Elizabeth Larson's research on "children's work,"[35] she confirms:

"From the parents' view, work is seen primarily as a character-building occupation that develops a sense of responsibility. More than 72 percent of the parents gave this reason for assigning their child chores.[36] Another 25 percent of parents described the child's duty to do chores as essential to integrating family and was part of being a family member. [...] Reciprocity in family work was learned by children as young as 5 years of age.[37]"

Chipping in toward the care of their home helps kids learn about their family's expectations and values. It also builds life skills they take with them when they go off to school and help clean up toys, or eat at a friend's house and clear their plate from the table, or co-exist with a college roommate years down the road. Taking care of shared spaces together *is* good etiquette.

It's awesome to teach your kids to chip in from a young age, but sometimes it just feels easier to do the job yourself. Sure, in theory, you want your four-year-old to clear their dinner plate from the table. But in practice, you really don't want to clean up the crumbs that tumbled off their plate and onto the floor. This can be especially challenging for Constellations and a certain type of Fireball parent, who wants things to be done a certain way. These parents ask themselves, *What's the point of showing a child to sweep if I'll just have to do it again myself?*

When young kids do chores, it's not really about the outcome. It's about your child learning a new skill by imitating you. When a toddler sweeps, you might not end up with a cleaner floor, but you do end up with a child that has superior gross motor skills, a sense of independence, and a feeling of pride in their contribution to the family.

So even if you'd rather have a root canal than guide your toddler through tidying the playroom, just remember: it's all part of teaching invaluable life skills!

Chores by Age

Age	Tasks
2–3 years old	• Pick up toys and books • Put trash in garbage can or recyclables in bin • Put dirty clothes in hamper

3–4 years old	• All of the above, plus... • Dust • Wipe counters • Wipe spills • Pull weeds • Take sheets off bed • Unpack groceries
4–5 years old	• All of the above, plus... • Set table • Make bed • Fold and put away simple laundry items, like facecloths • Water plants • Empty dishwasher of silverware, plastic dishes, and cups • Put sorted clothes in washer or dryer

EVIE'S Tip on Hunting for Toys

One area where you can almost always count on kids to shine is in collecting their toys. By the end of the week, your kid has probably deposited toys in every room of the house. That's why I like to hand each child a basket (even a laundry basket) and ask them to collect all their things from each room. It feels a little like a scavenger hunt, so it's fun enough for even really young kids, and it helps you corral the toys. Now, are you going to be able to get your kid to put all the toys back in their labeled bins? Yeah right. Remember, we're going for progress, not perfection.

"Pretty much as soon as my son became a toddler, I just felt like our house had to be set up so he could do things for himself. I've always thought that my goal is to raise a person who's a functioning adult in society, so I think that has to start early. For example, a couple of years ago when he was three or four, I redid his closet so it would be convenient for him to dress himself in the morning. We put in a double-hanging rod, I hung up a lot of his outfits, and then I used one of those shoe pockets that goes over the door to store his underwear rolled up like little towels, his hairbrush, and grooming stuff for hair. And on the other door, I hung a mirror.

So in the morning, when he was younger, I would kind of supervise and walk him through each step. I would say, 'Okay, let's pick out your outfit.' He'd get dressed and I'd say, 'Okay, check yourself out in the mirror.' But now in the morning, I just say, 'Get dressed for school,' and he goes in, takes his pajamas off, puts all his clothes on, brushes his hair, and he's ready to go. He has to be able to take care of himself, and it's got to begin now."

—**Anonymous**, Crescent, mom of one

THE FRONT-DOOR VIEW

You can't always control what's happening in every corner of your house. You might think your home is "visitor-ready," only to discover your kid left a little surprise in the potty. Ick. But even when you're not expecting guests, you can get away with a multitude of sins by following this one simple rule: Focus on the front-door view.

Try this: step outside your house and look in from the front door. Does it look cluttered and overwhelming?

Well, that's the first impression you're giving everyone who comes by, from the person delivering your pizza to the friend returning your baby carrier. If you only have five minutes to clean and tidy your home, we vote for focusing on the front-door view.

Following this rule means thinking strategically about where the messes and the clutter can live in your house until you have a chance to deal with them. If there's a way to do a job or store an item in a place that's not visible from the front door, that's the way to go.

SARAH'S Story

I have a small but stylish entrance into my home. There are three labeled cubbies to one side of the front door, where the big kids keep their backpacks, and there are baskets underneath for shoes. That space can get cluttered super fast. So when I'm expecting last-minute company, my first stop is that front-door area. My kids and I scoop up shoes, jackets, and extra papers, and tidy it all up. I do a quick vacuum and wipe down the floor, and all of a sudden, my entrance is ready for company!

DING DONG: SURPRISE! SOMEONE'S HERE.

Shoot! You just got a call that someone's on their way and your house is *so* not ready. What now?

You have an hour to prepare	First of all, don't overwhelm yourself. Be strategic! What can you achieve quickly that'll have the biggest effect visually? This isn't the time to start worrying about cobwebs on the light fixtures. Go for low-hanging fruit: • Toss dirty dishes from the table or sink into the dishwasher (if you have that luxury) • Clear off kitchen counters • Push chairs in at the table (you'd be surprised how big of an effect that has!) • Hide laundry back in a hamper, laundry room, or closet • Close the doors to bedrooms that aren't ready for guests and don't need to be • Toss toys away—they don't have to be organized, they just need a home • Clean and sanitize toilet, bathroom counters, and sink, and check any diaper-changing areas • Neatly stack paperwork, mail, and other clutter

You have twenty minutes to prepare	You could make the case that getting twenty minutes' notice is worse than no notice at all, because it's not really enough time to tidy up but you still feel like you have to try! Here's what to prioritize: • Clear dishes from the table and counters and set them in the sink or dishwasher • Check the bathrooms and diaper-changing areas for anything gross or smelly • Toss your clutter on your bed and close the door. It'll be your little secret... • If your kids are old enough to have toys out, they're probably old enough to help clean them up. If not, don't stress. A few scattered toys are to be expected in a house with young kids
The doorbell just rang with no warning	The best thing you can do now is say nothing. Don't draw attention to problem areas in your home, like the sink overflowing with dishes. If you don't point them out, maybe they won't notice and will think nothing of it. If you do point it out, you're just welcoming judgment!

> "Nothing inspires cleanliness more than an unexpected guest."
> —**Radhika Mundra**

Did You Ace the Quiz?

So what about your mother-in-law's pop-in visit? If your mother-in-law shows up unannounced for a visit with your new baby, game over. You've got to go with **C. Accept the inevitable**. Don't make yourself crazy trying to tidy up as she approaches the front door. Just take a deep breath, put on a smile, and say hello. Feel free to tell her the baby is *finally* napping and you were *just* about to hop into the shower—she might take the hint that she's arriving at a supremely bad time. If not, welcome her in without pointing out the mess or your un-showered state. That's on her. If you show up without warning to a house with a new baby, this is the risk you run. And if it really bothers her, maybe she'll offer to help out with those dishes in the sink!

PREPARING YOUR HOME FOR GUESTS

Sometimes you're caught off guard when the doorbell rings. Other times, you knowingly welcome family, friends, acquaintances, and even *strangers* into your home. Inviting people over means you'll have visitors eating in your kitchen, using your bathroom, sitting on your furniture, using your diaper-changing station, and playing with your kids' toys. *That'll be no big deal*...said no host ever. So how do you get your house ready?

Think of all the places your guests will probably go during their visit. For instance:

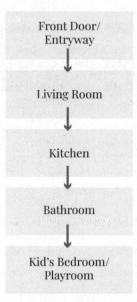

Does that mean you have to vacuum dust bunnies from under the bed in the guest room or even make your own bed? Nope. Check the list of "must-do" chores below and focus on the areas of your home that you know your guests will visit.

Most of the time, it's totally doable to close doors and make whole rooms off-limits! This gives you and your child a safe place to tuck things away that you don't intend to share. Just make sure you have a conversation with your kids about not playing in certain spaces. Otherwise, you might end up in a game of hide-and-seek that takes you and your guests right to that pile of dirty laundry you were hiding in your closet!

Once you've narrowed down the areas of your house that need attention, prioritize. Make a plan for **Must-**

Do, **Should-Do**, and **Would be Nice to Do** items. That'll look different based on who's coming to your house and what they're there for. Cleaning up toys matters way less when you're hosting toddlers that'll trash the place in two minutes, and cookie decorating calls for a way cleaner kitchen than an outdoor pool party. Here's a sample plan for a playdate with a couple of preschool friends and their parents.

Priorities When Preparing for Guests

Must-Do	• Clear and wipe down kitchen sink, counters, and table • Clean and sanitize toilet, bathroom counter, and sink, and check any diaper-changing areas • Make beds in rooms guests will visit • Put dirty clothes into a hamper • Clean floors where kids will be playing
Should-Do	• Tidy toys (but don't kill yourself!) • Clear clutter • Take out kitchen trash (a Must-Do if it's smelly)
Would be Nice to Do	• Fold and put away that laundry piled on your bed (otherwise, just shut the door) • Wipe sticky fingerprints off the refrigerator door • Empty small trash bins from bathrooms and bedrooms • Dust obvious surfaces (think dark furniture tops, not fan blades)

What's really most important is that your home is not a distraction from everything else you're doing to host and entertain your guests. If you're going through the effort of hosting your new parent group for an informal brunch, you don't want them to leave thinking about how bad your nursery smelled because you forgot to empty the diaper bin. The cleanliness and tidiness of your home shouldn't detract from your guests' (or your) experience.

A Note to Perfectionists

Listen, we know some of you reading this suffer from the same thinking that can plague us—that your house can never really be clean or tidy *enough*, so it's impossible to entertain. This just isn't true. It's like every summer when you feel nervous about showing up at the pool in your bathing suit because your body isn't "beach-ready," but then you look around and realize that no one at the pool looks like a supermodel! It's the same thing with your home: does it look like it belongs in a magazine? Probably not. Does that matter to anyone else? Not a bit, so get over it and invite some friends over.

Use (Three of) Your Senses to Clean Your Home

Coming into a new environment can be an assault on the senses, especially when the space was "designed" by a family rather than an interior designer who intentionally creates public spaces to be inoffensive and inviting. When you're getting your home ready for guests, try to experience your space like an outsider, using these three senses:

1. **Touch:** What are the surfaces in your home that you and your guests regularly touch? Think of things from the ground up: floors, chairs and toilets, tables and counters, handles and knobs. Are they clean? Is your couch covered in dog hair? Would you want to put your behind on your toilet if you were a stranger in this house?

2. **Sight:** What do you see around your house? Where are the spots that look cluttered or visually overwhelming? Where are the messes you've stopped noticing that an outsider would see?

3. **Smell:** Do the smells in your house repel or attract guests? The next time you walk into your home after a few hours away, take a deep breath. What do you smell? Is it a food smell? That's usually okay, as long as it's not reheated fish. Ugh. Is it an animal or bathroom smell? That's not okay. Time to root it out and eliminate it.

3 Things at Your House that Can Scare Other Parents Away

Guns: Maybe your family owns guns. Maybe they're locked up tighter than Fort Knox, or maybe your kids grew up in a house where guns were always sitting out, but they learned from a very early age that they can never, *ever* touch guns. Regardless of how your family treats firearms, lots of people who'll come into your home are afraid of them and you need to respect that.

If you do own one or more guns, put them away under lock and key when you're having guests over. If you ever get asked whether you own guns, don't take the question as an insult—it's no different than asking if you have a pool in the backyard that poses a drowning hazard for little kids. Take the time to reassure others that all of your guns and ammunition are locked away from little hands. If you're comfortable, you can even offer to show your guests where they're stored. Remember, hosting is about your adult guest's comfort, not your own convenience.

Dogs: Pets are part of the family, so it makes sense that many would bristle at the idea of tucking their dogs away just because they've got a guest in the house. We convince ourselves that our dogs are harmless, so there's nothing to worry about. But again, this isn't about you. Maybe your guest had a negative experience with a dog, or maybe they just don't want your dog humping their leg. Either way, if a guest of any age expresses concern about your dog, or even looks freaked out, put your pup in another room for the duration of the visit, assuming this isn't an overnight or long-term guest.

Pools: Pools are an amazing luxury. They're also an incredible drowning hazard, especially for young kids. According to the Centers for Disease Control and Prevention, approximately ten people die by drowning in the United States each and every day,[38] and the Consumer Product Safety Commission reports that, "74 [percent] of drowning incidents for children younger than [fifteen] between 2015 and 2017 occurred in residential locations."[39] If you're a pool owner, take special precautions when hosting families with young kids, and be sure to communicate with other parents about expectations and safety rules.

IF CLEANING YOUR HOUSE MAKES YOU CRAZY

Everyone has responsibilities that they could really do without. Maybe the drudgery of domestic chores is making you miserable. Maybe you've got deadlines at work that make dirty toilets dead last on your priority list, or maybe the unequal distribution of housework in your home is breeding resentment. After all, studies still show that "on an average day, 22 percent of men did housework—such as cleaning or laundry—compared with 46 percent of women."[40]

If you're sacrificing your sanity or your relationships for your home, hiring someone to help you clean, organize, or both, might be what saves you. If that's not possible for you right now, get clear about your priorities with your partner. When each person actually says *out loud* what they need in their home, they often unveil a disparity in expectations.

One partner will say that bath towels should be swapped out every other day, the other will say it's only necessary once a week. One wants to empty the bathroom waste bin once a week, the other wants to empty it when it's actually full (read: overflowing). It's the stupid little things that can make you crazy, especially when you're using up so much energy raising young kids. Parenting already requires so much give and take—you don't need another thing to bicker about!

If you discover that you're the designated neat freak in the relationship, poll your friends to see if you have higher standards than most, and if you do: (1) lower your expectations, or (2) understand you'll have to carry a bigger load than your partner. You can't make them believe mopping the floors every week is important if they don't believe in even owning a mop!

If, however, your friends (and this book) prove your point that your partner is a total slob, ask them for help—but do it tactfully. Resist the urge to completely unleash your frustrations about the division of labor being one-sided and ask yourself these questions that listeners of our podcast will recognize: What's the desired outcome? What's the best way to achieve it? Putting your partner on the defensive won't help. Telling them they're a slob won't help. As much as you may want to throw that mop in their face and scream, "Go mop the kitchen floor," remember that etiquette starts at home. How would you like to be asked (*told*) to take on a new chore toward the upkeep of your home? You know the old adage, "It's not what you say. It's how you say it"? Yup.

What This Isn't About

You know what keeping a presentable home *isn't* about?

1. How big your house is
2. How fancy or new your house or your furniture is
3. What neighborhood your house is in
4. Whether you have money for a housekeeper

Pride in your home has *nothing* to do with wealth or privilege. It's about caring for the things you own, whether you have a mansion or a hut, a sectional sofa or a single hand-me-down seat. Some of the neatest homes we've ever been in were the most modest. Take pride in your home, whatever it may be.

DON'T FORGET YOUR MOBILE HOME!

No, not literally your "mobile home." We're talking about your vehicle—your car, your truck, or your minivan. Parents spend so much time toting kids around, and for every person that swore up and down they were never, ever going to let their kids eat in the car, there's a parent whose minivan is full of goldfish cracker crumbs. Moldy sippy cups under the front seats, sticky fingerprints on the door handles, small toys in all the cup holders, enough food debris under your kids' car seats to sustain a small ant colony—that's just life with children.

But what about when you've got a guest in your car? That's when you start apologizing: "Sorry for the mess! Let me clear that seat off for you. Hold on while I move this to the trunk."

No one's expecting your car to look like it just rolled off the showroom floor, but a few little tricks will keep it presentable for riders, young and old:

- No milk, juice, or soda in the car, just water. That's the only way you can be sure those spills won't end up being sticky or smelly.
- Just in case, keep wipes on hand. Baby wipes work miracles on dirty hands and dirty dashboards.

- Stick to dry snacks. Sure, pretzels are going to leave crumbs in every crevice, but that's way less complicated to deal with than a squeeze-pack worth of yogurt mushed into your upholstery.

- Exit the vehicle with your trash. Instead of letting napkins, wrappers, and other garbage pile up in your car, make a habit of taking it with you when you hop out, even if that means a pocket full of dirty tissues. And get your kids to do the same. This is the family vehicle—you've all got to help take care of it! A trick Sarah uses: "Everyone pick up three things on your way out!"

Real-Life Sticky Social Situation:
Unwanted Advice

I have a friend who considers herself a minimalist, and every time she comes to my house she tries to tell me how much better I'd feel if I read such and such book, or got rid of this and that. At first, I would try to ask questions just to be polite. But honestly, I'm not interested in her opinion of the way I keep my home and I'm getting annoyed. How can I tell her to back off?

Dealing with a friend who has a lot of opinions can be a huge challenge—even a deal breaker for lots of friendships. If you've tried the polite route and it's not working, it's time for Plan B: honesty. Because really, the state of your home is shouldn't be a constant talking point. Unless you're literally living in a home that belongs in an episode of *Hoarders*, she should probably mind her own business. But saying so can be tricky. Try something like, "I'm so glad minimalism speaks to you. I know it's really popular, but my house makes me happy just the way it is." And if she brings it up again: "Yup, still not interested! You know me."

HOME AURORAS AND TWILIGHTS

How is your Parenting Perspective helping you shine or holding you back in your own home?

Crescent

Childhood is precious, and you're helping your kids build so many wonderful memories inside their own home. You let them take over the living room with their forts and make rocket ships out of the sheets on their beds. You've likely given lots of thought to the layout of your home and your furniture, to maximize the amount of space your kids have to play. You also probably have colorful bins where each toy is sorted, labeled, and made accessible. Crescents don't get bogged down by cleaning up toys all day. Instead, they get on the floor and play with those toys alongside their kids. When hosting, you cater to your littlest guests, cleaning surfaces they'll touch and dreaming up games and activities they'll adore.

Watch out for: Guilt about bringing your kids back down to earth with rules and expectations. It's healthy for kids to know that after they play, they've got to clean up. Pitching in builds personal responsibility and family values. Should a guest arrive at that moment of peak play, when the house is a disaster, focus on the positive: talk about how much fun you're having and invite your visitor to join in!

Fireball

There are actually two types of Fireballs when it comes to the home!

1. Because there are so many expectations outside the home, you really look to your home as a haven. Maybe you believe in batching chores and efficiency, not worrying about every little dish

in the sink or that dog hair on the couch. You're the most likely of the bunch to find balance by enforcing chores for your kids and dividing them with your partner.

Watch out for: Those first impressions. Take an outsider's perspective every once in a while and check in on the state of your home. Sure, it's just the way *you* like it. But when you're inviting someone new over, you may need to make adjustments to ensure they're comfortable, too. For example, you wouldn't want to miss out on an amazing friendship because you kept your two Great Danes loose when your visitor was clearly uncomfortable.

2. Or maybe you're the type of Fireball who can only find calm in your house when everything feels *just right*. Again, your home is your haven. But in this case, you're not seeking a respite from outside expectations. You've established your own special preferences. That might mean no toys in the living room, decorative pillows on all the beds, or a pristine personal space (like an office or a bedroom), so you always have a place to go to breathe. This type of Fireball keeps their common areas guest-ready because order pleases *them*, not for the sake of any guests!

    Watch out for: Rigidity. Sure, you have a way that you like things to be done, and it makes perfect sense to you. But don't forget to pause and ask yourself how the standards you've set are working out for the rest of your family and your guests. Are you reluctant to welcome friends and family because they might "mess things up"? That's when you know your home is actually holding you back.

Constellation

Constellations do their very best to keep their home pop-in ready. Heaven forbid someone thinks you can't keep a clean home! Ha! You take real pride in the appearance of your personal space, and you're modeling this well for your kids. Instead of viewing your home as a completely private space, you see it as almost an extension of the public sphere. Friends, family, acquaintances, and even strangers will come through your home at one time or another, so it should reflect well on you.

Watch out for: Perfectionism. It's nice to have a clean and tidy home, but everyone knows you have real human beings living there. A witness to a living room full of toys isn't the end of the world. And understand that just because you prioritize a tidy home doesn't mean everyone else in your home does, too. Don't let the mess make you miserable or grouchy with the people you love.

Constellations also need reassurance that it's okay to enforce their house rules, even with guests. If your family doesn't wear their shoes indoors, you can definitely ask guests to remove theirs. If you don't let your kids jump on their beds, you can certainly tell your little guests that they can't either. Constellations are always trying to be sensitive to other people's needs, but it's okay to express your preferences in your own home.

CHAPTER 6

Personal Appearance: Showering Isn't Optional

PARENTING POP QUIZ

It's the day of your family's annual fall photoshoot. You've got a gorgeous late afternoon session booked, which gives you just enough time to sneak out to buy yourself a new outfit and get a haircut. When your sitter arrives, the baby is napping and your two big kids are munching on snacks in front of the TV. All is well, and you feel like you're absolutely nailing this single parenting thing!

As your hairstylist makes their first cuts, your phone rings. It's your babysitter. She says the big kids are fighting like crazy and the baby won't stop crying for you. What do you do?

A. Speak to your big kids and remind them of the expectations you set before you left. Then, tell the sitter to snuggle the baby and distract the kids by playing outside. You're not heading home early over regular kid stuff. You deserve to look and feel great in these photos.

B. Ask your stylist to finish up as quickly as possible so you can get home. It was probably crazy to think you'd have time for hair and new clothes.

C. Apologize to your sitter for your kids acting up and promise you'll pay extra if they can hold down the fort until your haircut is finished. Then, apologize to your hairstylist for interrupting *their* work. Tell them all about the report from your sitter as a passive way of asking your stylist to hurry so you can get home.

D. Leave immediately to go home and take care of this chaos.

Keep reading for the correct answer!

EVIE'S Rant

If I were you and I'd just finished perusing this book's table of contents, I'd skip right to this chapter. *Personal Appearance? Is this parenting book seriously trying to tell me how to dress? Are you for real?* As a feminist, I'd bristle at the thought. Just one generation ago, women had to *force* society to accept their right to dress as they pleased, whether that meant pantsuits or miniskirts.[41] For thousands of years, men set guidelines for what women should wear as another way to control them and limit their role in society. We get that, so please understand that we aren't here to tell you to wear heels to the grocery store and a string of pearls each day (or ever!).

Reading about the etiquette of your personal appearance when you're an overworked, overwhelmed parent of young kids might be a turn-off. *As if I need another thing to worry about!* You, like many parents, may have come to think of your appearance as something you maintain *only* for the benefit of others. But guess what...it's not.

The ironic thing is, the social isolation and quarantining that kept us home during the coronavirus pandemic of 2020 taught us that we don't necessarily get ready for the day because we want to impress others. We get up, get dressed, fix our hair, even shave or put on makeup for *ourselves*. As one member of our community described so well:

> "I'm making a point in the mornings to get up before my daughter, work out, and grab a quick shower... I put on a little makeup and do something with my hair even if it is just a bun. Doing something for myself, like my workout, before the demands of the day just helps my mood. I'm more giving of myself after this.... The hair and make-up is totally a personal thing for me. I feel more in my game when I catch my reflection in the mirror and I have a little makeup on."
> —**Jordan**, Crescent, mom of one

Why would a busy parent bother with this personal care routine if the only people she was going to see were her immediate family members? There are two really important answers to that question:

1. This is about self-care, the foundation of our

Parenting Pyramid. Parents are much too quick to put themselves so far down on their own priority lists that personal hygiene doesn't even make the cut, and that's not okay. We're here to tell you that you're *way* too important a member of both your family and society to not have enough time for a new haircut, a wardrobe refresh, or a long, hot soak in the bathtub. You *need* time to take care of yourself so you have the emotional reserves to care for your family.

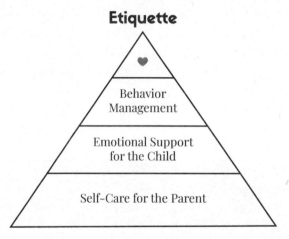

Etiquette

2. Getting dressed for the day instead of staying in your pajamas (even if you aren't ever going to leave your house or see anyone) can make you happier and more productive. "There's something called stimulus control where your behaviors are determined by a certain set of cues,"[42] so if you normally begin your day like Jordan—by exercising, showering, getting dressed, and doing your hair and makeup—keeping that routine (even as a stay-at-home parent or during a quarantine) creates a mindset of productivity,

normalcy, and stability. In this case, getting ready doesn't have anything to do with pleasing others; it has to do with your own mental health.

So even if the very premise of this chapter gives you pause, stick with us. Our goal isn't to make you look like you're ready for the red carpet or tea with the queen. But we *are* pushing back against feelings of being undeserving and the tendency to devalue ourselves through our personal appearance.

WHAT DOES YOUR PERSONAL APPEARANCE HAVE TO DO WITH ETIQUETTE?

Your personal appearance communicates to people around you how you feel about yourself, the people you're with, the environment, and the task at hand. You give people an impression of who you are with the clothes you wear, your posture, your hygiene, and even the expression on your face.

When you have "good manners," you think about how you affect other people. And whether you like it or not, the way you look *does* impact others. Consider your appearance in a professional context. Your team is meeting with a client to close a huge deal, and everyone is dressed in a suit except for the one guy who always shows up in a wrinkled button-down shirt, no matter the occasion. His hair is wind-blown and wild. He's even got a coffee stain on his shirt. What's he saying about the team? Is he making you look professional, capable, and focused? Probably not.

The thing is, people don't usually think of parenting as a team sport, so who are you really hurting by not looking like you just stepped off the runway? Well, as your kids get older, they might act like they don't know you if you show up to their school in a bathrobe and slippers. But you might also be affecting a team of parents in your community. Now, before you start rolling your eyes, hear us out.

Parents are always complaining about how the work we do is invisible. We don't get any respect and we don't get any thanks. But when we show up at school drop-off in our pajamas, someone inevitably looks at us and thinks, *Must be nice to be able to stay in your pajamas all day. They're probably headed home to scroll through Instagram and drink wine.* That person obviously doesn't have a clue, but that's the impression we just gave them—not only of ourselves, but of other parents, too.

On the one hand, society tells us not to carve out any time for yourself: looking good is selfish when you have a family to care for. But on the other, sending your kids to school looking photoshoot-ready when you haven't showered in three days signals that parents are unimportant, when that couldn't be further from the truth. That's why we need to reject the standard-issue Mom and Dad Uniforms.

MOM AND DAD UNIFORMS

Moms

- #messyhairdontcare
- The same three oversized (and over-loved) t-shirts or sweatshirts
- Ill-fitting leggings or pajama pants
- Dirty, old slip-on shoes
- Worn-out, tired looking diaper bag

Dads

- Worn-out college tee
- Gym shorts
- White tennis shoes and tube socks
- Fanny pack circa 1989
- Bucket hat for those long days on the playground
- And that same worn-out, tired looking diaper bag

What are you signaling to yourself, your children, and others when you adopt this all-too-familiar uniform of tired parents everywhere? Does this attire make you feel confident, capable, and valued? Not a chance. It probably makes you feel like you want to avoid your own reflection, and that's just not right. For goodness sake, you're doing one of the most important jobs ever! You're raising children to be well-adjusted members of society. You're caring for human beings at all hours of the day and night to make sure they're healthy, happy, clever, and caring.

If you had a role similar to parenting in another setting—say, in a classroom—would you wear sweatpants and a stained t-shirt to work? No way! First of all, you probably wouldn't get to keep your job if you dressed that way. There are expectations for how people in different professions are supposed to present themselves. It's easy to imagine a teacher in a button-down shirt, slacks, and loafers, but not in an outfit just a small step up from their pajamas.

Secondly, in a classroom setting, you'd choose nicer clothes because of the respect you have for the work you do. Just sit with that for a minute. When you respect the work you do, you show up as your best self, and your best self doesn't look like they just rolled out of bed.

So what are you telling everyone else about the work we do as parents if you choose the Mom or Dad Uniform?

Why We Choose the Mom or Dad Uniform

We've got two words for you: decision fatigue.

In 2012, President Obama told *Vanity Fair*:

> "You'll see I wear only gray or blue suits[...] I'm trying to pare down decisions. I don't want to make decisions about what I'm eating or wearing. Because I have too many other decisions to make.[43]"

Can't you totally relate?? It makes perfect sense! You find a uniform—something that's easy to wear and easy to launder—and you stick with it. That way you don't have to think about what to wear in the morning when there are a bajillion other things to decide, like...

- How long can you let the baby sleep before you'll be late for school?
- Do the kids need long sleeves or short sleeves today?
- What should you pack in their lunchboxes to make sure they're getting enough protein?

✎   Should you check the box to volunteer for the school field trip next month?

Seriously. The to-do list and the *to-decide* list are both endless. If common wisdom says the average adult makes 35,000 decisions each day, parents have got to make 50 percent more than that! And it's not like your decisions are trivial. One little error, like waking the baby up too early, can cause your whole day to spiral out of control.

With so much going on, lots of us do what feels easiest. We minimize the number of decisions we have to make each day. We stick to the six or seven healthy dinners we know we can throw together in thirty minutes. We streamline our friend list, because who has time to keep up with their fifteen closest college buddies? And we stop thinking about what we wear, even if it means walking around in a t-shirt that's old enough to have holes in the armpits.

Settling on a uniform might work well if you're the ruler of the free world and your wardrobe consists of suits (I'm guessing *that guy* doesn't have any trouble with self-expression or self-worth!), but it doesn't always work well for parents. And even if you *were* going to pick a uniform, shouldn't it be something a little more... *elevated*?

SHOWERING ISN'T OPTIONAL

Researchers Shannon Trice-Black and Victoria A. Foster wanted to understand how motherhood changes women, as their priorities shift from themselves to their families:[44]

> "Observations of mothers and children in playgroups revealed mothers' continual denials of self and placement of family's needs and desires above their own.[45] The societal pressures to do this can result in situations where resources and time are spent on children's preferences and appearance to the neglect of mothers' needs.[46] In caring for a family, house, and job, the wants and needs of the self are often disregarded."

Although this study focused on women, if you're a Crescent mom *or* dad, this "continual denial of self" may sound especially familiar to you. Crescents can take on the role of caregiver so fully that they overlook their own needs. They prioritize their child's well-being and wishes so strongly that something else has to fall off their plate—and it's often themselves. If you're a Crescent, you might be the parent who hasn't had a haircut in forever even though you take your child to the barbershop religiously. Think back to the quiz question you answered in chapter 1:

How would you describe your personal style now that you're a parent?

A. I wear whatever's appropriate for the given activity.

B. I choose clothes that are casual and easy to move in.

C. I use the weekend to embrace my personal style.

Can you spot the Crescent answer now? It's **B. I choose clothes that are casual and easy to move in.** Crescents see themselves as practical in the department of physical appearance. *I need to be in clothes I can chase my kids in—especially at a dangerous place like the playground.* But look down at what you're wearing right now. Are your clothes "casual" but well-fitting, flattering, and clean? That's what we're going for.

In order for you to have the emotional reserves to care for your family's physical, mental, emotional, and social needs, you *have* to make time for yourself. This isn't just about your outfit. That's why we're giving you permission—a *nudge!*—to shower, shave, fix your hair, put on makeup (if that's your thing), *and* pick clothes that express who you are outside of parenthood, every single day. You're not "just" a mom or dad defined by sacrifice to your family and your work. You're a unique individual with preferences, interests, and a personal style that you *deserve* to cultivate.

SARAH'S Story of Dressing like a Crescent

When I was a mom of toddlers, I had to make a shift in how I dressed. Before kids, I wore accessories and kitten heels and shirts with cute, frivolous details. But I soon realized that these were impractical outfits for me at the playground. I always envied the moms in heels, but that gave me anxiety! If I had to run after one of my kids or catch them from falling, I couldn't move quickly in flip-flops, heels, or a skirt. So I'd grab jeans or leggings, an easy-to-move-in top, and always wore socks and sneakers. The irony is, I love fashion. I love coordinating outfits and wearing different things each day. But when I was in the throes of raising toddlers, I had to make sure I could move comfortably in my clothes. My outfits were always well-fitting and fashionable (because I love that!), but practical and easy to move in—especially my shoes. My motto was always "cute and practical," and that fit with my Crescent perspective.

What Moms Can Learn from Dads about Self-Care

In one study of dads, over 75 percent "reported positive changes to their health behaviors since becoming fathers," including "positive changes in diet, increased frequency of exercise and physical activity, [and] taking better care of themselves in general."[47] Interestingly, the US urban men interviewed in this relatively small study said that they take better care of themselves *because* they're dads. One father put it this way:

> "Yeah, yeah, it's not about me. It's about the life of your child, so I have to keep myself together to make sure I'm here for him. So I'd say my whole entire attitude to health is that it's not just about me anymore, it's about us."

Where the research shows women tend to deprioritize their own care when they become mothers, this study provides evidence that becoming a dad might actually drive men to become *more* invested in their health and well-being. The fathers interviewed recognized that caring for themselves allows them to set a good example for their kids, "participate in activities with their child, remain in good condition to provide for their child, and live a long life to see their child into adulthood."

So why the gender disparity? Do dads feel less societal pressure to deny their own needs? The answer's not clear, but what we do know is that dads make a pretty good case for self-care.

WHAT THIS ISN'T ABOUT

Body shape. Hairstyles. A certain type of clothing. We're not here to tell you that in order to look presentable, you need to take off all your baby weight, revamp your dad bod, or never wear sweatpants again. It's about encouraging you to remember what made you feel good *before* you became a parent. Maybe it was cowboy boots and a sundress, maybe it was a concert t-shirt and a mohawk. The point is, eke out a few minutes between diaper changes and sippy cup refills for a thought and an action on how you want to convey yourself through your physical appearance. We're betting that "I don't care about myself in the slightest" isn't what any of us are going for, even if society tells us it should be.

GOOD MOTHERS ARE SUPPOSED TO PUT THEMSELVES LAST, RIGHT?

(Dads, you're not off the hook here just because this section is about mothers. Actually, consider it mandatory reading. You're about to get an inside look at one of the stereotypes that makes parenting in public view so complex for mothers, so you can understand your partner better and help push back on these "good mom" and "bad mom" stereotypes.)

In their research on the "Sexuality of Women with Young Children," Trice-Black and Foster studied society's perceptions of mothers:[48]

> "[M]others "are reduced to asexual beings, as sex is the antithesis of archetypal motherhood images."[49] It appears that both men and women perceive a split between motherhood and sexuality.[50] The more sexual a woman is presented to be, the less she is perceived to be a good mother."

It's really no wonder that women with young children struggle with their identities. Trice-Black and Foster reported moms complaining of loss (I used to be a "strong, sexy, independent woman"), dissatisfaction ("I look like a harried, frumpy mom"), and disillusionment ("Maybe if being a mom was all I wanted in life, I might not care so much"). There's even a link between body-image dissatisfaction (including perceptions of attractiveness) and postpartum depression in the first year after giving birth.[51]

Everyone receives the message that good mothers put themselves last, and those sacrifices are made visible to the world through their physical appearances. Mothers are supposed to be so singularly focused on their children that their own sexuality vanishes. But these demonstrations of "sexuality" are tricky, because our patriarchal culture can define almost *anything* as sexual.

Under the "male gaze," a term coined by feminist film theorist Laura Mulvey, "the woman [is an] icon, displayed for the gaze and enjoyment of men, the active controllers of the look."[52] If a woman puts effort into her appearance in a traditional way, it's *obviously* done with an eye toward sexual attention, right? Red lipstick is "sexual." Painted fingernails are "sexual." High heels and hoop earrings and long eyelashes are "sexual." But scholars like Ann J. Cahill challenge these assumptions by asking, "under what conditions can feminine beautification practices escape the workings of patriarchal power?"

> "The process of beautification must be understood and experienced as existing *for the pleasure and delight of the beautifying woman.* Only when beautification meets this condition can it hope to escape the mantle of social coercion.[53] "

So what if you just *like* wearing red lipstick—no "coercion" involved? What if red lips were your signature look before you became a mom because they made you feel polished, powerful, and ready to take on anything? And what if you're thinking of picking up a new tube in "Fire Engine Red" on your next pharmacy run?

Well, now that's complicated. It turns out your lipstick is actually part of a beautification routine that's been sexualized by the male gaze, and don't forget: "**The more sexual a woman is presented to be, the less she is perceived to be a good mother.**" *Not okay.*

How unfair is it that mothers are only prized when they sacrifice themselves and internalize society's sexist interpretations of what motherhood *should* look like? Makes you wonder if we're dressing down and shirking past preferences of what to wear and how to look because we've internalized the message that prioritizing ourselves makes us bad moms.

Sexuality, as it's defined in our culture, is *not* in conflict with successful, loving parenting. But constant, unwavering self-sacrifice is.

> "As you grow older, you will discover that you have two hands. One for helping yourself, the other for helping others."
> **—Sam Levenson,** *In One Era and Out the Other*

DID YOU ACE THE QUIZ?

So what do you do if all your best laid plans are at risk of getting squashed by sibling squabbles on the home front? Stick with the program and go with option **A. Speak to your big kids, tell the sitter to snuggle the baby, and proceed with your plans**. This isn't *just* about looking great in your family photos. It's also about not setting two negative precedents for your kids:

1.   If you don't feel like being with your babysitter, act up and I'll stop whatever I'm doing to rush home.

2.   What I was doing out of the house (taking care of myself) wasn't all that important anyway.

These are *not* messages you want to send! Before you leave the house, when you're talking with your big kids about expectations, make sure they know how much it means to you to get this time for yourself. Explain that you need an opportunity to take care of yourself just like you take care of *them*. Will that ensure they don't misbehave with the sitter? No, but it'll plant the seed for the significance of your outing. That way, when you speak with them by phone from your stylist's chair, they really get that this is important to you and they need to shape up.

DOES YOUR WORK LOOK PASS MUSTER?

If you work outside the home, you might be thinking it's not *that* big a deal for you to adopt the Mom or Dad Uniform on the weekends, since you look so professional Monday through Friday. You don't wear sloppy, old clothes to the office! This bit about letting yourself go doesn't apply to you, right?

It's true that parents who work outside the home are held to a different standard for their personal appearance during the work week, one imposed by their employer and society at large. But even if your work provides you with a *true* uniform, the way you wear it might belie your professionalism. Your overgrown hair, the dark circles under your eyes, and your worn-out shoes might reveal how low you truly are on your own priority list.

The thing about your personal appearance is that it requires time and energy. And what are the hottest commodities for parents with young kids, especially those who also work outside the home? You guessed it. If you're expected to show up in a professional setting each day while juggling the demands of parenting, time is something you'll never have enough of. You may feel like you don't have time for a visit to the salon or barber shop. You don't have time to shop for new shoes. You don't have time to eat right, exercise, and get enough sleep. But what happens if you don't?

The consequences are real. You show up looking frazzled and exhausted. You look like the new parent that you are in a setting that can be totally unforgiving. Should your competence be measured by your clothes? Of course not. Should you be passed up for a promotion just because you have a baby keeping you up all night right now? Definitely not, especially since the challenges you face today as a new parent is temporary, whereas the long-term implications for your career are permanent.

But the reality is, how you show up physically is one important measuring stick of your capabilities and your readiness to take on challenges. If you give people the impression that you're completely overwhelmed, you can get passed up for projects and overlooked when there are new opportunities. When you show up at work looking polished, you look prepared.

SHOULD THERE BE STANDARDS FOR HOW PARENTS LOOK IN PUBLIC?

In April 2019, a Houston high school principal sent the internet into a tizzy when she started enforcing a dress code, not for students, but for adults entering the school.[54] The list of banned clothing included pajamas, leggings, short shorts, torn jeans, low-cut tops, and short dresses. The story caught our attention because parents aren't used to being told how to dress in that role. We all understand a dress code at work, at our place of worship, at formal events...but at our child's school? What's interesting is that your response to this dress code would likely depend on your Parenting Perspective.

If you're a Constellation, you'd probably be all for this principal setting some boundaries. Constellations value being dressed appropriately for every occasion. They prioritize their role within the tapestry of other parents and educators at a school, and they wouldn't want to stick out for being over- or underdressed. You're not likely to find a Constellation wearing short shorts and a crop top at school pickup, even though they might pick that outfit for a day at the beach. It's a Goldilocks situation—Constellations want their appearance to be *just right* for the environment. And because these parents value personal appearance, they sometimes take issue with others who don't. They might praise the principal for setting standards for parents who don't seem to "get" the rules.

If you're a Fireball, you'd probably be outraged if another adult who has no authority over you told you what to wear, especially in an environment as casual as a school. Fireballs prioritize their own needs, boundaries, and preferences, not what others think, so they wouldn't be thrilled to learn that their preferred outfit wasn't meeting someone else's standards. What's interesting about Fireballs is that they might show up at school in a totally "appropriate" outfit, but *not* because they were worried they might offend other parents, teachers, and administrators if they didn't.

Fireballs are just as likely to show up in their cozy pajamas for morning drop-off or those torn jeans the principal forbade at afternoon pickup. They choose what feels right for them over what feels right for everyone else.

If you're a Crescent, you'd probably be shocked to get an email from your child's principal telling you that you wouldn't be permitted into the school unless you were dressed appropriately. If you dropped your kids off at school wearing your pajamas because you spent the morning making bento box lunches for them, you'd be pretty pissed to hear your attire wasn't fit for the occasion. Like Fireballs, Crescents tend to think, *I'm not worrying about what everyone else is wearing, so surely they're not worrying about me.* This balance between not feeling tethered to society's expectations of your appearance and understanding that you truly *are* judged by how you look can be especially complicated for Fireballs and Crescents.

Whatever your position is on this principal's dress code for parents, it makes clear that even though you may *feel* invisible, you definitely aren't. You can't overlook how much people learn about you from your physical appearance (which is a whole hell of a lot!). Should there be written, formalized standards for what adults wear in public settings, like their child's school? That's probably overkill. But that means it's on us as parents to hold ourselves to a standard everyone can be proud of.

When we send our kids off to school, we make sure their teeth and hair are brushed, their faces are washed, and their clothes are clean and tidy. We want their outward appearance to reflect their respect

CHAPTER 6: PERSONAL APPEARANCE

for their teachers and school. If that's the lesson we want to teach, we need to model it for our kids, too. We should aim to walk out of the house looking at *least* as prepared for the day as our kids. And on special occasions, like their holiday concert or their preschool graduation ceremony, we want the way we look to signal that this is an important day. At teacher conferences, we want our physical appearance to demonstrate our respect for the work that our child's teacher does and the time they're taking to speak with us. Does that mean we have to show up wearing a three-piece suit? Absolutely not, but there's a reason that Houston principal banned pajamas.

EVIE'S Perspective on Prioritizing Yourself

Every day, I make the decision to set aside time to get myself ready. It's not an elaborate routine, but it lets me walk out into the world feeling like the best version of myself. Of course, society conditions us to believe that parents aren't supposed to be concerned with their physical appearance. If I take fifteen minutes to style my hair, I'm obviously stealing that time from my family. I mean, shouldn't I be reading my child a book? How selfish of me to set my family's needs aside in favor of my own vanity!

But the same way I tell my kids they *must* change out of their pajamas and wash up before school, I show them that I *must* get ready myself. It's not that mommy is being selfish when she says that she can't sit down and do this project with you right now, it's that she needs to get ready for the day the same way you did. When we show our kids that we prioritize our own care (and by extension, our appearance), we show them how to treat us. We're showing them that we're worthy of time and attention. Don't all parents deserve that?

SARAH'S Perspective on Prioritizing Yourself

I love looking nice. It's mostly for me, and I know that. But I also feel uncomfortable when I go out in the community without a thoughtful outfit and a little make-up. So even from the beginning of motherhood, I made the time to get ready before leaving the house. When my children were infants, they were always soothed by the hair dryer, and so as they bounced in their activity chairs, I styled my hair.

Now that my kids are older, they not only give me that time without complaint, but have also begun to copy that behavior I've modeled all those years. I often see my daughter choosing a coordinating headband, or my son thinking about the shirt he's going to wear, and I'm proud that they're learning this self-care so early on.

Deal-Breakers for the Day

These are the things you absolutely must do each and every day. Everything else is just icing on the cake.

- Shower
- Brush your teeth and hair
- Change out of whatever you slept in or wore yesterday

> ✎ Change into an outfit that is clean, well-fitting, and flattering

WHAT MOMS USED TO WEAR

There's something ironic about encouraging mothers to reject the standard Mom Uniform, prioritize their appearance, and embrace self-care when just two generations ago, moms were breaking free of a completely different Mom Uniform. Even if you're not a fan of 1950s sitcoms, you've probably heard of June Cleaver, the quintessential housewife and devoted mother from *Leave It to Beaver*. June was the kind of woman who wore perfectly coiffed hair, a full face of makeup, tailored clothes, pearls, and high heels all day. She exemplified what moms of that era were *supposed* to look like, according to etiquette of the day. She also might've kept a bottle of Valium in her apron pocket to manage the pressure.

What we see in shows like *Leave it to Beaver*, *Father Knows Best*, *The Adventures of Ozzie and Harriet*, and *I Love Lucy* is that mothers of that generation were expected to look polished, perfect, and perky at all times. While there are things far worse than being overdressed while vacuuming, it's a matter of how restrictive the social norms were and how very high the bar was for moms. Etiquette in the area of a mother's personal appearance was stifling.

We have the feminist movement to thank for a cultural shift. The politicization of appearance encouraged women and mothers to break out of the June

Cleaver mold many had come to see as oppressive and objectifying:

> "Feminists [...] were the first 1960s activists to connect gender-bending dress and hairstyles to an explicit politics of gender that challenged broader conceptions of sex roles and femininity. [...] [F]eminists who promoted the concept of freedom of choice in dress pushed American society to accept changing fashion styles for women. Many American women, inspired in part by the rhetoric of the women's movement, fought for the freedom to wear pantsuits or miniskirts at workplaces and at schools, and by the 1970s many of these institutions began to accept these styles on women.[55]"

With all this ground gained, we can't be too careful about the way we talk about a mom's physical appearance. Sure, those 1950s housewives looked pretty good, and they probably felt confident about their appearance, but at what cost? At the cost of an incredibly narrow range of acceptable looks. At the cost of rigid gender norms. And at the cost of time and energy that could've been spent on other pursuits.

We're totally done with that June Cleaver-style, mid-century Mom Uniform. And we want to reassure you, no one on this side of the page is suggesting that we should ever return to that standard. We just know there's a happy medium between pajamas and pearls.

A Word on Makeup

Maybe makeup isn't for you. That's cool, no judgment. But it is for us. We both swear by a quick five-minute face to help us feel put-together, even during a quarantine.

When we talk to our kids about makeup, we tell them people wear it *if it makes them feel good*. It's not about making ourselves "beautiful." It's about making us happy when we look in the mirror. We don't feel happy when we see dark circles under our eyes, but we do feel happy when we see rosy cheeks or cat-eye eyeliner.

"Putting on our face" isn't about having poor self-esteem. It's an indication that we love ourselves enough to dedicate five minutes in the morning to our makeup so we can send our happiest selves out into the world. If you're looking for a quick and easy make-up routine, here's what works for us.

Evie's Five-Minute Face

1. Foundation to even skin tone, especially under the eyes
2. Liquid eye liner and mascara to define the lash line
3. Blush or bronzer for a little color

Sarah's Five-Minute Face

1. Hydration serum and sunscreen
2. Liquid foundation and under-eye concealer
3. Bronzer or highlighter and blush
4. Fashionable, colorful glasses

WHAT WOULD YOUR MOTHER SAY?

We've yet to meet a parent who doesn't care about how their child looks. Parents totally get how important physical appearance can be in the context of their kids. When children outgrow their outfits, we don't keep jamming their little bodies into too-small clothes. We go out and get new ones. When our kid's hair looks overgrown and shaggy, we don't just ignore the unsightly truth. We make time for a haircut. It's easy for us to have a critical eye for our kids, to make sure they're looking their best out in the world. So how come we don't give ourselves the same courtesy? When we build our children's wardrobes, we do it deliberately. And when the seasons change, we update their wardrobes. Moms and dads, we need to do the same!

THE ABSOLUTE CHEAPEST AND EASIEST WAYS TO LOOK AND FEEL BETTER (ACCORDING TO SCIENCE)

1. **Listen to your mother:** Stand up straight, pull your shoulders and chin back, and make yourself as tall as you can. Research shows that your posture is linked to your confidence and even your cognitive abilities.[56] It's true! Scientists actually studied how posture affects math performance, and they discovered that students who struggle with test anxiety, math difficulty, and "blanking out" could do simple math in their head more easily when they sat up straight.

2. **Say cheese:** Smile! The simple act of smiling can improve your mood, make you look more approachable (hello, new friends!), and if this is the sort of thing you care about, it can even make you look thinner and younger. When researchers at the University of Missouri-Kansas City showed college-age students faces with a variety of expressions—happy, sad, and neutral—"faces at the lower age levels were more likely to be categorized as old when they showed a sad facial expression compared to neutral expressions. Mirroring that, happy faces were more often judged as young at higher age levels than neutral faces."[57]

WHEN WAS THE LAST TIME YOU...

- Picked out a new piece of clothing you didn't absolutely need (that nursing bra doesn't count!)
- Worked out how you wanted, for as long as you wanted, because it made you feel strong and healthy
- Pulled your shoulders back and walked with a bit of swagger
- Had a haircut and hot-towel shave at your favorite barber shop
- Had a facial, wax, manicure, or massage

Sure, some traditional trademarks of a "polished look" may not be for you. Sarah doesn't usually wear jewelry because she has a toddler who pulls on it. Evie kind of hates having manicured nails because she feels like she has to preserve them. But is it *frivolous* to paint your nails when you're so busy raising young kids? Nope. Sometimes, it's just a good excuse to sit still and let them dry for an hour.

Make yourself a priority, because no one else will do it for you.

"I try to tell myself, *Others' opinions of me don't matter as long as I'm doing my best and have good hygiene. It shouldn't matter if I'm in old jeans and a t-shirt.* Then, when I dress 'cute,' 'on trend,' or whatever—actually fix my hair and makeup—I get a bunch of compliments. So it just reinforces the *You should care what people think of you* and *Whether or not they approve* narratives. On the other hand, when I look at other people, I'll always try to find something I like. I make a point to compliment something— hair, creative nails, cute handbag, great smile, funny personality. I like to make people feel good about themselves."
—**Melissa**, Constellation, mom of three

PERSONAL APPEARANCE AURORAS AND TWILIGHTS

How is your Parenting Perspective helping you shine or holding you back when it comes to your personal appearance?

Crescent

Whatever your personal style might have been before you became a parent, you now tend to prioritize your time with your kids over your time in the mirror. Your grooming routine is streamlined—you usually opt for a quick five-minute face, or an easy-care hair style. You choose clothing pieces that match well with each other, are easy to launder, and make it easy to sit on the floor to play blocks, or climb through a tube slide to extract a frightened toddler.

Watch out for: Remembering how it felt to put together a look that you absolutely loved. It's wonderful to prioritize your family, but when moms and dads feel like they've lost themselves to parenthood, their physical appearances are often a factor. One way to maintain your identity is by maintaining your appearance. If you prided yourself on your long hair before you became a parent, don't go and chop it all off after you give birth. If you had a standing appointment at the barber shop every other Friday night before you became a parent, try to keep it! Remember what made you feel good and make time for it, even in small doses.

Fireball

In the category of physical appearance, Fireballs can go either way. Although Fireballs excel at knowing what they need and carving out the time to feel whole as a person, that may or may not involve caring for their physical appearances in ways we'd typically associate with looking polished. Maybe you're a Fireball who feels refreshed and renewed when you make time for a mani-pedi. Or maybe you're a Fireball who'd much rather dedicate your free time to reading the latest best-seller.

Watch out for: Giving off the vibe that you're either too concerned with your looks, or not concerned enough. If you love to be completely put-together before venturing out to the grocery store, honor who you are, as long as your morning beauty routine doesn't involve setting a toddler in front of a screen for two hours (that hardly seems fair). Just know that others may perceive you as unrelatable or even judgmental of them. If you're the kind of person who would prefer to skip the shower and stay in your pajamas, revisit our **Deal Breakers for the Day**. We can't hold our children to higher hygiene standards than ourselves. Even if you feel invisible when you're out with your kids, you're not. How you look shows people how you feel about yourself and how to treat you.

Constellation

You've always taken pride in your appearance, and that hasn't changed since you became a parent. Before you get dressed, you think about what would be most appropriate for a given environment or activity. You probably haven't deviated from the grooming routines you had before becoming a mom or dad, since you still see them as part of what makes you shine in your community. Sure, your standards have shifted, but you still wake up each morning and make an effort to look presentable.

Watch out for: Unreasonable expectations, like *I can never leave my house in pajamas!* If you're headed to the emergency room, you most certainly can. This constant desire to look "presentable" can extend to a Constellation's children as well. Don't stress when your kids insist on dressing themselves and end up looking like explosions of colors and accessories. Actually, you might need to take a hint from them and give yourself permission to embrace styles or looks that aren't "appropriate" to some, but appeal to you.

Should I Leave the House Wearing This?

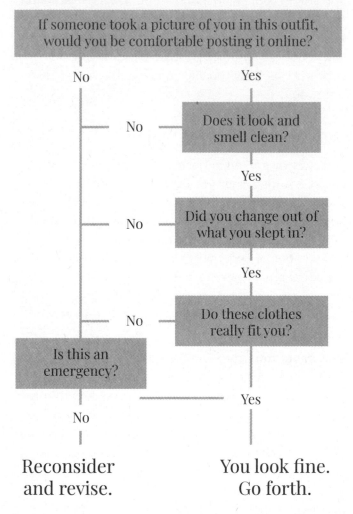

If someone took a picture of you in this outfit, would you be comfortable posting it online?

No — Yes

No — Does it look and smell clean?

Yes

No — Did you change out of what you slept in?

Yes

No — Do these clothes really fit you?

Is this an emergency?

Yes

No

Reconsider and revise.

You look fine. Go forth.

CHAPTER 7

School: There's No Honking in the Pickup Line

PARENTING POP QUIZ

It's seven thirty in the morning. You've got your baby in the bucket car seat, your three-year-old strapped into his five-point harness, and your six-year-old waiting at the ready. She's got her seat belt off and her backpack slung around her shoulders. She's crouched at the door of the minivan, ready to make her exit, and you're prepping her as your car inches closer to the drop-off point. "It's almost your turn. I love you! Have a wonderful day."

And then, when there are two cars left in front of you, she screeches. "MOM! I can't go to school! I forgot my bracelet!" She frantically darts around the car, looking for her puppy bracelet, the one she wears each day as her good luck charm. Your car seems to have a life of its own as you get closer to the teacher standing outside waiting to open the car door. "Honey, we have to go, I can see if I can find your bracelet for you after school." Your tone is gentle but urgent. It's a last-ditch effort, but you know she's like three seconds away from a total meltdown. And you also know the whole line is about to start honking at you if you don't *Keep. It. Moving.*

A teacher opens the door and gestures to your daughter, "Come on in, honey. There are people behind you." Your child is shaking her head and crying. "I can't go in yet. Where's my bracelet?" What do you do?

A. Pull into the parking lot and escort your child into the building once she's calmed down, even though it's frowned upon by the school.

B. Ease her out the door now so the other parents in line don't get even angrier.

C. Just give it a couple of minutes and hold up the line while you calm your child.

D. Get out of your car, mid-line, and call a teacher over to help you.

Can you guess which answer matches each Parenting Perspective?

A. **The Fireball Answer.** You're putting yourself first. You know it's against school policy to go in the building, but it's easier for you to pull over and sit in the parking lot while your kid finds the bracelet or finishes melting down. If it takes thirty minutes, so be it. Your kid will be late, but both you and your child will be satisfied with the outcome.

B. **The Constellation Answer.** You're so wrapped up in the stressors of the environment—all the other parents waiting in line, needing to rush off to the next phases of their day—that you act based on not wanting to inconvenience them. You may tell your daughter you'll look for the bracelet, but you don't give her much of a choice on whether or not to get out of the car. You may feel sad and upset afterward because your daughter left for school with high emotions, but you also wrestle with the fact that there was a line of parents behind you.

C. **The Crescent Answer.** You're thinking mostly about your child's comfort. You figure people will just get over it if they have to wait a few extra minutes, and when your kid exits the car, you'll feel okay. If it takes more than a few minutes, you may pull over to the parking lot, but you're going to try to address your child's concerns first.

D. **The wrong answer!** Ha! You definitely don't want to hold up other parents *and* interrupt the teacher who's handling the drop-off line.

Keep reading for the correct answer!

WHAT DO SCHOOL AND DAYCARE HAVE TO DO WITH ETIQUETTE?

When your child starts attending school, all of a sudden your world grows exponentially. Whereas before you were dealing with friends and family, now you're dealing with daycare workers, teachers, other parents, and other kids. People are asking you to do things, to participate in things, and to handle things you haven't had to worry about before. People are going to piss you off. You may even feel a little overwhelmed with everybody's expectations of you. You're also dealing with levels two and three of our Parenting Pyramid: expectations for your child's emotions and behavior.

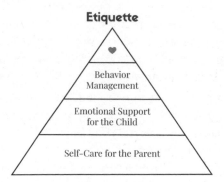

Etiquette

While they're at school, you're not there to coach them through their feelings, and *so much* is going to happen.

From school drop-off drama, to bullying, to the PTA, to teacher/parent relationships, to Saturday sports, you enter into a whole new chapter of *What the hell do I do now?* moments.

DID YOU ACE THE QUIZ?

In this case, it looks like your daughter is really upset, and it isn't something that can be solved in thirty seconds. It's okay to make people wait for a minute, but you can't hold up the line for too long. In this situation, you may start in Crescent mode (waiting in the drop-off line) and then slide into Fireball mode, ultimately choosing option **A. Pull into the parking lot and escort your child into the building once she's calmed down.**

Remember, it's okay to change perspectives based on what's happening around you—sometimes, you actually should! Your dominant perspective is the one you connected to in the quiz, but there will be times when you'll have to deliberately change perspectives mid-situation. This is exactly why the perspectives have strengths and weaknesses. It's interesting to note how you approach different situations.

While we're at it, there's no honking in the pickup line. Just because you're in a rush doesn't mean you get to judge what's going on in the car in front of you.

> "It really drives me nuts when parents are so fast to kick their kids out of the car or onto the bus. An extra five seconds to slow down during that time can be such a game-changer for our little humans! Keep in mind, most of the kids slowing the line down are young and can't move as fast as a teenager trying to get away from their parents ASAP! This one really irks me. You never know what's going on in someone's life or car! We all need to slow it down a little and be kind to each other!"
> —**Mary Anna**, Crescent, mom of two

COMMUNICATING WITH YOUR SCHOOL OR DAYCARE

Your school may send you daily (or even hourly) reports about how your child is doing. Or, you may have a quick check-in chat with your child's teacher at pickup and drop-off each day. It's worth finding out how each teacher likes to communicate, how often they plan to communicate, and what you can expect from each conversation.

The teacher will set boundaries on communication, but there will be times when you as the parent will need to initiate a chat. There are going to be easy conversations, like, "I think we left our lunchbox here yesterday," and hard conversations, such as, "My child is feeling bullied and I need your help." Feel confident in approaching the teacher with whatever you or your child needs. Most teachers want to help but can't if they don't know what's going on.

If you have a problem with a particular teacher, try to solve it with them first. Going over their head from the start will only make the problem worse, and they'll be upset that you didn't talk to them at all. And by the way, don't air your grievances on social media. Not cool.

How to Make Teachers Love You

Unless you're really lucky, you'll have to have at least one awkward conversation with a teacher during the school year. But if you use a couple of tricks *before* you get to that chat, you'll probably get a lot further with the tough stuff.

1. Send the teacher an email in the first two weeks of school, using the name their students call them (Mr. Smith or Ms. Anna), with a few thoughtful compliments. Maybe your child loves how funny they are, or the cozy reading corner they set up. Let them know. You've now positioned yourself well for your next interaction, which might not be as positive.

2. Be on time and follow the rules for pickup and drop-off. Say hello. Be kind.

3. Be prompt to conferences. Unless you've specifically asked to speak about a certain topic prior to the conference, save your big questions until you're at the end. The teacher may have already addressed some of your issues by then.

4. When sending an email or leaving a phone message, give the teacher at least a day to respond before sending a reminder. If they don't respond within 24–48 hours, definitely follow up!

5. If you have to talk about an awkward issue, start talking without attacking. "Jackson keeps telling me that there are kids screaming during center time and it's too loud. I wanted to get your perspective on it to see what you thought about that. Is that happening? Or does Jackson just need it to be really quiet for him to focus?"

Should I Tell My Child's Teacher about Any Unique Family Circumstances?

Some parents choose to let teachers know about their child's history because they want the curriculum to be inclusive, to make sure all types of families are included and portrayed in a positive light. Some parents choose not to disclose the information because they feel it's private. It's up to you! Your child may choose to share on their own when they get older. However, it's one thing to disclose that your family is unique in some way, it's a whole other thing to download your child's complete history. If it's necessary due to behavioral or learning concerns, go for it. Otherwise, it's your child's story and should be kept private.

DAYCARE DETAILS

Dropping off an infant or toddler for the whole day is a different scenario than catching the bus to kindergarten for a few hours. This place will be your child's home away from home, so it needs to feel that way for your child, for the provider, and for you. Trust is the most important connection—you two are a team and will be raising this child together. But there are also lots of logistics that need to be worked out so everyone stays happy.

- Be on time for pickup and drop-off, and if you're going to be late, make sure to call. Sometimes things at work happen. They're more likely to forgive a communicative and apologetic parent.

- If your child will be absent, let them know as early as possible.

- Drop off all the supplies your caregiver requests. Label everything, and make sure the school always has extra. (Think your baby will need three diapers today? Pack six! You could even send in about twenty and have them let you know when they're running low.)

- Get clarity on how you'll communicate with caregivers: when, how often, and by what method?

- Talk about discipline strategies and make sure you're on the same page.

- If your child has any food restrictions, make sure you've supplied the school with alternatives and clear instructions on what to avoid.

- Ask whether there are cameras in the facility. How often will you be able to access those camera feeds? Do they provide video, audio, or both?

✎   Make your payments on time.

✎   Say "thank you" often! Take an interest in what your caregiver has to say at pickup, and express gratitude every day. Give them specific compliments on what they're doing well. They'll feel important to you and your family. And they are! Always work together to make a plan that works for everyone.

WHAT TO DO WHEN SOMETHING AT DAYCARE OR SCHOOL NEEDS TO CHANGE

There will be times when communication seems way harder than it should be. Working with a daycare facility is a lot like being married: it requires a certain amount of trust and excellent communication. However, the biggest difference between your marriage and your relationship with your childcare provider is that you're the boss. You get the final word, but that doesn't mean you can run around giving orders and shouting when things don't get done your way.

It does mean that you get to set boundaries, especially if things aren't going the way you need them to. Some parents (especially Constellations!) may have to take a page from their Crescent friend's handbook and have that awkward conversation they've been avoiding. You are your child's advocate, and while you want to respect your childcare provider (you chose them, after all!), you also need to feel confident setting boundaries. You can be polite and gentle and still get your point across. It's not what you say, it's how you say it.

If the idea of having these little confrontations gives you a panic attack, here are some phrases to get you going. You can always send an email or text if a face-to-face approach seems too much.

- ✏ "I know most of the kids here are older than Alice, but she's only one and it's not healthy for her to eat fried or sugary foods. Could you please offer her the snacks I've packed? If she doesn't want them, I'll send in things I know she loves."

- ✏ "It looks like Luke's diaper was only changed twice today. I know he pooped once, but would it be possible to change his wet diaper three to four times?"

Sometimes you start with a question—a request—and switch to firmer language if you get pushback.

SARAH'S Story on Working with a Nanny

A few years ago, I started working with a nanny. (I always say "work with" versus "she works for me," because I view this relationship as a true partnership.) My husband works very long hours and travels, and with four kids and a job, I needed someone in my corner. I was so thankful for her and her help, and she did lots of awesome things—but of course, it wasn't perfect.

I'm usually a Crescent—a super advocate for my kids—but surprisingly, I was totally intimidated when talking to my nanny about anything I wanted to change. I didn't think I'd have such a hard time, but I didn't want her to think I wasn't thankful for what she was doing!

At first, I let a lot of things go because I was so nervous. Eventually, I tried texting, but that didn't create the "conversational environment" I wanted to nurture. So we sat down and had a few chats. I started by complimenting her with what I loved, and then moved to the easy changes. Ultimately, we had a few tough talks, especially when we disagreed. It didn't always end the way I wanted, but I learned from that. As I got more experience working with childcare providers, I set clearer expectations up front and talked about things when they first arose.

I approach things much earlier now, so the conversation isn't overwhelming. I've also grown a lot more confident in the decisions that I make for my children, so I'm not as tentative to discuss why I feel it's the right path to take. But I still always start with a compliment whenever I have to make a change. Positive talk goes a long way!

EVIE'S Story on Daycare Trouble

When I went back to work full-time, I enrolled my girls in an after-school program that included bus service from their school to a facility that also served as a daycare. At first, everything seemed to be going well. They were doing science experiments and cooking up treats and getting plenty of fresh air on the playground. But a few months in, something changed and the complaints started. "They won't let us talk at our tables."

"They never let us go to the art room anymore." And the worst? "The bus driver yelled at us today and told us that if we weren't quiet, she was going to leave us on the side of the road." My older daughter told me this threat actually brought my kindergartner to tears.

This was just one of those times when I went into full Crescent mode. Who on earth had they hired to drive this bus? What the hell was she threatening the kids for? I called the facility manager the very next day to let them know what had happened, according to both my kids. They were very apologetic and in no way denied events as my girls had described them. They said they'd speak to the driver to make sure it didn't happen again...but it did. So I called again and again, with each new concern, until we made the decision to pull our kids out. If regular communication, apologies, and promises to do better don't result in change, it's time to move on.

Most teachers will make a mistake at some point in the year. You might not like a class project, a homework assignment, or the way they handled a behavioral situation. If it's a one-time thing, you may be able to let it go. But if it's a chronic problem, you'll need to address it.

"I definitely feel that, because I'm a Crescent, I have a bit more confidence going to talk to teachers if there are issues. When my child was being affected emotionally and she was having anxiety and dread, I had no problem talking to the teachers to set some things up."
—**Cara**, Crescent, mom of three

Real-Life Sticky Social Situation: Napping Schedule

My ten-month-old goes to daycare five days a week. She was on a great schedule, with a two-hour nap in the afternoon from two to four in the afternoon. I pick her up at five o'clock, so she'd go to bed at seven. But recently, the daycare teachers have been letting her nap longer than two hours. They say that if they wake her up after two hours, she's cranky the rest of the afternoon. The other day they let her sleep for three and a half hours! When she does that, she doesn't go to bed until almost nine o'clock, and then I can't get her up the next day, not to mention the fact that I get zero down time at night. I'm okay if they go a little over two hours, but putting her down at one thirty and letting her sleep until almost five o'clock is ridiculous! How do I handle this?

There are two sides to this one. The daycare provider doesn't want to deal with a cranky baby, and you don't want a baby who goes to sleep at nine o'clock at night. It's important for the daycare provider to stay on your schedule, but it's also important for you to be flexible with their schedule. It sounds like your baby is with someone else about forty hours a week, so they should have a say in the changes of her schedule. That being said, a three-and-a-half-hour nap is really long! Babies do sometimes nap that long, but usually not every day.

Take it up with them by suggesting that they start her nap earlier, like around one o'clock, and let her sleep no later than four. That way, she can be active for four more hours and in bed by eight o'clock at the latest. Explain to your daycare providers why she needs to go to bed by eight, but also be open-minded to their suggestions for shifting her schedule so she doesn't get to bed at nine.

How to Handle It When Your Kid Gets in Trouble at School

You get the dreaded "Can I give you a call later?" message from your child's teacher. Or your child meets you at pickup with that look on their face, and you know they screwed up. The teacher tells you, in that kind but assertive voice, that your kid hit someone, bit someone, threw blocks at someone's head, whatever. You want to cry, but they keep going. This isn't the first time it's happened. In fact, your child has had to sit in time-out before for similar offenses.

Your first reaction is total embarrassment. What did *you* do wrong? Then, you're angry at your kid. Maybe you even lecture them in front of the teacher, just so they know you're doing something! On your way home, you wonder if your kid has been labeled one of *those* kids, and if that label will follow them forever. Your mind goes to dark, dark places.

As hard as that talk is to have, most kids will have challenges at some point in their school careers. That's okay, it's how they learn. It's embarrassing, but your kid isn't the first to ever have drama at school, and you can handle these situations with grace and confidence. The key is to work with the teacher to develop a strategy that works for everyone, and be consistent at home and at school. Let's go back to this little scenario one more time.

1. **The teacher meets you at the door/calls you on the phone.** Be open and present with them. Try not to give off angry body language, such as folded arms or an angry face. This conversation is awkward for the teacher, too.

2. **They start telling you all the bad stuff that happened today,** and you feel like melting into the floor.

    *   Listen and nod, don't talk. Let them finish and then ask clarifying questions. Some of this might be about venting.

    *   When they're finished, you can do a little digging. Start with one of our favorite questions: "What happened right before he threw a block at her?" Sometimes you'll find out that the teacher doesn't know what happened *right before*. Later, you might discover that another child instigated things. It's not an excuse, but it does provide context.

3. **Ask the teacher what strategies they used to help your child make better decisions.** Will this put the teacher "on the spot" a little? Yes, but that's okay. As long as your tone is gentle, you can ask tough questions. And make sure to ask what you can do at home to help, too. It's a team effort!

What to Do When Two Kids Are Fighting at School

"He hits me in line!"

"She takes my crayons every day!"

"He punched me when the teacher wasn't looking!"

"I told the teacher, but they aren't helping me!"

Ever heard these lines before? The hardest thing about dealing with conflict between two kids is that you aren't there, and you don't really know what happened. Your child tells you something, and if you're a Crescent, your immediate reaction is to save your child from whatever evil is lurking in the classroom. But there are always two sides to every story, and little kids don't always relay the full truth. If your child is telling you this more than a few days in a row, it's time to speak to the teacher. Friends with the parent? Approach them instead.

WHAT DO YOU SAY?

- ✎ **To the teacher:** "Julie loves school. (*Positive compliment first!*) But she seems bothered by Colin. She tells me that he's 'stealing' her glue sticks. I know he's probably not stealing them, but do you see any problem with them together? (*Talking without attacking.*) She's mentioned his name a few times to me now." You could also suggest that the teacher keep a look out for Colin and Julie, and ask to talk again in a few days. If the problem isn't fixed by then, ask if they could be kept apart for a little while. Hopefully the teacher will listen and validate, and take an actionable step to at least observe the kids together if they haven't noticed anything until now.

- ✎ **To a parent who's also a friend:** "It seems like Jack and Dell are having a hard time at school. Has Dell said anything to you about it? Jack says they're not getting along." Try to take the blame out of the equation. You don't really know what's going on with the two friends. If you're light on accusation, Dell's mom will be more likely to keep the conversation going. Maybe she'll shed some light on the situation. If so, you can talk to your child. If not, you can go into more detail about how your child is feeling.

IF YOUR CHILD MAY BE THE INSTIGATOR

No one wants to hear that their kid is causing problems, but the reality is, it's very common. If another parent approaches you about your child's behavior, the best thing to do is collect all the information you can. If that person is speaking respectfully, listen first, then say, "I'll be happy to talk to my daughter about what's going on. Can we speak again tomorrow?"

Later, ask your child what's happening. If necessary, speak with their teacher to get another perspective. Be sure to follow up with the other parent, and if you've gained any new information, feel free to bring it up in conversation. But:

- Keep conversation civilized and kind
- Look for solutions
- Ask for help, if needed

If a person approaches you aggressively, you don't have to participate. Respectfully ask that the parent cool down, and explain that you'd be happy to talk when they can speak to you more calmly. In the meantime, prepare for the conversation by speaking to your child or the teacher to find out what might be going on. You may need to set up a conversation involving school staff as mediators to keep the conversation civil.

Real-Life Sticky Social Situation:
Pushing on the Playground

> *My four-year-old tells me almost every day that there's another little boy who's pushing him down at recess. He said he told the teacher, but she's not doing anything about it. I want to get involved, but I'm not sure how to approach the teacher. I don't want her to think she's at fault, but I want to make sure my son isn't getting bullied. What do I do?*

Definitely approach the teacher! Send them a note or an email asking when would be a good time to talk. Pickup and drop-off are not the time to discuss big ticket items like this. The teacher will be more appreciative if you give them a heads-up on the topic and ask for a meeting time.

When you do meet, ask if they've noticed any issues between your child and this other little boy. If they say yes, you can fill them in on what your child has said. If they say no, explain that your child has been complaining for quite a while about the behavior, so you wanted to see if you could get their side of the story. Don't come at the teacher aggressively, and don't assume your child is telling 100 percent of the truth. There are two sides to every story. If they give you feedback you don't like or didn't expect, take a deep breath before you respond. More often than not, teachers are pretty objective and want everyone to feel safe and nurtured.

When You Feel Ignored, Disrespected, or Not Included

Maybe the teacher never responds to your emails. Maybe you don't feel like your culture, race, or family structure is represented in the classroom, or is being represented negatively. Maybe you're Jewish and the whole classroom is decorated for Christmas. Maybe you're African American and the only mention of Black culture all year is on Martin Luther King Jr. Day. If you feel you're being ignored, gently approach the teacher at pickup and ask to schedule a quick conference. She may just chat with you right then! If you schedule a conference, be prepared to gently, but directly, bring up your concerns and help establish an action plan to help your child succeed and broaden classroom views. Most teachers are child advocates, too, and want to find a way to support all the children in their classrooms.

If you feel like your culture, race, family structure, or religion isn't being included in the classroom, you need to have a private, serious conversation. Ask for a conference or phone call with the teacher where you'll have their full attention. Preschool and kindergarten are important places to learn, share, and be aware of differences, so don't feel shy about bringing up a lack of representation in the classroom! "Toddlers can recognize racial and gender differences. Preschoolers form their identities and are very interested in their similarities and differences from others. They are also aware of family structures and socio-economic statuses."[58] Kids notice differences from a young age, so following the archaic philosophy of "difference blindness" is not only unsuccessful, but can be detrimental to their long-term attitudes on diversity. Additionally, a child's culture needs to be honored in order for them to be academically and socially successful, especially if school is drastically different from their home life. Unfortunately, many children can be underrepresented in the classroom; as the parent, it's helpful for you to bring up these inequities.

Approaching the issue is the first step to a solution. If you're uncomfortable having the conversation with your child's teacher, bring someone along who can be an advocate for you. Most teachers want kids to feel supported at school! It may just be an oversight.

If you do bring up an area for improvement, be prepared for the teacher to ask for help. They may not know much about your culture or religion and may need help educating themselves and the students. Maybe you have books or toys you could donate, or activities to share. Be open and gentle when you talk to the teacher. Hopefully, they'll be just as open with you and ready to make some changes.

Handling That Awkward "All About Me" School Project

Your three-year-old comes bounding home with a big "All About Me and My Family" poster. He's supposed to fill in all the blanks, describing his family and where he was born. He's super excited. You're not. Now you've got to figure out where to put stepmom, stepdad, biological mom, and biological dad. Do you include biological dad, even if your son only sees him once a year? What if your child is adopted? Do you include his whole birth story in this tiny preschool family tree project?

If your child is very young, you may not have to address any complications at all. You can write in his immediate family, who lives in his house, and call that the boundary. If they're older and understand their family's dynamics, ask them who they'd like to include in the project.

But always remember the "Rule of No": you don't have to explain your entire family story to anyone. If your child is adopted and you don't want to share that, don't. If you don't want to participate in the project at all, write a quick note and explain that you'd rather do something else, or nothing at all. No reason necessary. It may feel uncomfortable to not give a reason, but family histories can be private. Most teachers will understand.

VOLUNTEERING AND PTA POLITICS

Teachers are always looking for parents to host classroom parties, volunteer for fundraisers, or even make copies and laminate posters. Most schools ask for volunteers throughout the school year to join or head the PTA. The volunteer list beckons to be filled, and by the second week of school, you've already been asked to host the Halloween Party and lead the holiday toy donation program!

It's easy to get wrapped up in "teacher asks" and think you have to sign up for something. Some schools actually require each family to volunteer in some capacity. But here's a secret (*and this is very important*):

unless it's mandatory, you do *not* have to sign up for anything. You don't have to justify yourself. *You can just say no.* Be polite, but firm. Don't worry about offering an explanation. If things change in the future and you want to volunteer then, there will always be opportunities.

On the other hand, saying no is only an option if there are other parents who enjoy this stuff and sign up, so you don't have to. If no one steps up to host your kid's preschool holiday party, guess what? There might not be one! Wouldn't that be sad? If you fall into this camp of eager volunteers, ask yourself this: Are you saying yes because of your Constellation tendencies? Do you feel like it's your civic duty to say yes, even when you know you've already got too much on your plate? If this sounds like you, give yourself permission to say, "I can't right now." The "right now" will help you feel like you aren't letting the teacher or your child down with a hard "no," just putting off new obligations.

And If You Do Say Yes?

If the PTA is your thing, that's awesome! These parents help guide schools' major social and fundraising events throughout the year. They help determine how funds are spent, and they advise the administration on new programs, both before and after implementation. Say yes to a position on the PTA only if you have the time and mental reserves to devote to the group.

Here are some ways to rock your PTA position:

- Understand the time commitment and duties of your position. How often does the PTA meet? What are the big events throughout the school year? What will your part be in running them? Again, make sure you know what you're committing to!

- Get to know your predecessor. Some roles in the PTA can be very specialized, such as planning large events with equipment, vendors, and gaggles of volunteers to coordinate. Even if your background is in event-planning, try to connect with the person who had the position before you to see if they can offer advice.

- Don't use your role on the PTA as leverage at the school. Whether it's putting in a special request for a teacher assignment or sneaking in to use the copy machine for personal reasons, don't assume your role on the PTA gives you or your child special privileges.

- Remain above the fray by staying out of PTA politics. The fact is, the vast majority of parents who volunteer for these roles are lovely, caring people who want to do right by their kids and the community. But every once in a while, parents get involved as part of a power grab, and working with them can be a real challenge. Do your best to interact in a professional manner (even when they don't return the favor), because these relationships within your child's school are important, and negative interactions can quickly become fodder for gossip.

- Remember, even though you're not employed by the school, you're still a representative of it in some tangential way. You also represent the other parents in your community as a member of the PTA. Let this guide your actions (in person *and* online) when it comes to speaking about teachers, administrators, and school programs.

Frequent PTA Q&A

Q. Can I bring younger children to volunteer events?

A. If it's a group activity, such as stuffing envelopes or making class goody bags, you sure can! If you're co-hosting a class party, check with the teacher first. The answer is usually no.

Q. What if I hate it, or something happens and I can't continue? Can I quit halfway through the year?

A. Because replacements aren't always available, especially mid-year, think twice about taking a position if you're not sure you'll be able to see it through. On the other hand, things happen. Don't let the off-chance that something *might* come up prevent you from volunteering in the first place! If you do need to step down, the best thing to do is to help find a replacement, if possible.

Q. What if there's a *total b----* on the board and her attitude is too much for everyone?

A. Approach her gently, one-on-one, and ask how things are going for her, in life and in the PTA. Sometimes just getting someone talking will reveal a battle you didn't know they were fighting. If she knows you're on her side, maybe she will be kinder to those around her.

Little Ways to Help Out at Your Child's School If You Can't Commit to a "Big Ask"

- Volunteer for Career Day
- Bring items the teacher needs, such as tissues, crayons, wipes, or party decorations and snacks
- Support them on social media
- Participate in a fundraiser
- Help decorate for a school function
- Participate in "Trunk or Treat" on Halloween
- Come in to teach the class about a special holiday tradition in your family

Real-Life Sticky Social Situation:
Pushy Party Planners

I'm on the oversight board for my three-year-old's preschool and recently, a parent has been pushing for healthier food offerings at preschool events and class parties. He piloted a meat-and-cheese party with his daughter's class, which went well. We also agreed to offer fruit-and-veggie platters instead of cookie platters at the family gatherings after the winter and end-of-year sing-alongs.

My problem, however, is that he essentially wants to take the template from his daughter's party and have the preschool mandate it as the class party menu for all classes at all parties. He wants to scrap our traditional Muffins with Mom and Donuts with Dad events, and remove pizza from our Family Fun Nights. From his viewpoint, any sugary treat "does acute damage" and shouldn't be allowed. He follows the Keto diet, so all carbs—even whole grains—are out (he didn't explicitly say this, but there are no grains on his menu, and he went on a mini-tirade against tortillas). A child bringing treats to share for their birthday, or contributing a favorite treat to the class party, would be a "no." He makes a passionate argument that even foods most people see as "healthy" (like yogurt and granola or apples) are actually bad, and he has the data to prove it.

Am I wrong in fighting this as too extreme and/or dictatorial? It is difficult to argue against healthy eating, and that's not what I'm trying to do. So

> *what can I say to this very vocal dad who is honestly trying to do what he thinks is best for his daughter? None of us think a mini-cupcake is healthy. But there's reasonable disagreement (isn't there?) as to whether it has an occasional place at preschool. As a parent who allows my kids to have yogurt and apples, I see him at the extremity, and I'm not prepared to dictate the exact menu for class parties—the menu is typically up to the teacher and class parent. I am willing to strongly encourage room parents to consider more fruits and veggies instead of cookies, and to give his menu as an example for ideas. Donuts with Dad is going to be the next big contention point, because it's a beloved preschool event, but my offer to simply add additional healthy choices (having a big fruit platter in addition to the donuts) wasn't "enough."*

This crusading dad does have a point. There's way too much sugar in kids' diets, and controlling the food at preschool events is one strategy to cut the sugar and teach our kids healthy eating habits. Honestly, the people who eat the food at those events are mostly the kids. Donuts for Dads isn't really about dads eating donuts—it's just about the time spent together, and the cute crafts kids give their dads. So maybe a few of these events can be revamped.

That being said, his ideas are probably too much of an extreme change for one year. It does put you in an unusual position. You want to advocate for what the other parents want, but he's also *very* vocal. So what to do? Maybe have him do some research to find out how many of the parents agree with him. What changes would they like to see implemented? Have him create a written survey so you can both find out what families want and need, and make your changes gradually from there.

TEACHER GIFTS

When must you give gifts? Never. (Didn't expect that one, did you?) It's true! You don't actually *have* to give a teacher a present *at any point* in the school year. However, typical gift-giving happens during the winter holidays, Teacher Appreciation Week, and/or the end of the school year. You can pick one of those occasions and give a gift. You can also give gifts to some teachers for the winter holiday, and to other teachers on a different occasion.

Gifts for daycare providers and teachers can add up super fast, so you'll have to set boundaries. But just in case you're wondering who you can skip on the gift list, let's play a little game called *Who Do I Have to Gift?*

Who Do I Have to Gift?

Q. Do I need to gift the bus driver?

A. No, but that would be really nice. They put up with a lot.

Q. Do I need to gift the "extra" teachers, like music and PE?

A. No, unless your child has a favorite.

Q. The guidance counselor has gone out of her way this year for my child. What about her?

A. Sounds like a great time to give a gift.

Q. What about my child's ballet teacher? We go once a week for one hour.

A. No.

Q. What about my child's swim instructor?

A. No.

Q. What about the front desk receptionist at the school? She's always so nice.

A. No.

Q. What about my child's after-school babysitter?

A. A little bonus would be really nice, if you can swing it.

There's a theme here, and that's the word "no." You never have to give anyone a gift. If you want to, go for it. It will be much appreciated. You could pick your child's favorite teachers and gift them, but don't feel like you have to spend hundreds of dollars gifting every adult your child comes in contact with. If you have multiple children, this can become super costly! Do what you can. If you love a teacher but can't afford a gift, a really nice note on beautiful stationery is an awesome option. Trust us—from two classroom teachers—notes like those are kept for years.

Ideas for Perfect Teacher Gifts!

- A $5–$10 gift card (movies, Starbucks, Target, grocery store)
- New game or book for the classroom
- Stationery
- Scented candle or essential oils
- Cozy scarf, mittens, or hat
- Baseball cap for a local or favorite sports team
- Favorite candies or treats
- Tumbler or coffee mug, especially one that's personalized
- If you're super crafty, anything homemade that *isn't* food
- A heartfelt note

What Not to Gift Teachers

- Homemade goodies: You never know about allergies or dietary restrictions.
- Cash: It's okay for an extracurricular coach or teacher, but not for a classroom teacher.
- Christmas tree ornaments: Don't assume the teacher has a tree.
- Alcohol: Just not the best message to send.
- The "My kid drew you a picture" gift, unless it also comes with a gift card. With an actual gift, it's a nice gesture; without, it just looks cheesy.

What about Group Gifts?

Sometimes you're asked to contribute to a group gift for a teacher. Parents sometimes do this for Teacher Appreciation Week, or if the teacher is about to welcome a new baby. In that case, do you have to contribute? Yeah, you do. It looks like you're totally skirting your responsibility if you don't. If you can't hack the requested amount, discreetly tell the organizer you can give a certain amount and that's it. No explanation needed!

WANT TO HITCH A RIDE?

Carpooling has become less and less common over the years due to car seat restrictions. But if you have a vehicle big enough for carpooling and extra car seats, it can be a game-changer, especially if you have other little ones at home who you don't want to drag out of the house unnecessarily. If you're invited to participate in a carpool but can't reciprocate, offer gas money or free babysitting in return. Even if your friend doesn't take you up on the offer, the thought goes a long way.

If you don't feel comfortable carpooling for one reason or another—you don't know the family well, you don't trust their driving, whatever!—don't feel pressured. Even if you're a Constellation, you have every right to say "No, thank you." But if you're always offering to drive, yet you're unwilling to put your child in someone else's car, be prepared for the possibility of an awkward conversation.

EVIE'S Perspective on Carpooling

When I was a girl, my family was in a terrible car accident, which has made me very cautious about driving, car safety, and more specifically, car seats. I check safety ratings before buying them, follow all the state guidelines, and have had them inspected and professionally installed. I've realized over the years that I'm *much* more cautious about this stuff than most people, which can make carpooling an issue. The only way it works for me is if I'm able to ask enough questions to put my mind at ease.

Being that I'm a Constellation, this usually feels obnoxious. I always feel like there's a real danger of other parents feeling judged when I ask questions that imply my child may not be safe riding with them. On the other hand, my kids' safety in cars is so important to me that I have a tendency to act more like a Crescent: I'm super protective! So to balance my need for reassurance with my natural instinct to not offend, I have to start the conversation with what makes me tick.

All parents have something they obsess over, whether it be car seat safety, water safety, sun safety, or something else. We've all had some negative experience that makes us way more cautious than the average parent, and that's okay. When the topic of carpooling comes up, I try to give an explanation for why I am the way I am that's a little self-deprecating, to offset any twinges of judgment that might come through for the other parent:

"I was in an awful car accident as a kid, so I'm a little crazy about car safety. Do you mind if I ask a few questions?"

It's my way of saying, "This isn't about you. It's about me." Now that my kids ride in booster seats and strap themselves in using a seat belt rather than car seat straps, I worry a lot less. But even now, I have to fight worry off. When I really don't get a good vibe about something, I politely decline, make up an excuse, and drive my own kid.

SPORTS AND ACTIVITIES

It's nine o'clock on a Saturday morning and you're pulling up to the soccer field. You drop off the juice boxes and pretzel packs you brought for the team's after-game snack and encourage your three-year-old to join their friends. They're all running around the field in some sort of controlled chaos, with balls flying in every direction, but they're having fun. Three is a little young to start activities, but it seems like everyone is signed up for something. Plus, your newly potty-trained preschooler really likes kicking the ball around, so maybe soccer is their thing.

Your child might not be in school yet, but once you officially "sign up" for something, you face all the same challenges school parents face. You may be right next to your child in all those parent/child classes, but there's still lots of fun new drama around the corner!

Playing Well with Others

Let's review the basics:

- Try to be on time, but if you're late, don't stress too much. These kids are really little and things happen. If you can't make it, try to let the coach know.

- You're not required to disclose any special needs your child may have, but if you think it will help, have a private chat with the coach.

- Grab that sports gear before the first game. If your child refuses to wear the shin guards or the protective cup because they're so uncomfortable, check with the coach to see if it's okay to skip them. Be prepared to sit out of the game, though. Since the goal is to set good safety habits early, they may say no.

- If at all possible, sign up for the snack list and bring a snack when you're supposed to. This one is harder to say no to, since your child will be consuming snacks and drinks provided by other families each week. However, if you won't be participating, or if you can't bring a snack, let the team parent know so they don't put you on the schedule. If your child is sick on your snack week, you don't have to show up just to hand out orange slices and Gatorade. It's okay!

Cheer On!

- It's totally okay to cheer on your child! Be sure to cheer on other kids, too.

- Is your kid the star of the show? Awesome! But if you keep getting compliments from everyone around you, find something nice and genuine to say about their children as well.

- Follow the coach's rules as best you can. If they don't want parents on the field, stay on the sidelines.

- Keep your other kids off the field/court/floor. They could get hurt, and it's not their time.

- Got an issue with the coach? If it's a one-time thing, let it go. Lots of these adults are working on a volunteer basis, so cut them a break. If the issues persist, bring it up delicately, away from other parents and kids, and when the coach isn't busy doing something else.

- Say "thank you" after each practice and game, and at the end of the season. Encourage your child to say "thank you" as well. It's nice to end the season with small gifts for the coach and assistant coach, but you don't have to! (Remember?)

Real-Life Sticky Social Situation:
Grandma's Too Competitive

Our almost-three-year-old started soccer this spring. The families are all wonderful and excellent at understanding that this is just for fun. The kids all share their balls during practice, and we have a fantastic volunteer coach. Some kids need some extra coaxing to go out on the field, some parents get out on the field and run around with their three- or four-year-old, and some need a snack break right in the middle of a game. It is a very lighthearted and supportive group.

My in-laws have attended every game. They have a standing invitation. My husband and I really appreciate their love and support of our daughter. They are always very positive with our daughter and think she is the best. The problem is that my mother-in-law is very judgmental of the other parents. It is totally uncomfortable! For example: one of the other three-year-olds was having some major anxiety about playing in the first game. The amazing mom was juggling twin eighteen-month-olds and her three-year-old solo at the first game. Dad came later, but she was holding it down until he got there. The little boy was crying and refusing to go out on the field. His mom got right out there and played along with him. I thought it was so great to see a mom recognize her son's anxiety and help encourage him. My mother-in-law [MIL] took it upon herself to loudly say to this mother, "Mom, maybe he's just not ready. He's going to make the other kids nervous!" I know the other mom totally heard. Ugh! I could not let my MIL parent-shame this mom, so I told her to be quiet because it's peewee soccer and everyone is here to have fun. I also said we didn't know this mother or child, nor did we know this child's needs. My MIL was not so happy about this comment, but it did the trick for that game. However, the comments have not stopped.

She passive-aggressively told another mom that her son was borrowing our daughter's ball too much and that she should bring a ball for practice. And just recently, she complained that the other team had too many parents helping their children during the game. Again, these comments are not just directed toward us, but to the entire soccer field so everyone can hear.

This has gotten so out of control that the other parents have apologized to me about things. One mom said, "Oh, I feel so bad. I should have brought a ball." Another said, "I hope my son didn't make your daughter feel upset because he was crying." Both times I immediately told them that it was no big deal and tried to play it off with grace. These parents must think we are crazy judgmental. I do not share my MIL's opinions on these topics, but this is a reflection on our family. Our daughter is definitely not perfect and has had many meltdowns about various soccer-related things. My goodness, these children are young!

I know this should be something my husband addresses, since it is his mother. However, my husband is very kind and struggles to stand up

> *to his mom. He has tried to say things to her in the moment, but it always comes off as a gentle suggestion. My MIL doesn't listen to him. I have less trouble with confrontation, but she is still my MIL and I walk a thin line between keeping the peace and standing up for what I think is right. Please help! We are just starting organized sports and have a long road ahead of us.*

Super sticky! You're totally right to be standing up for the other parents in this situation. The kids are really young, and all these struggles are very natural for kids learning how to play a new sport! But the mother-in-law/daughter-in-law relationship is very delicate. You may need to have a gentle chat when you're not at a game. It's *so* hard to bring up awkward topics, but if it helps, start with a compliment: "We love having you at the games." Then, lead into a light piece of feedback: "Sometimes I agree with your comments, but maybe you could whisper them into my ear? These kids are so little. Even your sweet granddaughter makes mistakes sometimes, right? I know we all just want them to have fun at this age." If you have a fun relationship, you could always throw in a joke or two. Enlist your husband's help, and maybe if you both say it, she'll listen. But be prepared for her to be embarrassed and skip a game or two while she recovers.

PARENT/CHILD CLASSES

Maybe you signed up for a parent/child gymnastics, ballet, or swim class. These activities make for awesome outings because the facilities are made for young families. The teachers are understanding, the equipment is safe and stimulating, and it can be a great place to make some new friends. Most of the time, these classes are a really fun way to spend an hour with your child. But every so often, something goes awry.

My kid just spit up all over the mat!

> ▸ That's okay! These places deal with things like this all the time. Ask for a wipe and clean it up. Don't be offended when they follow up with some disinfectant.

She's throwing a huge temper tantrum in the middle of the class!

> ▸ Comfort her however you need to. If it's a big room, you can always try to distract her in a different area, but don't feel like you have to leave the class the moment your child makes a peep.

My kid just pooped in the pool!

> ▸ There's an unfortunate situation. Maybe the swim diaper didn't fit, maybe you didn't think you needed one, or maybe your kid just had an accident. Either way, the pool will shut down now while they clean and re-balance the chemicals. Your best route here? Apologize and take your child home. It happens, but do your best to make sure you always follow the hygiene rules of a public pool (swim diapers on babies, no communicable diseases, etc.).

My kid keeps grabbing/biting/pushing other kids!

> ▸ Definitely stay on top of this one. If you see your child scooting over to another little buddy just so he can grab them by the hair, sweep your child up

before they get there. If you don't make it in time, just pull them away gently and apologize. Most other parents are understanding. Just be aware and stop it as soon as you can.

My kid isn't sharing the balls, and they just pushed another kid out of the way to get a turn on the balance beam!

▶ That's typical for this age group!! Many kids don't know how to properly share their toys until they're over the age of five! As far as taking turns, that skill comes when they're around three and a half to four years old. Learning how to share and take turns are huge parts of attending preschool and many other activities. That's why you're here. Certainly, talk to your child, but don't stress too much. If your child is the one getting pushed around, talk to the instructor and let them know what you need for your child to feel more comfortable.

SCHOOL AURORAS AND TWILIGHTS

How is your Parenting Perspective helping you shine or holding you back at your child's school, daycare, or extracurriculars?

Crescent

Maybe you're at the school a lot and volunteer to be as involved as possible. You're the first one to find out the emergency strategies of the schools, and you talk to your kids a lot about their social and emotional needs.

Or maybe you stay clear of volunteering, but are still very aware of your child's day-to-day progress. You're probably very comfortable approaching teachers with challenges or issues and feel ready to talk through solutions, but you steer clear of sharing too much with other parents—you're a natural protector and don't want your child's life broadcast throughout the school. You also feel comfortable bringing up issues of lack of representation in the classroom. In fact, you may offer to be an advocate for a more timid friend!

Watch out for: Your motivations. Yes, you're super involved, but why? Is it because you don't trust your child's school? Is it because you feel like you have to see everything that's going on? Every so often, take a step back and reevaluate your "why." Also, remember that many teachers are Crescents, and therefore sensitive and protective. Be open-minded and ready for their solutions, too.

Fireball

When it comes to managing school interactions, you're great at putting on your own oxygen mask first, so you rock the "Rule of No." You help out when you can, but you don't get upset if you can't be at a school party or field trip. You don't feel pressured to buy teachers gifts for every little holiday. And you talk to your kids about school, but don't stress too much. You trust that if there's a really big issue, the teacher will let you know.

You also might be the first to suggest a carpool, because you know that'll make it easier on everyone. Your strength is in streamlining. You're comfortable with what you prioritize and you don't think twice about your decisions.

Watch out for: Staying too distant. It's great to know your limits, but sometimes you may have to step outside your comfort zone and pitch in toward a common goal. Asking questions (like *why* the school is holding another fundraiser and *what* the funds will be used for) may help you feel more motivated. You might also have a tendency to wonder aloud why other parents worry so much or make the seemingly draining decisions they do. Just stay open-minded, because you never know what past experience drives another person's behavior.

Constellation

You love to be involved at your child's school because you always want to be helpful. Raising kids takes a team effort, and you see yourself as a valuable member of the team. Teachers, administrators, and volunteer organizations know they can count on you when they put out the call for help! You're generous with your time, and you're a thoughtful gift-giver. At your child's activities, you make a point of coaching them on being a good sport, sharing, and cooperating with teammates.

Watch out for: School burnout! You're dying to say no, but you just can't. It seems like everyone around you needs something, and you often find yourself signing up for more than you can handle. Don't forget: you can say no! You may also struggle to have difficult conversations with teachers, caregivers, and especially other parents. You might spend hours planning out exactly what you're going to say for what will end up being a two-minute conversation! Know that your caring, generous tone can go a long way when words fail you.

CHAPTER 8

Social Media: Should I Share That?

OUR GENERATION IS IN A POSITION THAT NO other generation has ever been in, nor will ever be in. Xennial parents (those in the micro-generation between Gen Xers and millennials, born roughly from 1977 to 1983) grew up with the inception of the internet. We grew up with AOL and chat rooms, but chose when to create our own online identities. We created our own social profiles in high school, college, or beyond, and hand-picked the photos and life events we wanted to share. We're the first generation to create our own personal brands.

Naturally, when we became parents, we just continued with this trend and shared photos of our babies. Social platforms became the viewing space for birth announcements and newborn photo-sharing, and eventually grew into a place to vent about our exhaustion, ask for advice, or document our daily adventures as parents. In doing so, we created our kids' personal brands for them.

WHY DO WE SHARE SO MUCH?

Why do parents feel so compelled to share their children's lives on social media? A March 2015 survey by C.S. Mott Children's Hospital at the University of Michigan found that, among the 72 percent of parents who discussed parenting on social media, the act of sharing "made them feel less alone." "[M]any said sharing helped them worry less and gave them advice from other parents. The most common topics they discussed included kids' sleep, nutrition, discipline, behavior problems, and daycare and preschool."[59]

And that makes sense. From the onset of trying to conceive, the internet is there to help you overcome every obstacle. From fertility, to breastfeeding apps, to apps that scrapbook for you, there's always a reason to pull out your phone. And while you're at it, you can easily document and record something. It's only natural that this habit would translate to seeking advice and support for all the gray areas that come with parenting.

We share because we want help, advice, validation, and support. We share because parenting is isolating, thankless, and difficult, and sometimes we need someone to say, "You're doing a great job!" We want someone to see all the hard work we're putting in to raise kind, thoughtful, adorable members of society. If our child does something cute/funny/smart, and no one hears about it...*did it really even happen?*

We also share because we have our trusted networks at our fingertips. When we have a question, we don't have to call five separate friends—we can quickly post and get lots of opinions and solutions within minutes, and we instantly feel more confident. As Dr. Wendy Sue Swanson, pediatrician and executive director of digital health at Seattle's Children's Hospital, says, "There's this peer-to-peer nature of health care these days with a profound opportunity for parents to learn helpful tips, safety and prevention efforts, pro-vaccine messages and all kinds of other messages from other parents in their social communities."[60] Parents look for voices of people they trust when they're making big decisions about their children's futures, and often those people are found on social media. "They're getting nurtured by people they've already preselected that they trust," Dr. Swanson adds.

Parents who use social media for advice and knowledge ask the most intimate and personal questions about their children's lives. And this is not in vain—there are thousands of networks whose sole purpose is to help and advise. We may be alone all day with our toddlers, but the internet is there for us, to answer any question or concern we may have. "71 [percent] of all parents on social media try to respond if they know the answer to a question posed by someone in their online network."[61] Generally, communities are supportive and willing to share solutions and information.

Social media has even been shown to lessen the poverty gap, as the same information is available to anyone with an internet connection.[62] Parents are able to know more about child development than ever before—no longer do you have to traipse to the library to find the perfect book to answer your question, or wait until your next appointment with the pediatrician. It's all right there, as long as you're willing to share.

WHAT DOES SOCIAL MEDIA HAVE TO DO WITH ETIQUETTE?

The online world is a parallel universe to real life. In social media land, we can take photos and videos to show details of experiences that could never come across in a conversation. As they say, a picture is worth a thousand words. Instead of just saying, "My three-year-old used markers to color all over his face!" we can take a photo of it in all its colorful, messy toddler glory, show our friends, and get a much better, more authentic reaction. Right?

When you decide to create that social media post, the sentiment changes from, "I've got to tell you this story!" to the question of, "Should I share this story with the internet?" Many stories you tell in real-life conversations may be embarrassing or private. If you share them at a playdate, their shelf life is short and their spread is limited. They may get repeated a few times and then forgotten. But when you share that exact same story on a social media platform, complete with a photo or video, it may live on forever.

Even if you delete something you shared, you'll never know if someone took a screenshot and sent it to someone else, or turned it into a meme. That may sound a little creepy...and it kind of is! Of course, you can lock down your profile with as much privacy as you want, but that doesn't mean your posts are actually *private*. Your stories about your child could be seen by thousands (even millions) of people!

In the decade between 2010–2020, the world of social media erupted. Ubiquitous platforms through which one could share every mundane and monumental detail of their life were widely accessible. By 2020, babies had hashtags before they were born. Children had YouTube channels before they could walk. Social media became their baby book.

Parents talk about kids' private lives in public spaces, and children become the stars of their parent's accounts. With these choices at your literal fingertips, you need to be responsible and deliberate about what you're sharing and why you're sharing it. Is this photo appropriate? Is this video too vulnerable to share?

You also need to be aware of your language and conversations. Often, there's a false sense of anonymity when you comment on others' posts. Because you sit behind screens as you type, you may feel a little more relaxed about social boundaries. Would you actually be that judgmental in real life? Probably not—but throwing that comment into a group chat seems harmless enough, right?

After you read this chapter, you'll never look at social media the same way again.

GETTING CONSENT

As soon as you share that first photo of your cute babe curled up in your arms, you initiate their online identity without their consent—without their ability to know if they even *want* to have an online profile.

You continue to live your story, and you post your children's pictures as your supporting characters. But where does the line get drawn? When do your children stop being pieces of your story and start being the main characters of their own? When do you have to start asking your kids if they want their photos out there for the world to see?

You could argue that, from the moment chilren are born, they're the stars of their own story. You're *their* supporting actor. But since they can't post for themselves so early in life, you give them that opportunity by using your accounts to share their lives.

Many younger parents actually feel they're doing their child an important service by providing them with so many memories and stories online. In their minds, the antiquated, tedious photo album has now been replaced by everlasting photos and videos in a cloud, all with accompanying comments that tell a story.[63] Some parents even plan their child's name around a cute Twitter handle or URL. They don't worry about consent, because this is the way of the future. Just as they post their own lives on social media, their children will grow up with this cultural norm, too.

> "Sometimes I wish social media was around when I was little, because I only have one small album of my own baby photos. And I don't think it would've negatively affected me today to have had them [on social media]. I think it would be cool to know what my mom was thinking and what I was doing on this day twenty-three years ago when I was one."
> —**Andie**, Crescent, mom of one

Andie sees social media as an opportunity—a place to document her son's life, not only for his future self and his understanding of her motivations as a mom, but also as a place to connect with long-distance family:

> "My family lives across the country and they miss a lot of the special moments. I post a lot. It does feel like a scrapbook they can go and look at. And then, when they do see [my son], they understand where he's at developmentally and his likes and dislikes."

Social media provides parents with the opportunity to give children a multi-layered understanding of their childhood. When they try to remember life as a child, they'll be able to look at detailed notes and photos from their parents that will provide them with a window back in time! You can't deny how cool that is.

The other side of the coin, though, is that some parents are unnecessarily (sometimes irresponsibly) posting kids' images all over the internet. Can an infant, toddler, or preschooler give consent? Of course not! But can a teenager get upset that his whole childhood is online for everyone to see? Yes. You have a huge responsibility here, and you need to be thoughtful and deliberate when you use social media. Whether it's a Facebook post, Instagram story, or blog post, there are so many ways to post a child's likeness and story online. And whether you're creating their online baby book or just posting a cute photo to share with friends, there are definitely some dos and don'ts. After all, "90 percent of children have been featured on social media" by their second birthday.[64]

With that statistic leading the way, keep their interests at the forefront of your mind.

ANNOUNCING THE ARRIVAL OF A NEW BABY

Has anyone noticed that beautiful birth announcements on specialized stationery have given way to carefully curated social media posts, always with a sweetly-staged newborn photo included?

- Thou shalt not announce a new baby's arrival on any social media network if you're not the parent. This is the mother or father's pleasure. It's also completely inappropriate to call or text others with the child's birth, name, and stats unless given explicit permission by the parent.

- Unless you want to get your head bitten off by a new mom, don't post photos of a woman who's just given birth (unless that mother has given you specific permission to use the photos). It's a delicate time, and a new mom might not want photos she privately texted to be made totally public.

- If you visit new parents in the hospital and snap a picture of yourself holding the baby, ask before posting. A little consideration can go a long way. New parents are sensitive and have a right to be.

- If you'd like to celebrate an achievement such as pregnancy, arrival of baby, gender announcement, or even a baby milestone, that's completely okay! Do this however you'd like. Many people favor an electronic announcement over a paper one, so go for it!

- Sharing a professional photo of your baby? Some photographers require an online tag, and some don't. Check with your photographer, and even if they say you don't have to, it's a really kind gesture to give them a shout out!

Real-Life Sticky Social Situation:
Stealing My Birth Announcement

My sister announced our baby's birth before we did! When our daughter was born, my husband and I wanted to enjoy her and wait a few days before announcing her birth on social media. But my younger sister (who doesn't have kids) either didn't realize or didn't care, and she announced the baby's birth before we had the chance. I had congratulations all over Facebook and I hadn't even announced it yet! I was so mad. Am I being totally old-fashioned to want to keep her birth off social media for a few days? Should I confront my sister about what she did?

You absolutely have the right to be upset! That was a very special and unique moment, and she took it from you. If you want to confront her, you definitely wouldn't be off-base. You might start with, "I was kind of surprised to see that announcement of Grace's birth on your account. We hadn't really told anyone yet." Even though the secret's out, do still make your own announcement! Not everyone will have seen hers, and this is a very magical moment for your family.

TALKING ABOUT ADOPTION ON SOCIAL MEDIA

Adoption is beautiful and traumatic. It's one family's greatest loss and another family's greatest gain. It's a complex and delicate process with many steps that all have to be respected. If you're adopting or know someone going through the process, there's so much you may want to talk about and share. But the rules are even more important in this scenario, for the protection of what's called the Adoption Triad: the baby, the biological parents, and the adoptive parents.

If You're a Family in the Process of Adopting

- If you're raising money to support an adoption, you can use social media to announce a fundraising page. Be sensitive with your language when you talk about raising money. For example, "Help us to expand our family through adoption" is appropriate language. "Donate to our adoption fund" is insensitive and makes the prospective child sound like a commodity. Avoid overwhelming your friends with constant asks for money, and don't private message them with direct requests for contributions.

- If you're adopting, be very deliberate with the timing of your social media posts. Some families choose to announce that they're on the adoption journey before they've been matched, but that can result in lots of questions you may not be ready to answer.

- Avoid "savior" status updates. You don't want it to look like you're "rescuing a baby." Things like, "This baby is so lucky to be with us!" are completely inappropriate. These types of updates are a big faux pas and insensitive to the adoption triad.

- Once you bring your baby home, don't post on Facebook until the TPR (termination of parental rights) has been signed. Some states have a waiting period, so hold off until that has passed as well. Once you do post, be respectful of the birth parents and their role in the adoption triad. The birth parents might not see the post, but someday the child will, and it's important to keep your language appropriate and kind.

- Don't post anything about the child's backstory on a generalized social media page. This is absolutely an invasion of privacy. If you need advice and want to look toward a specialized online group, you may need to divulge some details, but keep it as general as possible.

- It's also insensitive to the adoption process to celebrate a "gotcha day" online. "Gotcha day" is celebrated by some adoptive families in recognition of the day the child came to stay with their forever family. However, when this day is made very public, it's insensitive to the biological family, who lost this child on the very same day. Putting up a "gotcha day" post online, where it will live forever, is not fair to the child or first family.

- Speaking of birth parents, if you ever refer to them online, do not use the abbreviation "BM." This term has a disrespectful connotation. Better to use the term "expectant mom" prior to giving birth, and "first mom" after the birth.

- Fostering a child? Use a sticker to cover the child's face and don't use the child's name in your posts. Privacy is key here.

If You're Supporting a Friend or Family Member Who's on the Adoption Journey

When you have a friend or family member going through the adoption journey, it's important to be sensitive to the highs and lows of the process. This is especially important on social media. So first, do as much research as you can about what your friend is going through (whether they're a first parent or an adoptive parent). Follow their lead on social media. First moms or dads may not post anything about the birth of their child, or they may post photos of their child with their adoptive family. Comment with discretion. Adoptive moms may announce the birth way after they've told you in person, and that's when you can write a congratulatory post.

You may be curious about their choices or the process. Find a time to ask delicately—certainly not on social media. These conversations are best done over text or in person. Finally, if you know someone who has placed their baby for adoption, don't tag them in stories about adoption or foster care. They might not want to share their story.

PARENTING IN THE AGE OF "SHARENTING"

Do you "overshare"? Do you know someone who does? What does "oversharing" mean to you? The National Poll on Children's Health done by C.S. Mott Children's Hospital at the University of Michigan found that 75 percent of parents think that *other* parents overshare.[65] What could that mean? Anything from inappropriate photos, to posting too often, to divulging too much private information could all be categorized as oversharing.

Before you post, here are two general rules:

1. If you wouldn't put a photo of yourself doing that same thing on social media, don't do it to your kid.

2. Think about your "why" before posting. Sometimes we post to show solidarity. Sometimes we post to share cuteness. Sometimes we post to celebrate or mourn. Sometimes we post because we need a compliment or validation. All of these things are legitimate reasons, but it's important to not go too far in one direction. If you're constantly posting only to get validation that you're doing this whole parenting thing right, you may need some more real-life validation from your partner or family instead. You know what we're talking about…there are always a few people who post every perfect thing they do for their kids, with the sole purpose of getting a compliment. This is a little much, and will eventually overwhelm your followers.

Should You Share That?

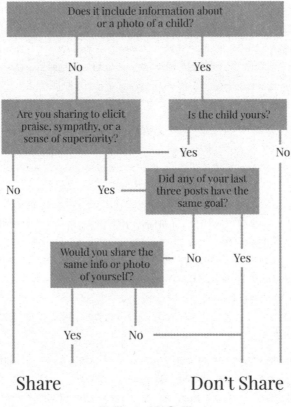

Does it include information about or a photo of a child?

No — Are you sharing to elicit praise, sympathy, or a sense of superiority?

Yes — Is the child yours?

Yes — Did any of your last three posts have the same goal?

No

No — Would you share the same info or photo of yourself?

No

Yes

No

Yes

Yes

Share

Don't Share

BE NICE

Part of social media's seductiveness is that it's so easy to relate to others. When we read a personal story about a mom up all night, or a toddler learning to walk, we feel connected by shared experiences. We feel this desire to like the post, comment that we're going through the same thing, and create solidarity with our friends.

But sometimes, we also feel a temptation to judge. *Oh...that car seat strap doesn't look right—should I say something?* Sometimes, we get too comfortable sitting behind a screen, preaching and posturing, and we forget to be nice. Sometimes we get pulled into heated philosophical debates: breast vs. bottle, c-section vs. vaginal, working mom vs. stay-at-home mom...it's all the same.

Here's a tip: Ask yourself, "Would I say these words I'm about to write to this person's face?" If the answer is no, reconsider and revise. If the answer is yes, keep the dialogue kind and considerate. Getting into an argument online will only cause you stress and frustration, and could possibly cost you friends. It will not improve the lives of anyone involved. There's no winning. There's also the risk that your online actions will have real-world consequences, especially when you have a false sense of anonymity. IP addresses can be traced back to you—we've seen people get burned this way.

If you're active on social media and post on a regular basis, remember that it's a give-and-take relationship. Since you want and enjoy interaction on your posts, it's kind to comment and interact with your friend's posts, too. The more you interact, the more people will interact with you. Building community is what online profiles are all about.

DON'T BE THAT PARENT— HERE WE GO AGAIN

You know how your mom used to say, "If you can't say anything nice, don't say anything at all"? That rule obviously applies to adults' online interactions, too. Unfortunately, just as playgroups can bring out annoying little quirks, social media has this way of bringing out other undesirable qualities! Here are the many types of annoying parents you'll find on social media. We've all got "friends" like these commenters. Who do you recognize? Are you guilty of any of these? (It's okay—we won't tell.)

- ✎ **The One-Upper:** You might remember this pesky friend from your playgroup (see our "Don't Be That Parent" list in the communication chapter on page 109). Well, they've got the same MO online. You know when a brand-new mom posts about how tired she is? This mom will respond with something like, "Just wait until you have two!" *Just shut up.*

- ✎ **The Passive-Aggressive Perfect Parent:** One dad posts a photo of his kids having ice cream and this commenter responds with, "So cute! My kids wouldn't eat that even if I tried, since we don't eat sugar! #welovehealthyfood" *Seriously, #soobnoxious.*

- ✎ **The Professor:** Cute kid in a car seat, and they say, "You might want to refer back to your owner's manual so you can adjust those straps correctly! #knowbetterdobetter" Please. If you really have to give life-saving advice (perhaps related to a car seat) do so privately and with some humility. But don't use that hashtag. Good lord. Might as well just write, "I'm a better parent than you." Remember the karma police? Yeah, they got your number now. "People in glass houses" and all that.

✎ **The Hijacker:** Photo of a kid at the beach for the first time, and they chime in with, "Yes, us too!" complete with three photos of their baby decked out head to toe in Lilly Pulitzer. Response is okay here, but nix the photos. Time and place. Not here, not now. Get your own thread.

✎ **The "Can't Stop, Won't Stop":** Every post is about their child. They have at least three photos of their baby in his car seat just from last Tuesday, and they document every last moment—from his messy diaper to his first smile—for all the world to comment on. *Not even grandma cares that much.*

✎ **The Saleslady:** Sure, many people sell makeup/skincare/fitness/vitamins/nail polish, and they love it. Please keep the posts brief and pepper in lots of other personal posts. You want your friends to know you as a person, not just by the products you sell, right?

PARENTING POP QUIZ

An old friend posts a picture of his newborn in a crib with a bunch of stuffed animals and blankets around the baby. You know this is totally unsafe. Do you say something?

A. Send him a private message about how this is a SIDS (Sudden Infant Death Syndrome) risk with some info on SIDS, so he knows you're for real.

B. Ignore it. He probably knows it's dangerous and just posted the photo for cuteness.

C. Comment on the post saying that the baby is cute, and then cheerfully remind him that those blankets are unsafe.

D. Wait to see what others do. If no one else comments, you're going to!

Keep reading for the correct answer!

WHAT NOT TO SHARE

- No posting of naked children, ever. And no covering their privates with a sticker. Even in stories that erase after twenty-four hours. Talk about an invasion of privacy!

- Potty training your child? Please don't post a photo of them on the potty for the whole world to see. Put a picture of yourself on the toilet instead! Oh wait, you wouldn't do that? Of course not! If you really want to share your toilet-training journey, write something generic— minus the number of times they peed on the floor, wet their pants during errands, or needed new underwear at preschool.

- If your child has a tantrum or is upset, please don't snap a picture and share it. That's a true emotion your child is feeling, and it's not fair for it to be plastered everywhere.

- Sick child? It's okay to ask for well wishes or prayers for your child to heal quickly. However, think twice before posting a photo of a sick child looking pale and exhausted, or throwing up.

Even posting a photo of a child sleeping is an invasion of their privacy.

- If your child got in trouble at school, don't post anything about it publicly. This is your child's business. If you want to confide in a few friends (which we all need!), chat privately.

- Speaking of school, first day photos are cute! First day photos that explain the name, address, and exact location of the school are not. Be wary of any photo that showcases personal information about exactly where your child spends a lot of time. Safety first.

- Lastly, don't over-post. One cute photo of your three-month-old in their car seat is fine. Ten at slightly different angles, or six posts a day? Too much.

EVIE'S Story on Not Always Following the Rules

When my baby was just a few days old, we had a photographer document our six-pound peanut curled up in her birthday suit, snoozing on blankets, baskets, and other props. Have I ever posted those *unbelievably adorable* photos of my 1) naked and 2) sleeping baby on social media, breaking two of our rules? I sure have.

I can't say why, but something feels different about posting a photo of a naked newborn versus a naked big kid. And something feels different about posting a photo of a sleeping newborn with her tiny, pursed rosebud lips versus a sleeping ten-year-old with their mouth agape. Maybe it has something to do with how much she looked like a little doll, or maybe she was just so young that I hadn't given her agency in my own mind yet. I hadn't yet realized she might someday resent me for sharing those photos.

Will our kids come to see this sharing as an act of love and pride, or an invasion of their privacy? We have a ways to go before the votes are cast, but it's something to think about before we press "Post."

DID YOU ACE THE QUIZ?

Sometimes people post cute photos on social media knowing they don't "look" safe. This is a perfect example. New parents are reminded by many experts not to put blankets or stuffies in a crib, but they sure do make for an adorable photo. Now, that doesn't mean you can't say anything, but it does depend on your relationship.

If it's a family member or super close friend, you could send a private message with a quip, "Cute pic, but you know that's not safe, right?" They'll probably write back saying that they know, and that the baby doesn't sleep this way. If they ask why, then you can share some info on SIDS. However, if this is a friend you haven't spoken to in years, you should probably go with choice **B. Ignore it.** There are lots of other people closer to your friend in real life who will probably reach out with a reminder, and he doesn't need to hear it from you as well. If he posts *another* photo like that, then gently nudge him in the right direction by maybe going with option **A. Send him a private message about how this is a SIDS risk**.

SHOULD YOU TELL YOUR CHILD WHAT YOU'RE SHARING?

Your child is playing with Play-Doh and they just made the cutest little pizza. You ask them to hold it up and snap a pic.

Your daughter just looks too cute holding her purse and wearing her sunglasses. You snap a selfie with her before the two of you run into the grocery store.

These photos are the little things that make up your day and tell your story on social media. But how much do you tell your young child about what you're actually doing with that cute photo? There are two schools of thought here.

1. **You don't tell them anything.** They know you took the photo, but they don't know the next step— they have no idea you then posted it on social media for friends and family to like or comment on. Once they're elementary school-age, you start to introduce the idea of social media, slowly and gently. They probably start learning from friends at this point anyway, so you may as well get there first.

2. **You tell your child you're going to put this photo up for friends and family to see, and maybe someone will say something nice.** When someone does, you read that comment to your child.

If you choose option one, you're not getting any sort of consent from your child. But can you really get consent about this from a child five or younger? If you don't tell them anything, are you breaking some sort of trust with them?

If you choose option two and do tell them, you run the risk of them constantly asking you to take a photo to "show people" or get likes and comments. Now you have a child who's already seeking external validation for how they look and what they do. Is that the path you want to take?

Either way, the answer isn't clear. We're navigating rocky territory by even having the option to showcase our child's entire life online. The results of our choices, good or bad, won't be clear for at least a decade or two, so the best we can do for now is be respectful of our children when we post about them, be responsible about the descriptions we use, and be introspective about our choices. And just like anything else we do, we're the model for our children's learning and behavior. Kids do what they see, not what we say. Make the choices that are best for your family.

EVIE'S Social Media Philosophy

My social media experience and my parenting journey collided right after I had my first baby, when I posted photos of my daughter's birth on our private, password-protected website for our long-distance family to see. One of those photos was taken right after I'd given birth, before our baby was even swaddled, so she was naked and her whole body was visible. I'd thought nothing of posting the photo on a private website, but it wasn't long before my phone rang. It was my mom.

She was calling to tell me, in the gentlest way possible, that I might want to reconsider including that particular photo in our online album. "I know we're the only ones who are supposed to be able to see that picture, but you just never know if some sicko might get it." She was right. I was stunned. That thought had never crossed my mind. I knew my mother was treading lightly, telling a hormonal, brand-new mom to take down a photo of her baby. But I also knew that she was totally right. And aside from the possibility that an innocent photo like that could get into the wrong hands, it made me pause to consider the implications for my child's privacy. Who was I to be posting naked photos of anyone online? What had I been thinking?

That little foray into problematic posting set the stage for a lot more reflection on what I'd post on social media and elsewhere online. But the honest truth is, when my kids were babies and toddlers and I could snap a photo and post it without them having the slightest inkling of what I was doing, I used to do it much more often. I'd write about my kids on our first mommy blog and post their photos *all the time,* because I felt like it was my story to tell. I'd share updates about their birthdays and first days of preschool on Facebook, because I knew my family and closest friends got joy out of engaging in our lives that way. But now that my kids are in elementary school and they have a vague sense of social media and its uses, I think long and hard before I post anything.

Is it fair to tell the world it's my child's birthday today? I don't share my date of birth for all the world to see, even if just for the risk of a stolen identity!

Is it fair to post a photo of her that will elicit a whole bunch of comments she's not able to see? Or should I show her all the compliments she receives? That's problematic in its own way, as we struggle not to raise kids who live for likes.

I'm sure my perspective on posting to social media will continue to evolve, but right now, my sweet spot is posting photos of our family. Somehow, a picture of me and one of the kids or one of our family of four feels more like I'm telling a story about my life (which the kids are a part of), rather than me making them take center stage without their knowledge, understanding, or consent.

SARAH'S Social Media Philosophy

I'm a Crescent in real life and online. I'm not afraid to admit that I like to control when and where my kids' photos and stories are on the internet. I do post photos of my kids on one of my accounts, but not the other. I always choose photos that put them in a flattering light and don't share their personal challenges with the online world. I do, however, hold trusted friends accountable for those things! I'm totally *that* parent who will text my friend and ask them to take a photo of my child down if I didn't okay it first. Sometimes I do say yes, and other times I say no. It depends on where it's going, honestly. I'm usually okay with Instagram stories, but not Facebook posts. My husband is active duty military, so we've always had to be a little more protective with our children's photos online.

I also haven't told my kids too much about social media. They know that I take photos, and recently with my older two (at ages ten and seven), I've started asking permission and respecting their decisions. But I don't tell them that people will be commenting. I usually just say, "Is it okay to put this up so friends and family can see?" I feel that I've used very strong discretion with which photos I've shared over the years and don't think that any of them are disrespectful or embarrassing.

Sometimes, I actually wonder if I should have posted more. I look at younger parents who use social media as baby books and wonder if in twenty years, that will be the norm. Maybe my kids will feel left out because every moment isn't available for them online. I hope my yearly traditional photo album is enough, because I'm just not comfortable sharing every little thing with the world.

IS SOCIAL MEDIA INVITED TO PARTIES AND PLAYDATES?

Had a great playdate? Cool! Want to share a photo of your child and all their friends in the sandbox? Not cool! Don't post a photo of anyone else's child on social media without explicit permission—even if you don't tag your friend! And respect your friend if they says no, or if they ask you not to tag them.

If your friend posts a photo of your child without your permission, you have every right to tell them to take it down, untag you, or both. This goes for babysitters, too. When you hire a caretaker for your child, be sure to go over your social media rules with them.

Playdate and Party Particulars

- Conversations you had on a playdate stay there. It's not okay to post a family's private information online.

- Drama in your playgroup? Totally typical. Keep it in the playgroup. It's not okay to post a mean-girl comment after everyone gets home, or passive-aggressively share a quote you think speaks to the misbehavior or injustices you've witnessed.

- Don't discuss holiday magic on any social media forum a child may see. This could accidently happen when you're posting about a Santa visit to a holiday party, a group Easter egg hunt, or an especially creative Elf on the Shelf moment. You never know what kids are reading and you don't want to be the one spilling the beans!

- Posting photos of your child's birthday party online is sticky. You might end up hurting the feelings of people who didn't get invited. Plus, you really do need permission from everyone in the photo before you hit share. Use discretion.

- It's okay to shout-out a friend online after they've given your child a gift. (More on appropriate ways to say "thank you" on page 125). But if you do it for one, do it for all.

Real-Life Sticky Social Situation:
Pictures Posted without Permission

I love hanging out with my neighbor and her toddler. I bring over my two-year-old and we always do the cutest things. Pumpkin painting, snowflake decorating—you name it, she does it. She's super crafty and fun. The problem is, she always puts tons of photos on her craft blog after we go home, and she's never asked me first. Honestly, I think it's because she wants kudos for all her cute projects. I'm not a huge online sharer and feel uncomfortable with my toddler's photo everywhere for people to comment on. How can I tell her that I love spending time with her, but I don't love all those pictures posted online?

Your kid, your right to say no! We've definitely been in this position before. It's uncomfortable, but it's a necessary conversation. Tell your friend that, as much as you love her and her super cute projects, you feel weird about your child's photo living on her blog. Maybe she's using that playdate time as a chance to get content, but that isn't fair to you. She needs your explicit permission. Tell her that maybe next time she can photograph your child's hands, but not their actual face. This way she gets her photos, and you get your privacy.

And if you choose to post photos of your own child doing the craft on your social media accounts, that's your business. It doesn't mean you've given your friend permission to do the same.

Supporting Friends through the Tough Stuff

Occasionally, your child or someone else's child will go through something really hard—an illness, a failure, or something even more traumatic. Obviously, you set boundaries on what you'll share online for your own child. But how do you support a friend?

- Follow their lead. If they post a diagnosis online, it's okay to ask about their child online. If they don't, keep it private.
- If they ask for "general prayers," it's okay to respond that you'll think of them or pray for them. It's not okay to ask why.
- Don't ask specific questions online for all to see.
- If their child is dealing with a chronic illness and they've set up a social media page in their honor, the rules change a little. In this case, with the child's permission, it's okay to post photos. What if they have a sick infant or toddler that can't give permission? Follow the parents' lead and be very careful with what you choose to share.

MANNERS FOR ONLINE GROUPS

- Keep the group's privacy in mind. Some groups are closed, so only members can see the content. That's your cue to keep the conversation in the group. Many group conversations are filled with sensitive and private issues. Don't go sharing content elsewhere! Other groups are open, which means whatever you post is much more likely to get shared outside the group. Share wisely!

- Stay on topic. If you're a member of a support group for adoptive families, that probably isn't the right place to share your favorite tuna casserole recipe. Honor the nature of the group and stick to the common bond you all share.

- Starting a meal train or fundraiser for a family in the group? That's totally okay. However, keep the family's privacy in mind. Maybe they're okay with letting other families in the group know that they had a baby, but not okay sharing that they had an emergency c-section and are having trouble recovering. Also, please don't share their address with the entire group. The coordinator of the group usually has the personal info and shares it with each volunteer as necessary.

- Skip the self-promotion. Whether you've joined the multi-level marketing world, you just started a blog, or you're launching a photography side gig, promote yourself on your personal profile, not in groups (unless there's a specific call for your product or service).

- Don't necessarily tag friends in the group (or outside of it) if their family is going through a difficult experience similar to one you see being discussed. They may not want to be "outed" like that.

- If you're offended by a conversation, think before you post. Is it really worth getting embroiled in a battle over this particular issue? People say a whole hell of a lot of nasty stuff in these groups, and while you might want to share another perspective, it might not be worth the days of heartburn associated with getting slaughtered on social media. Pick your battles.

SOCIAL MEDIA AND SCHOOL

- Don't like your child's teacher? Don't like an assignment or a grade your child got? Don't you dare post your grievance online. Take the mature route and talk to the teacher or the administrators, or call your bestie to vent. Don't make it public. If you use the internet to vent your frustrations, you're: 1) trying to embarrass the school when you should be addressing your concern in a much more professional manner, and 2) teaching your child that gossip is the way to solve problems.

- Did something really awful happen at school and you feel you've *got* to call your local news station or write a long blog post? Resist the urge. Don't make your child the headline of the six o'clock news.

- Want to post a photo or a video of your child shining at school? If it's just your child, it's okay. But if any other children or adults are in the photos or videos, you must get their verbal permission.

- Try not to overdose on the many moments your child is a shining star. #anothertrophy, #ineedanothershelf, #mykidsarockstar all get to be too much.

Are you a community leader? PTA president, teacher, local government employee? That's a double-edged sword. You have influence and everyone is watching you, especially on social media. People are looking to you as an example, so the rules are even more important for you. How uncouth would it look for the PTA president to bad-mouth a teacher all over her public page? And sadly for you, each picture and post you put up will be scrutinized, so keep your posts classy—no keg stand pics from a wild weekend away! When you take on a leadership role in the community, what you do and say speaks for that community.

Can I Friend...?

Q. Can you friend your child's daycare or school teacher?

A. Not usually. If you have a formal relationship with the teacher, don't friend them on social media. If you have a more informal relationship, or this teacher has taught more than one of your children, it's probably okay to reach out. However, if the teacher extends a friendship request to you, go for it!

Q. Can you friend the principal or anyone else in an administrative role?

A. Nope.

Q. Can you friend the PTA president?

A. Yes, if you're actually friends or at least acquaintances. Otherwise, there's usually a PTA Facebook page or group you can join.

Q. Can you friend your child's nanny?

A. Yes. This is an intimate relationship, and you probably want her on your friend list!

Q. What about babysitters?

A. Yes! And if you want to snoop a little before you friend/hire them, we totally understand!

TIME TO UNFOLLOW SOMEONE

Just not feeling it anymore? For whatever reason, you've decided to thin the herd and you're cutting friends left and right.

Q. Do I have to tell them?

A. Nope.

Q. What if I see them, like, tomorrow?

A. They're not going to ask you because social media life is a parallel universe to actual life. (So weird right?) And if you've gone so far as to unfriend them, they've probably really pissed you off somehow, so don't worry about it.

Q. Can I unfriend someone because their kid was a jerk to my kid?

A. Sure, but kids make up and move on, so you might want to hold off and just unfollow for now.

Q. What if we make up in three months and then I want to be their friend again? Can I re-request them?

A. Yes, but it's a little awkward. The act of re-friending might elicit a comment—really a question—from your friend. Are you prepared with an answer? If you're uncomfortable with that, try to not unfriend them in the first place, unless you're absolutely sure that you're done.

SOCIAL MEDIA AURORAS AND TWILIGHTS

How is your Parenting Perspective helping you shine or holding you back on social media?

Crescent

As the type of parent who puts their child's needs first, Crescents are usually very deliberate about social media posts. When you post a photo, you think about your child first. Would they be embarrassed to see this online in a few years? If the answer is yes, you keep the photo to yourself. You also may not be comfortable airing all your own business on social media, so you have strong boundaries on what you will and will not share. Every time your friend snaps a photo of your child, you make a mental note to check if it will end up on social media later. If it does, you have no issue sending a quick text asking for that photo to be removed. Your child, your choice.

Watch out for: Pressuring your friends to make decisions like you do. You may not want your child's photo in everyone's Instagram story, but every family gets to make their own choices. You can politely ask that your child not be included without judging others for their decisions.

Fireball

A Fireball's social media posts are usually relatable, funny, and click-worthy. You don't just post pictures of your kids being adorable, you also share articles that interest you, photos of you and *your* adventures, and laugh-out-loud memes that capture the hilarious side of parenting. People love your candid online personality and #nofilter conversations. You're real and you don't glamorize or romanticize the life of a parent. You may have lots of followers because people think you "get them." Fireballs are so needed in a world of picture-perfect, impossible-to-achieve, totally staged photos!

Watch out for: Inappropriate photos or too much info. You may think a photo is funny, but in reality, it would be embarrassing if your child saw it IRL. Keep those potty pics or kiddie meltdown moments to yourself, even if they get a laugh. They're not worth sharing at your child's expense.

Constellation

You're usually very thoughtful when it comes to social media. You recognize that there are lots of unspoken rules about what, when, and how much to post, and you try hard to follow them. Maybe you agonize over posting photos of your child's Halloween party because you don't want to hurt others who weren't invited. Maybe you can't sleep at night because you're worried about whether to approach a friend about something dangerous you saw in one of their photos. Constellations see the online spats others engage in and make a conscious decision not to engage. Sometimes that means you post less than others, seeking only the lighter parts of social media— opportunities to send congratulations, click "Like," or comment on an adorable baby.

Watch out for: Feeling disrespected. It's okay to say "no, thank you"! If something makes you uncomfortable, use some of the language we suggested and tell your friend or family to take that photo down.

Conclusion

IT'S IMPOSSIBLE FOR US TO PREDICT EVERY situation we'll be in with our children and how we'll react. That's one of the best things about kids—their unpredictability! But where other parenting books try to help you manage your child's behavior in a bubble and thrive through their developmental milestones, we pop the bubble and cover all the stuff that happens in between. Your baby may have just started reaching out to grab the thing he wants to look at, but what happens when he pulls all the candy off the shelf in the grocery store checkout line? In that moment, it's about your reaction. What should you do? What should you say to your child and the cashier?

Parenting *is* public. Much of the time we spend with our kids—especially as they get older—is in the community. We go to daycares, schools, stores, places of worship, birthday parties, and even weddings. We interact with family, friends, and strangers all the time, and those interactions set the foundation for what your child learns about being a good member of the community. Parenting is all about raising well-adjusted members of society, and those lessons start early, with every interaction and outing you have. There are literally *thousands* of potential interactions every day that give you the chance to model, teach, and reinforce manners and character. In this book, you've learned how to handle all sorts of dilemmas with grace and confidence, so you can model for your children how to become kind, considerate adults.

Remember that Parenting Pyramid from the beginning of the book? Etiquette is the pinnacle for a reason. You've got to prioritize yourself to have the energy and patience to fill your child's emotional cup. Once your child feels emotionally safe and secure, you can establish boundaries for their behavior. Then and only then can you focus on etiquette and manners, because you've created space for it! The pyramid is in the shape of an iceberg on purpose. People only see the tip—the manners you and your child show the world. But before you get there, you've put in countless hours of invisible work to be successful.

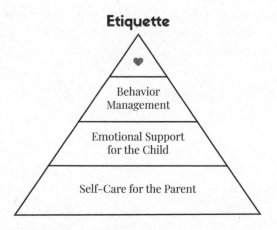

THE PARENTING PYRAMID reminds us that, as much as this book is about laying the groundwork for your children, it's also just as much about *you*. What kind of parent are you? When we know ourselves and we know *why* we make certain choices, it's much easier to predict our reactions and behaviors because we understand our motivations. That's when your Parenting Perspective comes in. After reading this book, you're probably pretty comfortable with who you are as a mom or dad. But here are a few extra nuggets to provide some insight into your friendships and your marriage, as well as highlight areas for growth.

CRESCENT

A Crescent is the type of parent whose first question is, "How will this impact my child?" From being annoyed at the lack of a public bathroom in a store to wondering if the long checkout line will interfere with naptime, the Crescent parent will always consider their child's needs first. A Crescent is also a natural advocate for kids and can often predict their needs and emotions before anything blows up into a full-fledged meltdown.

What Makes a Crescent a Good Friend

Don't want to walk to the car in the rain after a fun trip to the children's museum? Your Crescent friend will bring the car to the front door. Your three-year-old is hungry and you forgot a snack? A Crescent is there with three different types of Goldfish and an extra water bottle. This is the person who will ask the uncomfortable questions that everyone is wondering but won't dare to ask. "Are there guns in your home? What adults will be there during the playdate?" Crescents will be the first to advocate for your children or pull them away from an uncomfortable situation.

You've got to have a Crescent in your life. They are caregivers and helpers to all those in their social circle.

If You're Co-Parenting with a Crescent

Get ready for lots of passionate conversations! Crescents are excellent at reading their kids' needs and will jump to their rescue if they feel like it's necessary—which will be often! They may actually need to be pulled back a little, as their need to "do something" can be overwhelming. They'll fight to the death with their partner about the best route to take when faced with parenting obstacles and will not back down easily.

Crescent Pitfalls

Crescents' need to help their children can become frustrating because they tend to think they need to jump to the rescue. Crescents might benefit from a little nudging when it comes to giving their kids room to grow and make mistakes. They may not want to say yes to the playdate with the school friend they've never met, but it's probably a good independence exercise for their child.

FIREBALL

A Fireball knows and understands that parenting is a marathon, not a sprint. Their biggest question is, "Does this work for me and my family?" They're excellent boundary-setters and know how to identify stressors and remove them. These are usually more experienced parents—those who've been around the block and know that they have to fill their own cup first before they're of any use to their children.

What Makes a Fireball a Good Friend

It's really important to have a few friends who are Fireballs, especially if you're a new parent! These are the friends who will say, "You can go out on a date night. Your baby will be fine!" or, "It's okay to take some time for yourself and read a book, workout, whatever. You're worth it." Fireballs know that identities are not lost once someone becomes a parent. They'll constantly challenge you to set your own goals and say no to things that make your family feel stress or discomfort. Keep this person around—they may frustrate you at times, but know that these are the friends who have *your* best interests at heart!

If You're Co-Parenting with a Fireball

Get ready for some date nights soon after the baby's arrival. Your partner might push you to find time for date nights, even if it's the last thing on your mind. They may ask if you've made time to do the things you find enjoyable, such as reading or exercising. They may even insist that the children not sleep in the grown-up bed, because everyone's sleep is important. If you're a Crescent, these requests might seem super frustrating and may even cause conflict, which you'll manage with lots of conversation and compromise.

Fireball Pitfalls

Fireballs can come across as aloof and unfriendly, even selfish at times. Because they're so good at setting boundaries, they may look like they're ignoring others' needs, or not prioritizing the things they "should" be. This can be really hard for others to understand. It's important for Fireballs to jump out of their comfort zones every once in a while and do things that aren't on their priority list, to show consideration and generosity to those around them.

CONSTELLATION

Constellations recognize that they're part of a community and really want to make sure everyone in their family is a model member. The question running through their mind is, "How are my choices impacting everyone around me?" They take pride in being thoughtful and considerate, and work hard to make people around them feel comfortable. This means Constellations often worry about how their family might be negatively affecting others. "Is my child being too loud or too wild? Will that mom think my floors are clean enough for her child to play on? Have I offered enough snack choices at the playdate?"

What Makes a Constellation a Good Friend

When it comes to friends who are flexible and eager to please, Constellations are your go-to. Need to work a coffee date around your child's preschool schedule? No problem. Maybe you need a friend to bring some groceries by when your family has the flu? Ask a Constellation. Thinking of inviting a family with young kids to your wedding? Pray the parents are Constellations! They'll always think of their friends' comfort first and are usually very generous and flexible with their time.

If You're Co-Parenting with a Constellation

Get ready for lots of talks about how children should behave in public. Because Constellations are *so* in tune with how others perceive their brood, they usually have high expectations for the kids when you go out. You'll probably get lots of compliments, so soak them in!

Constellation Pitfalls

Constellations can be so concerned with other people's judgment that they miss their own kids' needs right in front of them. They may have to be reminded that it's okay to "ask" to skip the bathroom line if their kid is having an emergency, or to skip dusting the ceiling fans before hosting. They also have a tendency to pay too much attention to what other people's kids are up to. It can be hard for Constellations to keep their mouths shut when it comes to correcting the behavior of their own kids, as well as everyone else's.

WHAT WE HOPE YOU LEARNED

1. **Be confident!** You know what's best for your child. If you know your child is going to cry for a

few minutes in the stroller before falling asleep, ignore the stares from other shoppers that say, *Pick up that baby!* When you make a decision, know why you've made it. You know who you are, what Parenting Perspective you identify with, and why you're making these choices.

2. Use your **Parenting Perspective** to make and strengthen your **connections**. Find friends who prioritize what you prioritize. Need a friend who lives down the street and isn't overprotective about playing in other families' backyards? Look for those Fireballs. Need a friend who will chat at the playground while you follow your two-year-olds around? Look for Crescents. Need a friend to host your baby shower? Look for Constellations.

3. Even though we all identify with one of the Parenting Perspectives, it's important to know that **these categories are fluid**. A parent may be a Crescent in the first few years of their child's life and then grow into a Fireball as their kids get older. It's also important to be able to turn off your primary Parenting Perspective and turn on another one based on what's happening around you.

4. Build your **character**. There are usually lots of "correct" ways to handle a sticky situation. But as you've seen throughout this book, there are "wrong" ways, too. Sadly, parents often find themselves on the "wrong" side because they don't have a plan for prioritizing their needs, their child's, and everyone else's. When situations sneak up on us, it's easy to do what feels *easy* instead of what's right. But those long-unspoken rules of this public parenting game are clearer now because we know how to be considerate

without being a pushover or a nervous wreck.

So, the next time your child has a temper tantrum at the bank, or screams on an airplane, or pushes someone down at the playground, or won't pick up toys at someone else's house...or you don't know what to wear to preschool open house, or when to text your new friend, or what to serve at your child's birthday party...

Take a deep breath.
Be confident.
Know who you are.

Love,

EVIE AND SARAH

PS

WE HOPE YOU LOVED THIS BOOK AS MUCH AS we loved sharing it with you, but the conversation doesn't stop here! Be sure to find us on www. evieandsarah.com, where you can read more of our advice, listen to episodes of our podcast, subscribe to our newsletter, and join our Facebook Group (Talking Modern Manners for Moms & Dads). That group is home to tons of parents and caregivers just like you, who are thoughtful, analytical, deliberate, and incredibly kind. You totally belong there with us.

We'd love to hear from you about anything you read in this book, or your own unique sticky situation. We're always here to help, whether by answering your question on our podcast, weighing in on Facebook, or through one of our coaching programs. Feel free to email us at hi@evieandsarah.com.

Lastly, if you loved this book, please take a few minutes to rate and review it on Amazon. It would really mean a lot to us. Thanks so much!

Acknowledgments

SARAH: I'd like to first acknowledge my best friend and the other half of this project: Evie Granville. From early morning check-in phone calls, to late-night marathon editing sessions, to eruptions of laughter over the stories we tell in this book, this process has just been so much fun. Writing a book with your best friend requires openness, honesty, vulnerability, and kindness. Thank you for always being my friend first and my co-author second. As we always say, our strengths balance perfectly; where I falter, you stand tall. I am so thankful to be in business with my bestie.

And to my loving, supportive husband, who's been cheering me on since the day he met me, and who always listens to my dreams and makes me feel like I can accomplish anything. A special thank-you to my little inspirations, my sweethearts and little loves— my four spectacular children. My experiences with them set the stage for this book long before it was a tangible idea. They are silly, creative, imaginative and unpredictable—I love them deeply every day. And thank you to Debora. You have helped me more than you know. Finally, to my parents, who've been reading my writing since I was nine years old, and who have always encouraged me to keep writing, keep trying, and to always have more than enough food at the dinner table.

EVIE: When Sarah knocked on my door nine years ago, we caught each other at such vulnerable moments on our parenting journeys and clung onto each other through so many ups and downs. I could never have guessed how strong our bond would become. I could never have known how much she would teach me about myself and my parenting. And I would never have believed a book and a business could grow out of our friendship. Everyone deserves a Sarah in their life. Thank you for always being there and for always saying "Yes!"

Much love to my girls, whose kindheartedness and youthful optimism remind me that people are inherently good, and "etiquette" is just a fancy word for being nice. Thank you for being patient and always seeing the best in me. I love being your mom every day. To my husband, thank you for having faith in all my craziest schemes, for giving me room to fly, and for growing alongside me. I'm eternally grateful to my parents who have been a foundation of stability, love, and support. They first showed me the power of manners with their endless generosity. I loved growing up in a house where there was always room at the table for one more.

TOGETHER, we'd like to acknowledge the first person who believed in us: our agent, Regina Ryan. She's been with us from the beginning, reminding us that we had important things to say and believing in us when we weren't sure we believed in ourselves. Her commitment and dedication to this project have been unmatched, and we are forever grateful for her support and confidence in our vision.

We want to especially thank the team at Mango Publishing, specifically our editor, Natasha Vera, who worked tirelessly on our drafts and prepared this book to meet the world. Thank you also to Hannah Paulsen, who created and managed the book's marketing, and to the design team who created multiple iterations of the cover as we searched for the perfect look and feel.

Thank you also to Thomas Christiansen, who edited our podcast so we could focus on the book, our publicist Joanne McCall for helping us identify our core audience and our main message, and to our brilliant business coach Julia Aquino-Serrano, who cheered us on, shifted our mindset, gave us clarity, and propelled us forward.

We'd also like to thank The Little Gym community, especially Sarah Romanowski, Betsy Williams, Ann Sleigher, and El and Randy Garver. Thank you for your support, your podcast listens, your submitted questions, your social media shares, and your unwavering love.

We are beyond grateful to our readers and listeners, and specifically to two groups without which this book would not have been possible. First, the "P's and Q's Society," our small but mighty Facebook super group who is always the first to show support and solidarity. We are so grateful for every share, every podcast review, and every question you submitted. And to our larger Facebook discussion group, "Talking Modern Manners for Moms and Dads." We thank you for every engaging, analytical, and delightful conversation; every opinion you shared for our book research; and every sticky situation that you trusted us with. This book is for you.

Finally, to our contributors. We're so thankful for your time, your attention, your thoughtfully written answers and phone interviews. To Cara, Andie, Laura, Jordan, Erin, Chloe, Melissa, Mary Anna, and Debora—we appreciate your candor and honesty as you told the stories we all need to hear.

Modern Manners for Moms & Dads

1. How does this book differ from other parenting books you've read?

2. Do you think it's true that parents have a reputation for being "totally oblivious jerks" (page 11)? If so, is that reputation well deserved?

3. How did your social circle change when you became a parent? Did relationship-building become more difficult once you had kids?

4. What's your Parenting Perspective according to the quiz in chapter one (Crescent, Fireball, or Constellation)? Which descriptors for your Perspective did you find most/least accurate (page 37)?

5. What is your partner's parenting perspective? How about your best friend? How does your perspective and theirs contribute to the strengths and challenges of your relationship?

6. Which level of the Parenting Pyramid (page 15) do you spend most of your time and energy working on? Have you established stable foundational layers?

7. What's the most embarrassing thing that's ever happened to you as a parent? How did you handle it?

8. Which research finding from the book surprised you the most?

9. Did the book inspire you to change any of your parenting choices? Which ones?

10. How do you think subscribing to this book's advice will change your relationships with your child(ren), partner, friends, family, and strangers?

About the Authors

Sarah Davis, Ed.D., and **Evie Granville, M.Ed.,** are best friends and moms to six children between their two families. With their combined expertise in early child development, education, communication, and etiquette, they teach parents research-based strategies based on their "Solar System Parenting Framework." This method provides a powerful social advantage linked to relationship-building, self-awareness, and stronger, more resilient parenting. Their advice stems from their professional experience in the classroom, their research, and their "hands-on training" as mothers.

Sarah earned her doctorate in Curriculum and Instruction from Texas A&M. She earned her Masters of Education from the University of San Diego, and her Bachelor's from Skidmore College. She is the parent to four children and a proud military spouse. Evie lives outside Boston with her husband and two girls. She graduated with honors from Columbia University and earned her master's degree in Secondary Education from George Mason University.

Their advice on *Modern Manners for Moms and Dads* has been featured by *Parents, MSN, The Washington Post, Associated Press, Reader's Digest*, and other major media outlets.

Index

Bibliography

Adam, Emma K., Meghan E. Quinn, Royette Tavernier, Mollie
    T. McQuillan, Katie A. Dahlke, and Kristen E. Gilbert.
    "Diurnal Cortisol Slopes and Mental and Physical Health
    Outcomes: A Systematic Review and Meta-Analysis."
    Psychoneuroendocrinology 83 (September 2017): 25–41.
    https://doi.org/10.1016/j.psyneuen.2017.05.018.

Arnold, Andrew. "How Millennials Use Social Media to Become
    More Competent Parents." *Forbes*, March 5, 2018. https://
    www.forbes.com/sites/andrewarnold/2018/03/05/the-
    connected-parent-how-millennials-use-social-media-
    to-become-more-competent-parents/#5b846c6770a3.

Arnold, Jeanne E., Anthony P. Graesch, Elinor Ochs, and Enzo
    Ragazzini. *Life at Home in the Twenty-first Century:
    32 Families Open Their Doors.* Los Angeles: Cotsen
    Institute of Archaeology Press, 2012.

Artis, Berna, and Jill Telford. "Creating and Celebrating
    Diversity in Preschool Classrooms: How to Connect
    Children's Learning to Their Real Life Experiences."
    Presentation from the District of Columbia Office of the
    State Superintendent of Education. https://osse.dc.gov/
    sites/default/files/dc/sites/osse/publication/attachments/
    DEL_Cultural%20and%20Linguistic%20Diversity_
    Creating%20and%20Celebrating%20Diversity.pdf.

Bell, Patrick. "Industry Trends: Baby." *ECRM* (blog), February
    26, 2016. https://ecrm.marketgate.com/blog/2016/02/
    Industry-Trends-Baby.aspx.

Benard, Bonnie. "Fostering Resiliency in Kids: Protective
    Factors in the Family, School, and Community." Position
    paper, Western Regional Center for Drug-Free Schools

and Communities, 1991. https://files.eric.ed.gov/fulltext/
ED335781.pdf.

Cahill, Ann J. "Feminist Pleasure and Feminine Beautification."
Hypatia 18, no. 4 (Fall/Winter 2003): 42–64. https://doi.
org/10.1111/j.1527-2001.2003.tb01412.x.

Cartledge, Gwendolyn, and JoAnne Fellows Milburn, eds.
*Teaching Social Skills to Children And Youth: Innovative
Approaches.* Boston: Allyn & Bacon, 1995.

Centers for Disease Control and Prevention. "Unintentional
Drowning: Get the Facts." Home and Recreational
Safety. Last modified April 28, 2016. https://www.cdc.gov/
homeandrecreationalsafety/water-safety/waterinjuries-
factsheet.html.

Collett, Jessica L. "What Kind of Mother Am I? Impression
Management and the Social Construction of
Motherhood." *Symbolic Interaction* 28, no. 3 (Summer
2005): 327–347. https://doi.org/10.1525/si.2005.28.3.327.

Cowen, Emory L., Andreas Pederson, Haroutun Babigian,
Louis D. Isso, and Mary Anne Trost. "Long-Term Follow-
up of Early Detected Vulnerable Children." *Journal of
Consulting and Clinical Psychology* 41, no. 3 (December
1973): 438–446. https://doi.org/10.1037/h0035373.

C.S. Mott Children's Hospital. "Parents on Social Media: Likes
and Dislikes of Sharenting." *National Poll on Children's
Health* 23, no. 2 (March 16, 2015). https://mottpoll.org/
sites/default/files/documents/031615_sharenting_0.pdf.

Decluttr. "Survey Finds 54 Percent of Americans are
Overwhelmed with Clutter and Don't Know What to Do
with It." Cision PR Newswire. January 13, 2015. https://
www.prnewswire.com/news-releases/survey-finds-54-
percent-of-americans-are-overwhelmed-with-clutter-
and-dont-know-what-to-do-with-it-300019518.html.

Dieleman, Lisa M., Bart Soenens, Maarten Vansteenkiste,
Peter Prinzie, Nele Laporte, and Sarah S. W. De Pauw.
"Daily Sources of Autonomy-Supportive and Controlling
Parenting in Mothers of Children with ASD: The Role

of Child Behavior and Mothers' Psychological Needs."
Journal of Autism and Developmental Disorders 49,
no. 2 (February 2019): 509–526. https://doi.org/10.1007/
s10803-018-3726-3.

Duggan, Maeve, Amanda Lenhart, Cliff Lampe, and Nicole
B. Ellison. "Parents and Social Media." Pew Research
Center. July, 16, 2015. https://www.pewinternet.
org/2015/07/16/parents-and-social-media/.

Elksnin, Nick, and Linda K. Elksnin. "Facilitating the Vocational
Success of Students with Mild Handicaps: The Need for
Job-Related Social Skills Training." *Journal of Vocational
Special Needs Education* 13, no. 2 (Winter 1991): 5–11.
ERIC.

Feuer, Jack. "The Clutter Culture." *UCLA Magazine*, July 1, 2012.
http://magazine.ucla.edu/features/the-clutter-culture/
index2.html.

Fisher, Anna V., Karrie E. Godwin, and Howard Seltman. "Visual
Environment, Attention Allocation, and Learning in
Young Children: When Too Much of a Good Thing May
Be Bad." *Psychological Science* 25, no. 7 (July 2014):
1362–1370. https://doi.org/10.1177/0956797614533801.

Friedman, Ariella, Hana Weinberg, and Ayala M. Pines.
"Sexuality and Motherhood: Mutually Exclusive in
Perception of Women." *Sex Roles* 38, no. 9–10 (May 1998):
781–800. https://doi.org/10.1023/A:1018873114523.

Garfield, Craig F., Anthony Isacco, and Wendy D. Bartlo. "Men's
Health and Fatherhood in the Urban Midwestern United
States." *International Journal of Men's Health* 9, no. 3
(Fall 2010): 161-174. https://doi.org/10.3149/jmh.0903.161.

Greene, Ross W., Joseph Biederman, Stephen V. Faraone,
Timothy E. Wilens, Eric Mick, and Heather K. Blier.
"Further Validation of Social Impairment as a Predictor
of Substance Use Disorders: Findings from a Sample
of Siblings of Boys with and without ADHD." *Journal
of Clinical Child Psychology* 28, no. 3 (1999): 349–354.
https://doi.org/10.1207/S15374424jccp280307.

Grolnick, Wendy S. *The Psychology of Parental Control: How Well-Meant Parenting Backfires*. Mahwah, NJ: Lawrence Erlbaum Associates, 2003.

Guendouzi, Jackie. "'I Feel Quite Organized this Morning': How Mothering Is Achieved through Talk." *Sexualities, Evolution, and Gender* 7, no. 1 (January 2005): 17–35. https://doi.org/10.1080/14616660500111107.

Haelle, Tara. "Do Parents Invade Children's Privacy When They Post Photos Online?" NPR. October 28, 2016. https://www.npr.org/sections/health-shots/2016/10/28/499595298/do-parents-invade-childrens-privacy-when-they-post-photos-online.

Hagner, David, Pat Rogan, and Stephen Murphy. "Facilitating Natural Supports in the Workplace: Strategies for Support Consultants." *Journal of Rehabilitation* 58, no. 1 (January 1992): 29–34. ProQuest.

Hamer, Mark, Emmanuel Stamatakis, and Andrew D. Steptoe. "Dose-Response Relationship between Physical Activity and Mental Health: The Scottish Health Survey." *British Journal of Sports Medicine* 43, no. 14 (April 2008): 1111–1114. https://doi.org/10.1136/bjsm.2008.046243.

Hass, Norah C., Trent D. Weston, and Seung-Lark Lim. "Be Happy Not Sad for Your Youth: The Effect of Emotional Expression on Age Perception." *PLOS One* 11, no. 3 (March 2016). https://doi.org/10.1371/journal.pone.0152093.

Hillman, Betty Luther. "'The Clothes I Wear Help Me to Know My Own Power': The Politics of Gender Presentation in the Era of Women's Liberation." *Frontiers: A Journal of Women's Studies* 34, no. 2 (June 2013): 155–185. https://doi.org/10.5250/fronjwomestud.34.2.0155.

Holohan, Meghan. "'Pause Before You Post': How to Share Your Kids' Photos Safely Online." TODAY. April 3, 2018. https://www.today.com/parents/kids-privacy-educates-parents-sharing-photos-online-t126349.

Howe, Neil. "Nothing's Too Good for My Baby." *Forbes*, November 30, 2016. https://www.forbes.com/sites/

neilhowe/2016/11/30/nothings-too-good-for-my-baby/#5c8e81d81ab6.

Isensee, Laura. "Houston High School's Dress Code for Parents Draws Pushback." Houston Public Media. April 24, 2019. https://www.houstonpublicmedia.org/articles/news/education-news/2019/04/24/330636/houston-high-schools-dress-code-for-parents-draws-pushback/.

Koçak, Aylin, Athanasios Mouratidis, Zehra Uçanok, Emre Selcuk, and Patrick T. Davies. "Need Satisfaction as a Mediator of Associations between Interparental Relationship Dimensions and Autonomy Supportive Parenting: A Weekly Diary Study." *Family Process*, early view (February 2020). https://doi.org/10.1111/famp.12523.

LaFrance, Adrienne. "What Happens to a Woman's Brain When She Becomes a Mother." *The Atlantic*, January 8, 2015. https://www.theatlantic.com/health/archive/2015/01/what-happens-to-a-womans-brain-when-she-becomes-a-mother/384179/.

Larson, Elizabeth A. "Children's Work: The Less-Considered Childhood Occupation." *AJOT: American Journal of Occupational Therapy* 58, no. 4 (January 2004): 369–379. https://doi.org/10.5014/ajot.58.4.369.

Lewis, Michael. "Obama's Way." *Vanity Fair*, September 11, 2012. https://www.vanityfair.com/news/2012/10/michael-lewis-profile-barack-obama.

Livingston, Gretchen, and Kim Parker. "8 Facts About American Dads." Pew Research Center. June 12, 2019. https://www.pewresearch.org/fact-tank/2019/06/12/fathers-day-facts/.

Martin, Joyce A., Brady E. Hamilton, Michelle J. K. Osterman, Sally C. Curtin, and T. J. Matthews. "Births: Final Data for 2013." *National Vital Statistics Reports* 64, no. 1 (January 2015): 1–65. https://www.ncbi.nlm.nih.gov/pubmed/25603115.

Masten, Anne S., and J. Douglas Coatsworth. "The Development of Competence in Favorable and Unfavorable Environments: Lessons from Research on

Successful Children." *American Psychologist* 53, no. 2
(February 1998): 205–220. https://doi.org/10.1037/0003-
066X.53.2.205.

Mayo Clinic Staff. "Friendships: Enrich Your Life and Improve
Your Health." Healthy Lifestyle: Adult Health. Last
modified August 24, 2019. https://www.mayoclinic.org/
healthy-lifestyle/adult-health/in-depth/friendships/art-
20044860.

McCay, Lauren O., and Denis W. Keyes. "Developing Social
Competence in the Inclusive Primary Classroom."
Childhood Education 78, no. 2 (Winter 2001/2002):
70–78. https://doi.org/10.1080/00094056.2002.10522707.

McMains, Stephanie, and Sabine Kastner. "Interactions of
Top-Down and Bottom-up Mechanisms in Human
Visual Cortex." *The Journal of Neuroscience* 31, no.
2 (January 2011): 587–597. https://doi.org/10.1523/
JNEUROSCI.3766-10.2011.

McPherson, Katie. "The Mental Health Benefits of Getting
Dressed for Work." HuffPost. April 20, 2020. https://www.
huffpost.com/entry/getting-dressed-work-mental-healt
h_l_5e98a6f3c5b619ebab8f496c.

Mulvey, Laura. "Visual Pleasure and Narrative Cinema." In *Film
Theory and Criticism: Introductory Readings,* edited by
Leo Braudy and Marshall Cohen, 833–844. New York:
Oxford University Press, 1999.

National Safety Council. "Drowning: It Can Happen in an
Instant." Water Safety. https://www.nsc.org/home-safety/
tools-resources/seasonal-safety/drowning.

National Sleep Foundation. *Bedroom Poll: Summary of
Findings.* Washington, DC: WBA Market Research, 2011.
https://www.sleepfoundation.org/sites/default/files/
inline-files/NSF_Bedroom_Poll_Report.pdf.

Parker, Jeffrey G. and Steven R. Asher. "Peer Relations
and Later Personal Adjustment: Are Low-Accepted
Children at Risk?" *Psychological Bulletin* 102, no. 3

(November 1987): 357–389. https://doi.org/10.1037/0033-
2909.102.3.357.

Pellegrini, A. D., and Carl D. Glickman. "Measuring
Kindergartners' Social Competence." *Young Children* 45,
no. 4 (May 1990): 40–44. JSTOR.

Peper, Erik, Richard Harvey, Lauren Mason, and I-Mei Lin. "Do
Better in Math: How Your Body Posture May Change
Stereotype Threat Response," *NeuroRegulation* 5, no. 2
(June 2018): 67–74. https://doi.org/10.15540/nr.5.2.67.

Saxbe, Darby E., and Rena Repetti. "No Place Like Home:
Home Tours Correlate with Daily Patterns of Mood
and Cortisol." *Personality & Social Psychology
Bulletin* 36, no. 1 (January 2010): 71–81. https://doi.
org/10.1177/0146167209352864.

Silveira, Marushka L., Karen A. Ertel, Nancy Dole, and Lisa
Chasan-Taber. "The Role of Body Image in Prenatal
and Postpartum Depression: A Critical Review of the
Literature." *Archives of Women's Mental Health* 18, no. 3,
(June 2015): 409–421. https://doi.org/10.1007/s00737-015-
0525-0.

St-Esprit, Meg. "How Millennial Parents are Reinventing
the Cherished Family Photo Album." *The Atlantic*,
December 7, 2018. https://www.theatlantic.com/family/
archive/2018/12/preserving-kids-photos-in-the-digital-
age/577579/.

Strain, Phillip S., and Samuel L. Odom. "Peer Social
Initiations: Effective Intervention for Social Skills
Development of Exceptional Children." *Exceptional
Children* 52, no. 6 (April 1986): 543–551. https://doi.
org/10.1177/001440298605200607.

Tardy, Rebecca W. "'But I *Am* a Good Mom': The Social
Construction of Motherhood through Health-Care
Conversations." *Journal of Contemporary Ethnography*
29, no. 4 (August 2000): 433–473. https://doi.
org/10.1177/089124100129023963.

Taylor, Angela R. "Social Competence and the Early School Transition: Risk and Protective Factors for African-American Children." *Education and Urban Society* 24, no. 1 (November 1991): 15–26. https://doi.org/10.1177/001312 4591024001002.

Trice-Black, Shannon, and Victoria A. Foster. "Sexuality of Women with Young Children: A Feminist Model of Mental Health Counseling." *Journal of Mental Health Counseling* 33, no. 2 (April 2011): 95–111. https://doi. org/10.17744/mehc.33.2.p1ht7pt2533n3g2r.

US Bureau of Labor Statistics. "American Time Use Survey Summary." Economic News Release. June 25, 2020. https://www.bls.gov/news.release/atus.nr0.htm.

van der Kaap-Deeder, Jolene, Maarten Vansteenkiste, Bart Soenens, Tom Loeys, Elien Mabbe, and Rafael Gargurevich. "Autonomy-Supportive Parenting and Autonomy-Supportive Sibling Interactions: The Role of Mothers' and Siblings' Psychological Need Satisfaction." *Personality and Social Psychology Bulletin* 41, no. 11 (September 2015): 1590–1604. https://doi. org/10.1177/0146167215602225.

Wang, Margaret C., Geneva D. Haertel, and Herbert J. Walberg. "What Helps Students Learn?" *Educational Leadership* 51, no. 4 (December 1993/January 1994): 74–79. Gale Academic OneFile.

Warton, Pamela M., and Jacqueline J. Goodnow. "The Nature of Responsibility: Children's Understanding of 'Your Job.'" *Child Development* 62, no. 1 (February 1991): 156–165. https://doi.org/10.1111/j.1467-8624.1991.tb01521.x.

White, Lynn K., and David B. Brinkerhoff. "Children's Work in the Family: Its Significance and Meaning." *Journal of Marriage and the Family* 43, no. 4 (November 1981): 789–798. https://doi.org/ 10.2307/351336.

Sources Consulted

Campbell, Rachel, Els Tobback, Liesbeth Delesie, Dirk
    Vogelaers, An Mariman, and Maarten Vansteenkiste.
    "Basic Psychological Need Experiences, Fatigue, and
    Sleep in Individuals with Unexplained Chronic Fatigue."
    Stress and Health 33, no. 7 (December 2017): 645–655.
    https://doi.org/10.1002/smi.2751.

Conger, Rand D., Gerald R. Patterson, and Xiaojia Ge. "It Takes
    Two to Replicate: A Mediational Model for the Impact
    of Parents' Stress on Adolescent Adjustment." *Child
    Development* 66, no. 1 (February 1995): 80–97. https://doi.
    org/10.1111/j.1467-8624.1995.tb00857.x.

Grolnick, Wendy S., Laura Weiss, Lee McKenzie, and Jeffrey
    Wrightman. "Contextual, Cognitive, and Adolescent
    Factors Associated with Parenting in Adolescence."
    Journal of Youth and Adolescence 25, no. 1 (February
    1996): 33–54. https://doi.org/10.1007/BF01537379.

Reis, Harry T., Kennon M. Sheldon, Shelly L. Gable,
    Joseph Roscoe, and Richard M. Ryan. "Daily Well-
    Being: The Role of Autonomy, Competence, and
    Relatedness." *Personality and Social Psychology
    Bulletin* 26, no. 4 (April 2000): 419–435. https://doi.
    org/10.1177/0146167200266002.

Ryan, Richard M., Jessey H. Bernstein, and Kirk Warren Brown.
    "Weekends, Work, and Well-Being: Psychological Need
    Satisfactions and Day of the Week Effects on Mood,
    Vitality, and Physical Symptoms." *Journal of Social
    and Clinical Psychology* 29, no. 1 (January 2010): 95–122.
    https://doi.org/10.1521/jscp.2010.29.1.95.

van der Kaap-Deeder, Jolene, Bart Soenens, Elien Mabbe, Lisa
Dieleman, Athanasios Mouratidis, Rachel Campbell, and
Maarten Vansteenkiste. "From Daily Need Experiences
to Autonomy-Supportive and Psychologically
Controlling Parenting Via Psychological Availability and
Stress." *Parenting: Science and Practice* 19, no. 3 (May
2019): 1–26. https://doi.org/10.1080/15295192.2019.1615791.

Weinstein, Netta, and Richard M. Ryan. "A Self-Determination
Theory Approach to Understanding Stress Incursion
and Responses." *Stress and Health* 27, no. 1 (February
2011): 4–17. https://doi.org/10.1002/smi.1368.

Endnotes

1   Dieleman et al., "Daily Sources," 509–526.

2   Dieleman et al., "Daily Sources," p. 512.

3   van der Kaap-Deeder et al., "Autonomy-Supportive Parenting," 1590–1604.

4   Koçak et al., "Need Satisfaction."

5   Grolnick, The Psychology of Parental Control: How Well-Meant Parenting Backfires.

6   McCay and Keyes, "Developing Social Competence," p. 70.

7   Benard, "Fostering Resiliency."

8   Taylor, "Social Competence," 15–26.

9   Cartledge and Milburn, Teaching Social Skills.

10   Masten and Coatsworth, "The Development," 205–220.

11   Pellegrini and Glickman, "Measuring," 40–44.

12   Wang, Haertel, and Walberg, "What Helps Students," 74–79.

13   Elksnin and Elksnin, "Facilitating the Vocational Success," 5–11.

14   Hagner, Rogan, and Murphy, "Facilitating Natural Supports," 29–34.

15   Greene et al., "Further Validation," 349–354.

16   Parker and Asher, "Peer Relations," 357–389.

17   Cowen et al., "Long-Term," 438–446.

18   Strain and Odom, "Peer Social Initiations," 543–551.

19   LaFrance, "What Happens."

20   Mayo Clinic Staff, "Friendships."

21   Livingston and Parker, "8 Facts."

22   Livingston and Parker, "8 Facts."

23   Bell, "Industry Trends."

24   Martin et al., "Births," 1–65.

25   Howe, "Nothing's Too Good."

26   Arnold et al., Life at Home, p. 36.

27   Feuer, "The Clutter Culture."

28   Decluttr, "Survey Finds."

29   Saxbe and Repetti, "No Place," 71-81.

30   Adam et al., "Diurnal," 25 41.

31   McMains and Kastner, "Interactions," p. 587.

32   Fisher, Godwin, and Seltman, "Visual Environment," p. 1362.

33   Hamer, Stamatakis, and Steptoe, "Dose-Response," p. 1111.

34   National Sleep Foundation, "Bedroom Poll," p. 18.

35   Larson, "Children's Work: The Less," p. 376.

36   White and Brinkerhoff, "Children's Work in the Family," 789–798.

37   Warton and Goodnow, "The Nature," 156–165.

38   Centers for Disease Control and Prevention, "Unintentional Drowning."

39   National Safety Council, "Drowning."

40   U.S. Bureau of Labor Statistics, "American Time Use."

41   Hillman, "The Clothes," 155–185.

42   McPherson, "The Mental Health."

43   Lewis, "Obama's Way."

44   Trice-Black and Foster, "Sexuality," p. 97.

45   Guendouzi, "I Feel Quite," 17–35.

46   Collett, "What Kind," 327–347.

47   Garfield, Isacco, and Bartlo, "Men's Health," 161–174.

48   Trice-Black and Foster, "Sexuality," p. 99.

49   Tardy, "But I Am," 433–473.

50   Friedman, Weinberg, and Pines, "Sexuality and Motherhood," 781–800.

51   Silveira et al., "The Role of Body Image," 409–421.

52   Mulvey, "Visual Pleasure," p. 840.

53   Cahill, "Feminist Pleasure," p. 59.

54   Isensee, "Houston High."

55   Hillman, "The Clothes," p. 156.

56   Peper et al., "Do Better," 67–74.

57   Hass, Weston, and Lim, "Be Happy."

58   Artis and Telford, "Creating and Celebrating."

59   Haelle, "Do Parents."

60   Haelle, "Do Parents."

61   Duggan et al., "Parents and Social Media."

62   Arnold, "How Millennials."

63   St-Esprit, "How Millennial Parents."

64   Holohan, "Pause Before."

65   C.S. Mott Children's Hospital, "Parents."

Mango Publishing, established in 2014, publishes an eclectic list of books by diverse authors—both new and established voices—on topics ranging from business, personal growth, women's empowerment, LGBTQ studies, health, and spirituality to history, popular culture, time management, decluttering, lifestyle, mental wellness, aging, and sustainable living. We were recently named 2019 *and* 2020's #1 fastest growing independent publisher by *Publishers Weekly*. Our success is driven by our main goal, which is to publish high quality books that will entertain readers as well as make a positive difference in their lives.

Our readers are our most important resource; we value your input, suggestions, and ideas. We'd love to hear from you—after all, we are publishing books for you!

Please stay in touch with us and follow us at:

Facebook: Mango Publishing

Twitter: @MangoPublishing

Instagram: @MangoPublishing

LinkedIn: Mango Publishing

Pinterest: Mango Publishing

Sign up for our newsletter at www.mangopublishinggroup.com and receive a free book!

Join us on Mango's journey to reinvent publishing, one book at a time.